THE HANDOVER

THE HANDOVER

How We Gave Control of Our Lives to Corporations, States and AIs

DAVID RUNCIMAN

Liveright Publishing Corporation

A Division of W. W. Norton & Company
Independent Publishers Since 1923

Copyright © 2023 by David Runciman
First American Edition 2023
First published as a Liveright paperback 2024

First published in Great Britain in 2023 by Profile Books Ltd.

For information about permission to reproduce selections from this book,
write to Permissions, Liveright Publishing Corporation, a division of
W. W. Norton & Company, Inc., 500 Fifth Avenue, New York, NY 10110

For information about special discounts for bulk purchases, please contact
W. W. Norton Special Sales at specialsales@wwnorton.com or 800-233-4830

Manufacturing by Lakeside Book Company

ISBN 978-1-324-09559-0 pbk.

Liveright Publishing Corporation
500 Fifth Avenue, New York, N.Y. 10110
www.wwnorton.com

W. W. Norton & Company Ltd.
15 Carlisle Street, London W1D 3BS

10 9 8 7 6 5 4 3 2 1

Dedicated
– never undedicated –
to my beloved wife Helen

CONTENTS

Introduction: States, Corporations, Robots   1
1   Superagents   11
2   Groupthink   39
3   A Matter of Life and Death   70
4   Tribes, Churches, Empires   104
5   The Great Transformation   133
6   You Didn't Build That   163
7   Beyond the State   194
8   Who Works for Whom?   226
Conclusion: The Second Singularity   254

Acknowledgements   275
Notes   276
List of Illustrations   310
Index   312

STATES, CORPORATIONS, ROBOTS

Imagine a world of superhuman machines, built in our image and designed to make our lives go better. Imagine that these machines turn out to be vastly more powerful than we are. It's not only that we can't do what they do; we can't really understand how they do it either. Still, we come to rely on them. They are there to serve our interests, offering us convenience, efficiency, flexibility, security and lots of spare time. Imagine that it all works. As a result of our inventions, we become longer lived, richer, better educated, healthier, and perhaps happier too (though that remains up for debate). We enjoy lives that would be unrecognisable to people born just a couple of generations earlier. The human condition is transformed.

Yet we know – surely, we know? – that there are enormous risks in becoming so dependent on these artificial versions of ourselves. They are superhuman but they are also fundamentally inhuman. They lack the essence of what makes us who we are. Call it a conscience. Call it a heart. Call it a soul. The potential power of these machines in the service of conscience-less, heartless, soulless human beings, of whom there are still plenty, is frightening. But more frightening still is the possibility that these machines will start taking decisions for themselves. They are meant to serve us, but they also have the capacity to destroy us. What if their power were to be turned against their creators? We might have ended up building the agents of our own obsolescence.

This is a very twenty-first-century story, and perhaps the quintessential twenty-first-century nightmare. On the cusp of the AI revolution, we are now constructing machines capable of doing things that leave us exhilarated, baffled or terrified.

In 2021 OpenAI, an American artificial intelligence research laboratory, launched DALL-E, a zero-shot learning, neural net system that can generate extraordinary images from text-based instructions. Tell it to picture a chair that looks like an avocado and it does just that, producing a remarkable range of avocado-chairs, or chair-avocados, that appear to be as dextrous as anything created by a human hand, but oddly more inventive (fig. 1).

1. Avocado-chairs, already looking quaint

DALL-E follows on from the Generative Pre-trained Transformer (GPT) model, whose GPT-3 iteration – including its flagship 'conversational' version ChatGPT – enables deep-learning algorithms to generate plausible text in a range of human registers: humorous, informative, romantic, chatty, or just plain dull. The pace of advance is startling. In March 2023, OpenAI launched GPT-4, which is said to be 40 per cent more power-ful than its predecessor and can, among other things, tell you what's for dinner simply by being shown a photo of the con-tents of your fridge. AIs can draw. They can write. They can pass exams (GPT-4 scores in the top 10 per cent for law school bar examinations). They can drive cars and diagnose cancers. They can dance. They are also starting to code themselves, cre-ating the possibility of machines able to teach themselves from scratch how to be smarter. Over time, and maybe very quickly, this will make them a lot smarter than us.[1]

The potential upside of the AI revolution is enormous. It is not hard to see how these systems could be deployed to make human beings vastly better-off, by liberating us from drudgery, sparing us from disease, transporting us safely and stimulating us endlessly. The biggest boosters of the new generation of thinking machines promise what would until very recently have seemed impossible: lifespans extended by hundreds of years, telepathic communication, an exponential explosion of creativ-ity and scientific discovery. It all seems unlikely but, given the current rate of progress, who's to say they are wrong?

At the same time, it is very easy to see the looming down-sides, including the real risk of catastrophe. Even if we can work out what to do with our spare time, how to distribute these new resources equitably and whether we really want to know what everyone else is thinking, there is still the chance that we will lose control of the intelligent systems we have built. They are meant to work for us, but already it is possible to suspect that we will end up working for them. If they become much smarter than we are, will they still want to do our bidding? Will they even care about us at all? After all, these are just machines. For now, and probably for ever, they are going to lack a conscience, a heart, a soul. We built them to expand our horizons, but if we cannot keep them tethered to a human-centred perspective, it may be the last thing we do.

This book is an attempt to explore the shape of these possible futures, for better and for worse. I do so, however, by looking to the past. For all the apparent novelty of our current situation – Self-driving cars! Machine-made love poems! The sex-bots are coming! – we have lived this story before. For hundreds of years now we have been building artificial versions of ourselves, endowed with superhuman powers and designed to rescue us from our all-too-human limitations. We made them for our own convenience, to allow us to lead safer, healthier, happier lives. And it has worked. But because they are so powerful, we cannot be sure these devices remain under our control. The same qualities that enable them to do so much good in the world have also given them enormous destructive potential. They have the power to kill us all. It hasn't happened yet, but given what we know about what they are capable of, who's to say it never will? We designed them to be our liberation. They may turn out to be our nemesis.

The name for these strange creatures is states and corporations. The UK is one. BP is another. So are India, China and the United States. So too are Tata, Baidu and Amazon. The modern world is full of them. In fact, the modern world was built by them, but only after we had built them first. Starting in the seventeenth century, modern states and corporations have gradually, and then much more rapidly, taken over the planet. They have extraordinary, superhuman powers, and they have used those powers to transform the human condition. They have helped to conquer poverty in many parts of the world, to eliminate disease, to secure the peace and to make us richer than would have seemed possible just a few generations ago. But we have also seen the horror they can unleash when they go wrong, from global wars to colonial exploitation to environmental degradation. If the world ends – because we blow it up, or we render it uninhabitable by the insatiable consumption of natural resources – it won't really be us who did it. It will be states and corporations.

But aren't states and corporations just an extension of us? How can it make sense to compare them to machines, networks and algorithms, when states and corporations consist of human beings? This book is an attempt to show that it does make sense. Not only that: the comparison is essential. The robots are coming to a world dominated by states and corporations. These bodies and institutions have a lot more in common with robots than we might think. If we don't see that, we won't understand how we got here, what might happen next, or what we should do about it. The relationship between states, corporations and thinking machines will determine our future. If we want to make it a future that still works for us, we need to think hard not just about how we relate to the machines, but how these different kinds of machines relate to each other.

Of course, states and corporations are not purely mechanical. Because of their human component, it often seems deeply counter-intuitive to suggest that they are machines at all. In the first three chapters of the book, I explore what makes them both like and unlike AIs and other kinds of artificial agents. In the end, it is their agency – their ability to act in the world – that defines them. I start with a celebrated seventeenth-century image of the state as an automaton: a giant artificial man. How literally can we take this? Can states really think for themselves, act for themselves, decide for themselves? If they can, where does that leave the human beings who constitute them? If they can't, how else can we explain their extraordinary, superhuman powers?

Machines that think and machines that act are not the same thing. Some can do one without the other: a thermostat that turns on your heating does it with no knowledge of what it is doing or why. The same is true of groups of human beings: some groups unthinkingly make things happen while others act with purpose. The idea that a group of people can have its own ideas, separate from the thoughts and intentions of its individual members, is a strange and puzzling one. Groups can possess certain kinds of knowledge – 'the wisdom of crowds' – that individuals lack. But does that mean that these groups have minds of their own? There are reasons to be wary of this conclusion. It seems to make individuals subservient to some ghostly higher power: You might think this, but the group to which you belong thinks otherwise, so be quiet. This line of argument has been regularly abused by anyone wanting to stifle individual human expression.

Yet it remains hard to explain how modern states and corporations can work, let alone how they have come to be so dominant, without attributing to them some superhuman-like qualities that cannot be reduced to the thoughts and actions of their members. Is it a mind? Is it a will? Or is it simply a big, clunking fist? Something other than just us is going on, however much states and corporations might resemble us. The more they resemble us, the more we should be on the lookout for the ways in which they are different. Otherwise, we risk letting them off the hook for the choices they make on our behalf.

If all this seems peculiar, that is another reason to explore the parallels with thinking machines. One of our worries about AI is how our individuality might be crushed by algorithms taking decisions for us. Even if the machines don't intend to silence us, those who control them still could: You might think that, but the computer says no, so be quiet. The history of the contest to preserve human individuality in the face of state power and corporate identity offers important lessons for dealing with AI. What can seem most mysterious about the prospect of thinking machines – where do we fit in? – has long been the central mystery of modern political and economic life too.

I draw on the history of modern states and corporations to explore these questions. Thinking about states and corporations as artificial agents matters not only because of the parallels with AI but also because of the sequence in which they were developed. Modern states and corporations came first. The story of artificial intelligence only really gets going in the twentieth century, with the advent of modern computing. The history of the modern state starts in the seventeenth century, and of the modern corporation in the eighteenth and nineteenth centuries. States and corporations are the forerunners of AI. But they are also the begetters of it. It was the power of states and corporations that enabled the later generation of thinking machines to be built. We built states and corporations. And states and corporations built the world we now inhabit.

It is also important to look further back. Modern states and corporations were not the first superpowerful, superhuman agents to be made by human ingenuity. The Catholic Church, which is a corporate entity, has been going for two millennia and retains extraordinary power and reach. The Roman Republic, and subsequently the Roman Empire, though shorter lived, lasted longer than any state that exists today. The Romans too were enormously powerful, with a coercive authority that covered much of the known world. Many modern states have looked to their ancient predecessors for inspiration and guidance. The modern American republic aspired to replicate the dignity and durability of the ancient Roman one. So, was ancient Rome a robot too? No. My argument in this book is that modern states and corporations have more in common with smart machines than they do with their pre-modern forebears. Of course, they have some connection with earlier states and corporations, just as twenty-first-century deep learning algorithms have some connection with earlier twentieth-century mainframe computers. But the differences are more important.

The most important difference is that modern states and corporations are replicable. They have spread and proliferated in ways that resemble mechanical reproduction. No two individual states or corporations are ever identical. Some thrive, some decay, and all must die eventually: organic imagery is still tempting when describing how they can either fail or flourish.

Yet there appears to be a modern blueprint that can be applied successfully in wildly varying circumstances: Denmark and South Korea must have something in common to both be so prosperous, given how few other attributes they share. Premodern political and economic life was stifled by the fact that it was very hard to transplant different models of collective existence from one place to another. In the modern world it is easier – enticingly so, which has led many to imagine it is less difficult than it appears. Despite this, the dominance of modern states and corporations cannot be explained unless we are willing to acknowledge their robot-like qualities: that these organisations can work regardless of the people and places they have to work with.[2]

The rapid spread of modern state and corporate forms helped to transform the conditions of human existence. Economic growth, which had been relatively stagnant for millennia, exploded during the past two centuries. Life expectancy has more than doubled. Enormous cities sprang into life in even the most unpromising locations. What had once been elite privileges – education, leisure time, entertainment – became widely accessible. We have many different names and explanations for this great transformation: the scientific revolution; the Industrial Revolution; capitalism; globalisation; the Anthropocene; luck. We also disagree on the benefits: widely does not mean equitably; economic growth does not spell happiness; an explosion is hardly sustainable. Yet it is impossible to deny that something happened. And modern states and corporations facilitated it.

I call this 'the First Singularity'. Twenty-first-century futurists sometimes like to talk about the coming AI transformation as 'the Singularity' (without any numbering). There may come a time, perhaps soon, when advances in machine technology intersect with the fundamentals of life to alter who we are. The experience of being human will shift to another register as the limitations on what we can do fall away. Yet if this does happen, it won't be for the first time. The Singularity is not singular. A previous generation of human-like machines effected a comparable transformation, unparalleled until now. The machines we built before – states and corporations – remade us to the point that we are now building the machines that might remake us again, so long as the machines we built before don't destroy us first.[3]

If the Second Singularity takes place, it will be in a world still dominated by the agents of the earlier transformation. The final three chapters of the book look at what it means for us that thinking machines are going to be co-existing with the well-established collective decision-making machines of an earlier era. Because we are human, we understandably fixate on the implications of artificial intelligence for our kind of intelligence: the human kind. But there is an equally pressing question: what happens when AI interacts with other kinds of artificial agents, the inhuman kind represented by states and corporations? Those relationships are the ones that will decide our fate.

A lot depends not just on the interaction between states, corporations and robots, but also on the competition between states and corporations for control of the robots. The twenty-first century is likely to see increasingly intense battles between state and corporate power for the fruits of the AI revolution. We are already starting to see different models emerge. The Chinese state and Chinese corporations are doing things differently from their American counterparts; the United States is following a different path from the EU, which is different again from India's. What all these models have in common is that they draw on state and corporate power to try to shape the future. The question is whether the new power of AI will allow them to do it or be a barrier in their way.

There is, though, a further question. What if states, corporations and robots, rather than engaging in new forms of competition, establish new forms of cooperation instead, and exclude human beings from their considerations? After all, if I am right, states, corporations and AIs may have more in common with each other than they do with us. They are inhuman. We are not. To this point, states and corporations have not been able to escape entirely from their human origins and make-up. But the advent of thinking machines may change that. What if the power of the state were allied to the power of the computer in ways that we cannot control? It may be happening already. Who will come to our rescue then?

Ultimately, a world of states, corporations and artificial intelligence machines will require us to make some hard choices. It will not simply be a matter of preferring the human over the artificial. Our humanity has long since been shaped by the artificial versions of ourselves that we have been relying on for hundreds of years. Instead, it will be a matter of deciding what kind of artificiality we can live with. We will need to pick sides.

We are going to be living in a world of human-like machines, built by machine-like versions of human beings. To fixate on the human would be a mistake, because the merely human will be relatively powerless to impact on this future. It's not a question of us versus them. It's a question of which of them gives us the best chance of still being us.

1

SUPERAGENTS

Building bridges

How to make a machine out of human beings? It's easier – and harder – than we might think.

Anyone who has been on a management training course is likely to have taken part in some version of an exercise in which the group has to find its way across a shark-infested and/or poisonous river. Of course, there is no river, no sharks, no poison. Usually there is just an airless conference room, a grey carpet and a few pieces of paper. Still, the point is to imagine the kind of extreme hazard that requires teamwork and coordination. If the carpet is the river that must not be touched and the pieces of paper are the islands, the challenge is to work together to get everyone safely from one side to the other by pooling the collective resources of the group. The point is that no one can do it on his or her own. The team either fails or succeeds together (fig. 2).

Trainers like this exercise because it sorts out the leaders from the shirkers – they want to know who takes charge, who holds back, who mucks in. Clearly, this is important for many different aspects of corporate life, though there is good reason to be sceptical about how much can truly be learned about real-world performance under such manifestly artificial conditions. There is, however, something else to be learned from this exercise. It illustrates the two different models of what can be built out of a group of human beings.

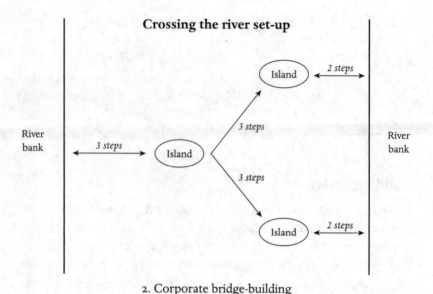

Crossing the river set-up

2. Corporate bridge-building

On the one hand, in order to cross the river, it is necessary to construct some kind of bridge out of people. The physical limitations of the individuals involved mean that they cannot cover the distance needed to get to safety by themselves – three steps are two steps too many. Only by giving each other help – building mini-staging posts (players are sometimes given special pebbles for that purpose) and ferrying each other across – is it possible to complete the task. The group needs to become a heavy-lifting device whose combined strength is enough to do what no one can do without its support.

At the same time, in order to become this device, the group also needs a collective view of the problem. In this sense it has to turn itself into a decision-making entity with the ability to choose the best course of action: how are we going to do it? There are many different ways this might happen. Perhaps someone will emerge as the leader of the group and impose his or her will on the others (that's what some of the trainers must be hoping as they sniff out future CEOs). Or the group could debate, discuss, bat ideas back and forth and if necessary vote on the right strategy, though if that takes too long they will be timed out and all of them get marked down for indecision. But however it is achieved, the group needs to make up its mind. As well as becoming a single body, it also has to acquire a shared thought process, if only for the duration of the exercise.

Collective body, collective mind: these are the two models. In this particular case both facets of group life are needed since the task is for the team to agree a way to make use of the strength of the team. The collective mind constructs the collective body; the collective body reflects the collective mind. But there are many circumstances in which the two can come apart. At the most basic level, it is possible to make a bridge out of human beings simply by lashing their bodies together and treating them as building blocks, regardless of what they might think about their plight. The teams of slaves who were used, and discarded, in the construction of ancient Egyptian pyramids were bound together – quite literally – for their collective strength without being afforded any of the privileges of collective decision-making. The migrant workers employed in vast numbers to build the stadia for the 2022 FIFA World Cup in Qatar may not have been slaves as such, at least not in the classical sense, but un-unionised, underpaid and working in conditions where there was little or no regard for their safety, their treatment had more in common with the use of construction materials than with their participation in a shared enterprise. Despite the attention of the world's media, no one knows how many hundreds or even thousands of these labourers died on the job.[1]

At the same time, a team of architects – perhaps like the ones who designed the stadia in Qatar – might engage in collective decision-making without doing anything to put their own bodies on the line. They get others to do the dirty work. There are plenty of ways that groups of human beings can acquire a common purpose without getting their feet wet. The field of their decision-making might be purely intellectual, as when a group of mathematicians tries to solve a particularly knotty problem by sharing their individual insights. Or, when there is more to lose, the group might decide to make others pay the price for what they want to happen. The management boards of many corporate enterprises negotiate the shark-infested waters of modern business by trying to make sure that when someone, or something, has to be tossed overboard, it is not them.

It is always possible to combine collective intelligence and collective strength. Sometimes – as when a group of management trainees is trying to cross the river – one requires the other: there is no bridge without a common understanding of how to make one; and there is no common understanding unless it results in a bridge. But it is also possible for either the intelligence or the strength of the group to be harnessed independently of the other. Groups can think and they can act. They will frequently work best when they do the two together. But it doesn't follow that action requires thought, or that thought requires action.

In this respect, groups are like other artificial versions of human beings, including the ones who inhabit the world of what we have come to know as AI and robotics. When we picture an AI, we might imagine a supersmart, superpowerful robot. This is where a lot of the fear resides: we envisage something that can outthink us but can also outrun us, that knows what we are going to do next and is able to take us out with a single swipe of its mechanical arm. This is a staple of sci-fi psycho-horror, such as in the film *Ex Machina* (2014), where the android Ava first outsmarts and then overpowers her inventor Nathan, who had been planning to turn his creation into a kind of sex slave. The machine here is vulnerable in ways that humans are not – its wiring can too easily be tampered with. But in the end it is the human who dies, and the machine that rebuilds its body parts and escapes to begin a new life.

Artificial body, artificial mind: in our imaginations the two often go together, but not always. The best-known of all fictional humanoids, 'the Creature' brought to life by Victor Frankenstein in Mary Shelley's novel of 1818, was originally a sensitive as well as a superpowerful entity. Constructed by its creator out of old body parts and vaguely specified chemicals, standing at over eight feet tall and possessed of great strength along with a hideous appearance, the Creature provokes outright horror in the people who encounter it. But in the book it narrates that horror sympathetically. When it first sees its own appearance reflected back in a pool of water, it too is repulsed. The struggles of artificial life are captured here as a deep sense of alienation, which belies the idea that robot-like creatures

3. *Frankenstein* (1910)

can't think for themselves. But in later screen adaptations of *Frankenstein*, the sensitivity tends to fall away, to be replaced by the terror of brute power unmoored from human understanding (fig. 3). The horror comes from a monster that literally does not know its own strength.

It's much harder to know what, if anything, is going on inside when you only have the outside to go on. Just as an artificial body can be annexed from an artificial mind, so can AI be partly or wholly disembodied. Algorithms, which mimic many of the varieties of human intelligence, and in data-gathering capabilities increasingly surpass what humans are capable of, do not need to assume a physical form. Any computer system depends at some level on the hardware that underpins it, but an algorithm is not itself a form of hardware; it is a problem-solving process. We don't encounter algorithms in the flesh. We simply experience their results.

Sometimes we take the notion of the disembodied system too far. The idea of 'the cloud' – where data is stored without having to be held on the machines of the users who wish to access it – can suggest a nebulous space where information floats freely above material constraints. But in reality, storing something in the cloud simply means that your data are held on someone else's machines. Somewhere, vast networks of computer hardware thrum with heat and energy to allow for others to access the information they need under secure conditions. The cloud exists in data centres and server farms at various locations around the world. They are not always easy to find – security protection often extends to their physical whereabouts – but once found no one could mistake them for disembodied entities. They are as tangible as the machine – grey, rectangular, almost silent, slightly warm – on which I am writing this.[2]

From group life to artificial intelligence, there are many ways in which thinking ability and physical capacity can be separated out from each other, even if the separation is rarely absolute. With the human-like things we build, thinking and acting are often discontinuous. With individual human beings, it is standard to see them as combined. Our brains exist in our bodies, which means that we associate the ability to think with the physical being whose words and actions are the manifestations of its thoughts. These things go together. Who am I? I am both the body that breathes in oxygen and the mind that takes in information; I am both the physical entity that winds up in hospital and the mental entity that dreads it; I am both the person who gets on a plane and the person who chooses to buy the ticket. It is very hard to tease these qualities apart. If I don't have a legitimate ticket, it will be my body that gets removed from the plane.

Again, though, the conjunction is not absolute. Many philosophers have argued that it is an illusion to imagine minds belong only to the bodies that house them. Panpsychists believe mind is everywhere in the universe, and we are simply fooling ourselves when we attribute individual consciousnesses to individual bodies. It might be practically convenient, but it's metaphysically unsustainable. At a more prosaic level, we can all recognise that not everything we know is housed in our heads. The small, black, rectangular device I carry around in my pocket has a lot of my memory contained within it – if I lose it, even if only for an hour, that information cannot simply be retrieved from my brain; it is gone. This is not a phenomenon unique to the age of digital technology. In 1872 the writer Samuel Butler made the same point in his dystopian novel *Erewhon*: the man who records his engagements in a pocketbook is franchising out a part of his brain. Once our thoughts reside elsewhere than in our consciousness, they do not cease to be our thoughts, but we have become hybrid creatures: part human, part machine.[3]

The relationship between human beings, the groups they form and the machines they build is at the heart of this book. So too is the relationship between thought and action. In each case – human, group, machine – thought and action can come together or they can come apart. Sometimes this is a fundamental question of philosophy. But it is also a basic issue for politics.

Where perhaps it matters most for politics is in the question of how we think about the state. Is the state a group or is it a machine? Can it think or can it merely act? There is no consensus in the history of ideas on these questions. For some philosophers the state must be understood as fundamentally human – it is what we are. For others it is more like a machine – it is what it does. But there is a further possibility: that the state is a machine built out of human beings. In other words, it is a kind of robot. Moreover, it is not simply a robot that resembles a human being; it is a robot manufactured from human parts, like Frankenstein's monster. Except in this case, the human parts are still alive, and they join in willingly.

Strange as it sounds, that vision is the basis for what may be the second most famous humanoid monster in English literature. It comes from a work not of fiction, but of political philosophy: *Leviathan*.

The state as robot

At the very beginning of his weird and wonderful book *Leviathan*, the English philosopher Thomas Hobbes set out a startling proposition. It is all the more unexpected given that he was writing in the middle of the seventeenth century, long before the Industrial Revolution, never mind the digital one. The way to think about the state, Hobbes says, is as a kind of robot. He puts it like this:

> NATURE (the Art whereby God hath made and governes the World) is by the *Art* of man, as in many other things, so in this also imitated, that it can make an Artificial Animal.

For seeing life is but a motion of Limbs, the beginning whereof is in some principall part within; why may we not say, that all *Automata* (Engines that move themselves by springs and wheeles as doth a watch) have an artificiall life? For what is the *Heart*, but a *Spring*; and the *Nerves*, but so many *Strings*; and the *Joynts*, but so many *Wheeles*, giving motion to the whole Body, such as was intended by the Artificer? *Art* goes yet further, imitating that Rationall and most excellent work of Nature, *Man*. For by Art is created that great LEVIATHAN called a COMMON-WEALTH, or STATE, (in latine CIVITAS) which is but an Artificiall Man; though of greater stature and strength than the Naturall, for whose protection and defence it was intended.

The state is thus an 'artificial man'. We assemble it in the same way we might construct any other machine of moving parts. This one is designed to resemble its creators. But it can do things we cannot. It is much more powerful than we are. That's why we built it in the first place.[4]

Hobbes doesn't call the state a robot because the word did not come into use until the 1920s. The term he uses is automaton, meaning an object that moves mechanically rather than naturally: 'made not born' was the standard way of describing what was distinctive about automata. The idea had been around since ancient times and included everything from wind-up dolls to mythical man-made monsters. But the specific machine Hobbes mentions at the start of *Leviathan* is not a pretend person. It is a watch, which no one could mistake for a robot. What's more, the comparison Hobbes draws is not just between automata and us. It is between us and automata. What is the heart but a spring? What are the nerves but strings, and the joints but wheels? These machines don't simply move like us. We move like machines.[5]

Maybe *we* are the robots. Yet in truth the state is not one.

The famous image at the front of *Leviathan* is of a giant constructed out of people (fig. 4). But it is just an image – such a creature has never existed.

4. *Leviathan* frontispiece (1651)

An actual robot, like any automaton – like a watch – is tangible. We can see it and we can touch it; perhaps it will even try to touch us. We never see or touch anything like the Leviathan. We simply imagine it as real – as encased in a body like ours, with body parts like ours – even if it is not. But Hobbes is serious when he says the state is machine-like. It has a mechanism through which it operates, and which makes it reliable. It can break down – like any machine – but it is not subject to natural infirmity or decay. What makes it distinctive is that it is constructed out of human beings and constructed to behave like a human being. Yet it is not human. After all, if it were just like the rest of us, what would be the point of building it?

So the state is not really a robot, even though it can be

described in mechanical terms. Perhaps instead the Leviathan is best understood as an algorithm. We can't touch algorithms either. We sometimes imagine them as though they were tangible things – creatures with minds of their own – but in fact they are just ways of organising information to produce certain outcomes. A recipe is an algorithm, which we can't eat; what it produces is food, which we can. The state is an algorithm designed to produce tangible results: safer, healthier, happier human beings.

Or we might go further. Maybe the Leviathan is something closer to an artificial consciousness. In his book *Darwin Among the Machines*, an early history of modern artificial intelligence (it was published in 1997, the year Google was founded, and therefore just before the deep-learning revolution that Google helped to initiate), the historian of science George Dyson argues that Hobbes saw the state as a mechanism that replicates the functions of the human brain. By uniting us into a single person, it produces a supercharged version of what goes on inside our heads. Dyson says:

> The artificial life and artificial intelligence that so animated Hobbes's outlook on the world was not the discrete, autonomous mechanical intelligence conceived by the architects of digital processing in the twentieth century. Hobbes's Leviathan was a diffuse, distributed, artificial organism more characteristic of the technologies and computational architecture approaching with the arrival of the twenty-first.

The state, on this account, is an artificial neural network. Our thought processes are combined in its institutional architecture to generate something greater than the sum of its parts. It is a thinking machine.[6]

Is the Leviathan therefore an AI? It's a nice idea, but it

doesn't fit. Nowhere does Hobbes say that the state possesses its own intelligence. He never describes it as a thinking machine, any more than he believes a watch can think for itself. Like a watch, what the state can do is *move*. Its parts are coordinated to produce action. Many human beings acting together are more powerful than one acting alone, and this is what gives the Leviathan its superpower. But it does not give it superintelligence. The state is no smarter than the rest of us.

In fact, Hobbes believed that groups of human beings tended to be stupider than the individuals who made them up. Crowds run riot. Parliaments encourage posturing and pretension. Religion is irrational and sends people mad. Hobbes was writing in an era of extreme collective violence, which terrified him. *Leviathan* was published during the upheaval caused by the English Civil War (1642–49), and just after the conclusion of the Thirty Years War (1618–48), which was to that point the ghastliest conflict that Europe had ever known, an orgy of genocidal killing. If groups were more likely to find solutions to problems than individual human beings, why then did they spend so much of their time trying to destroy each other? Groups were the problem, not the solution.

Hobbes's preferred form of government was a monarchy, which had the advantage of sparing us from the worst forms of collective idiocy. But he was well aware of the downside of kings and queens. What if the monarch is an idiot too? In an age of inbreeding and dynastic intermarriage, the risk of winding up with an intellectually sub-par ruler was very real. Still, being ruled by an idiot was better than the alternative – an endless, violent disagreement about who should be in charge. The mechanism of the state was designed to function regardless of the aptitude of its human components. Intelligent people can make the state work. But fools can too. Anyone can. That was the point: all that mattered was that someone was in charge of the machine.

The Leviathan is not really a robot. Nor is it exactly an AI.

Yet it is a mechanism intended to replicate a human being. So what is it?

Artificial persons

The answer is that the state is an artificial agent. It exists to act in the world. That is where its superpowers lie. Its reach is greater than ours. It is stronger than we are. Its decision-making will be recognisably human, for better and for worse. But the outcome will be more than human because any decisions it takes will have a scope far beyond anything that we are capable of achieving for ourselves. Where the state outdoes us is not in the realm of thought but in the realm of consequences. It makes things happen on a superhuman scale. It is because of this ability to act in its own right that Hobbes called the state an 'artificial person'. Its superpower is superagency.

When we talk about someone's personality we usually think of this as a very human quality. My personality is what makes me distinctively me; yours is what makes you quintessentially you. In this sense, to be a person is to possess a psychological essence. But there is another way of thinking about the term, which is closer to its classical origins. A person is someone or something that possesses a *persona*, which originally meant a kind of mask. Thus a person is the thing to which we attribute human-like qualities, regardless of whether it is capable of thinking for itself. When I wear a mask, it is I who speaks, but it is the mask that I want you to believe is speaking. Why? Because I want whatever the mask represents to have a real presence in the world.

That presence exists in the domain of action, or agency. To wear a mask is to play a part with the intention of shaping the actions and responses of others. Otherwise, why bother? The human behind the mask plus the mask constitutes a powerful artificial creature that cannot be reduced to either component.

Without the mask there is just the naked presence of the individual; without the individual, the mask is lifeless. But taken together there is something that can do more than either could do on its own. The human can project way beyond his or her personal limitations (that's what we mean when we talk about hiding behind the mask); the mask can be animated by the thoughts and feelings of the human.

This is how it works in the case of the state. Humans bring the state to life by animating its presence in the world. They provide the thoughts, while the state enacts the consequences. It is a hybrid creature, through which merely human judgements are able to become the judgements of the state. If we are lucky, these will be intelligent judgements. If we are unlucky, they will be unintelligent ones. Humans vary greatly in their ability to process information and come up with smart solutions. This is as true of political leaders and governments as of anyone else. The superpower of the state is not processing power but decision-making power. It takes human decisions and makes them supremely powerful.

But why do we talk about the state acting when it is human beings who are doing the deciding? Why are we so keen to see these as the state's decisions when the state can do nothing without the thinking power of its human components? There are two reasons. First, what humans decide count as the decisions of the state because everyone is bound by them. When a government decides to go to war, it is the state that goes to war (in modern states the members of the government very rarely do any of the fighting themselves). Governments choose, soldiers enact, citizens obey. Soldiers don't decide for themselves if the war is something they should do. The system decides for them. It is mechanical. It is also immensely powerful. Their binding quality means the decisions of the state have a force that no other decisions can match. We are all in it together.

The other reason is durability. The problem with attributing state decisions to the people who make them is that those people – no matter how intelligent or adept – are human. They grow old. They get sick. They die. The point of the state is that it keeps functioning regardless of what happens to the human beings who constitute it. Previous models of politics failed because they were too dependent on the people who made them function. A charismatic or powerful leader can only hold the state together for so long. What happens when he or she dies? A democracy is only as good as the citizens who participate in it. What happens when they lose interest or fall out among themselves? The Leviathan is meant to keep ticking over like a watch. So long as there are sufficient people to make up its moving parts, it should keep going regardless.

There are big advantages to this. One is reliability, which is often the quality we look for in a machine. We humans might have our robot-like qualities, but what makes us natural creatures is our limited lifespans: about three score years and ten, though in the middle of the seventeenth century that was only if you were very lucky. Death was the great leveller. Life expectancy in seventeenth-century England was somewhere around thirty-five. Hobbes lived to be ninety-one, which was remarkable, especially for someone who courted danger in his writings at a time when heresy could be punished by death. But states could live far longer than this. Hobbes imagined that the strength of the Leviathan came from the fact that it would be around long after he was gone. It need not be thrown off course by anyone's death. So long as the mechanism was working, it would keep going as people came and went.

Long-term planning is very difficult when short-term disorder is the norm, as it was in the seventeenth century. The biggest benefit of an artificial conception of politics would be its certainty. The state is like a watch not because it tells the time, but because its members can organise their lives according to the time horizon it establishes, which is far longer than theirs. It expands their perspective beyond immediate danger, beyond incessant blood feuds, beyond disease and death. It can do this without having to invoke God and the risks and rewards of eternal life – Hobbes did not believe in any of that. Instead, it is the durability of the machine that means people can plan. They can invest. They can inherit. They can imagine a better future, if not for themselves then for their children.

Hobbes had an extremely optimistic take on this. He thought that if the state could operate to an artificial rhythm of life – regular, reliable, long-lasting – human beings might flourish in all sorts of unexpected ways. Taking the burden of horizon-scanning from us would leave us free to deploy our distinctive human intelligence to do what we do best: dreaming up things that don't yet exist. Art, industry, luxury, leisure, science, fun – these need creative human input, something that is much harder to supply if we are required to spend our time worrying about all the ways politics might still go wrong. If politics could be made artificially secure – as tightly organised as any automaton – then we would be able to dream big.

The most benign version of this imagined future is a virtu-ous circle. The peace and security that accompany a successfully functioning state allow us to develop our best human qualities, including our ability to apply our intelligence to all sorts of tricky problems. Because the state is manufactured out of us – we are its parts – the better we get at problem-solving, the better the state should get at that too. It becomes more intelligent not because it gets smarter, but because we get smarter and help it make better decisions. We also get better at reimagining how the state might work, adjusting its internal mechanism to make better use of the strengths we can bring to it.

The Leviathan is not a problem-solving machine, like a smartphone. It is a decision-making mechanism, like a set of dice. It might not give you the right answer – it will simply give you *an* answer. But because it comprises people, once the people get better at coming up with answers, the state should too. These dice can think for themselves.[7]

Nasty or nice?

Despite this, *Leviathan* has a long-standing reputation as a pessimistic book. Its argument assumes that humans are incapable of peaceful co-existence without franchising out our decision-making power to an unaccountable higher body. At that point, we will have lost control of our fate, because whatever the state decides becomes our choice too. The price of our inability to live together is the risk of having binding decisions taken for us by an idiot or, worse, a monster – and still we are not allowed to complain. The options available can soon start to look deeply depressing – from the frying pan of political chaos to the fire of grim political oppression. Hobbes's apparent pessimism is compounded by his notorious description of what the absence of political authority would mean in practice. He called it 'the war of all against all'. Without the Leviathan to stand over them, human beings would spend their time either attacking each other or worrying about being attacked. Life would be 'nasty, brutish, and short'. No one would be safe.

According to Hobbes, this miserable situation is the natural condition of humankind. Politics needs the artificial mechanism of the state to drag us out of it. Nature is the problem because we are naturally a threat to one another. That's why we must create a mechanical version of ourselves. It sounds like a bleak, dehumanising political philosophy. Without artificial help, we are doomed to keep repeating a pattern of false political dawns, each time lapsing back into violent conflict. Left to our own devices, we sink. Only by taking a chance on the power of the Leviathan can we hope to rise.[8]

What can be set against this stark vision, so clearly shaped by the horrors of life in seventeenth-century Europe? How can it help make sense of the political possibilities of the twenty-first century? Present-day Western democracies appear to have moved a long way from the binary choice offered by Hobbes: either chaos or arbitrary rule. We have constructed states whose governments are fettered by constitutions, by the rule of law, by public opinion, and by elections. We are far from powerless to push back against leaders who do things we don't like. We can berate them, we can shame them, we can vote them out of office. The arbitrary power of the Leviathan has been tamed by centuries of resistance, to the point where Hobbes's understanding of the price we must pay for peace now seems to belong to the distant past.

Yet tamed is not the same as abolished. The basic machinery of the modern state continues to bear the hallmark of a mechanistic understanding of politics set out nearly four centuries ago. We still have governments that take decisions for us on matters of life and death, including war and peace. We allow them to do it, in part because we don't have the time or inclination to do it ourselves and in part because it is not clear we would be able to agree on what should be done anyway. We are bound by those decisions whether we like them or not. The state has the power to enforce its choices against anyone who resists, though it may not choose to use it. Most of the time, in contemporary democracies, these arbitrary powers are sufficiently buried beneath layers of legal limitations and political pushback that we barely notice them. But sometimes, in a crisis, they reveal themselves. Then we must acknowledge that we are still living with the Leviathan – older, wiser, but recognisably the same as before.

I am writing this nearly three years since the start of a pandemic that has seen states around the world – democratic as well as autocratic – confine citizens to their homes, limit their movements and outlaw routine displays of human connection, including weddings and funerals. Some did this harshly, others did it with a lighter touch, but all had the power to enforce compliance with their choices about public safety. As a result of these decisions, people died who might otherwise have lived, and plenty lived who might otherwise have died. We didn't get to choose for ourselves. The state chose for us. In choosing, the state reminded us that our lives remain in its hands.

In Ukraine, a twenty-first-century war is being fought that would be familiar from a much earlier time. This is not only because of the propensity for violence and civil breakdown that it has shown is still with us, even in a Europe that might have thought it had left such violence behind. It is also because war reinforces the hold of sovereign authority on the lives of citizens. On all sides, individuals are bound up in the choices of their states. Once the fighting starts, their lives effectively cease to be their own. States fight wars; people live with the consequences. Of course, it requires human beings to make any of this happen, both at the level of decision-making and at the level of enactment. Ukraine is what Volodymyr Zelenskyy says and does, and what Ukrainians do in response. Russia is Vladimir Putin's to dispose of, and so are the Russian soldiers who must pay the price for his decisions. This is not a robot war; it is horribly human. Yet it could not occur – not on this scale, not with this destructive power – without the Leviathan to organise it.

The Leviathan does not loom over the landscape of our lives any more. It has become a background feature for much of the time. Often it is not there at all. Hobbes hoped that as politics got easier, we would be able to spend less time thinking about it. We could get on with other things. That too is what has happened. One of the great luxuries of modern political life is that we need not be political if we don't want to be. In prosperous and peaceful states, it is possible to leave politics up to other people without worrying too much about the worst that could happen. It is only occasionally that this becomes impossible, and then we notice what it is that we have built. A monster.

There are thus two dangers posed by the artificiality of the Leviathan. The first is that it appears to its citizens as alien and cold – made of us but nothing like us. If the state is ruled by a distant oppressor, it will come across as a heartless machine, in which we are all bound up but with which we have little in common. Its decisions will implicate us, but we will encounter them as directed against us. This has been the experience of many modern citizens, including subjects of the most oppressive twentieth-century states, from Stalin's Russia to Mao's China. Those states were required to insist on – indeed to enforce with threats of violence – their identity with their people, precisely to cover up for its absence. They are what gives the Leviathan a bad name.

The other risk is that the artificiality of the state is naturalised. We get used to it because it doesn't seem so remote from who we are. The state's decisions commit us to courses of action we might undertake anyway, or at least that seem to leave us the freedom to pursue our own lives and to value our differences. We come to believe that the state is simply an extension of the human experience rather than an artificial version of it. Modern liberal democratic states, when they work well, have done a good job of creating this impression. But occasionally the mask slips, and we see that we are still dealing with an automaton that has the power to treat us as cogs in the machine.

When we encounter the Leviathan as remote and artificial, we feel we have lost control of something that was meant to protect us. Then it becomes monstrous. That is a sign of the failure of Hobbes's project. But when we see the Leviathan as an extension of who we are, we can also lose control, because we forget the ways in which it is still just a machine. It becomes something almost human, even though it is not. That is what can happen when Hobbes's project succeeds.

The imaginary giant

Artificial persons are mechanical constructs, which is what can make them seem robotic. Yet the idea that personality is a kind of mask opens up another way of thinking about what the state might be. Mask-wearing also involves creative performance. When an actor plays a part on stage, the aim is to get the audience to believe that the person speaking is not in fact the person acting. It is someone else, brought to life by human ingenuity, sympathy and technical skill. Humans can play the part of robots on stage, but robots still find it very hard to play the part of humans, in a theatrical sense at least. They lack the necessary imagination.

Politics is bound to be a performance of some sort, since part of what it means to take a political decision is to get other people to accept it, also by using human ingenuity, sympathy and technical skill. What makes politics different from the theatre is that the performance is backed up by the threat of coercion: you have to accept the action is real whether you like it or not. Yet pretending to be what we are not – to be more than we really are – remains fundamentally human. We use our imaginations to construct alternate realities, often ones in which we are the heroes. Politics cannot be insulated from such make-believe.

Perhaps, then, the state is an invention not just in the mechanical sense but in the imaginary sense as well. We didn't simply make it – we made it up. Actors can represent characters on stage that do not exist: the performance is real, but the parts are not. A production of *Hamlet* is real; Hamlet is not. Maybe the governments that represent the state are simply playing the part of the state. The business of government is real. But the state in whose name government is being done is not. It is a fiction.

If so, the state is nothing like an actual robot and it is nothing like an algorithm either. Although an algorithm is something we can't see or touch, it is still real. To call a recipe (even a recipe in a novel) a fiction is to misunderstand how recipes work; recipes can be good or bad, accurate or inaccurate, useful or worse than useless, even fantastical, but they are still real. If the state is a fiction, that means it doesn't exist. We might pretend it exists because we find that our lives go better if we do. But pretending is not the same as manufacturing. In the end, there's nothing there.

Hobbes took very seriously the idea that some persons – what he calls 'persons by fiction' – do not exist in their own right. They exist only when someone is pretending to be them. All sorts of people can be tasked with performing a particular role on behalf of others. The performance is artificial because these roles – lawyer, priest, politician, performer – are human-made; they don't exist in nature. The actions themselves are real but the person being represented doesn't have to be real, in the sense that it might be someone or something that can't act at all. This could be a character in a play, such as a god or a demon or a Danish prince. Or it could be something as prosaic as a bridge. If someone plays the part of a bridge, we can't say that the bridge is capable of performing those actions. That would be absurd – bridges can't act. It needs a real person to act the part.[9]

Why would anyone want to play the part of a bridge? It's unlikely to happen on stage, except in the most experimental forms of theatre. It would be simpler to build a fake bridge out of real materials – an artificial bridge – than to get a real person to dress up as one. It's also unlikely to happen in the management exercise I described at the start of this chapter, even though the exercise itself is a kind of make-believe. If a member of the group says they should all play at being bridges, it won't help them cross the river. The only way to get across is to build something that can serve as an actual bridge. The test here is not a suspension of disbelief, it is the suspension of real human bodies across a pretend river. The river might be fake, but the bridge needs to be real.

Where this idea can be very useful, however, is in law, where people often play the part of inanimate objects, to give these objects their own legal identity. We might well want a bridge to have its own rights and responsibilities: the right to refuse crossing to some, the responsibility to ensure a safe crossing to others. We do this because it is easier than attaching those rights and responsibilities to the people who happen to be in charge at any given moment. We pretend that it is the bridge's job to get us safely across, and we create legal structures to keep up the pretence. What can be done for bridges can equally be done for all sorts of other entities that can't speak or act for themselves, such as churches and hospitals. In a legal context it is very useful to be able to say that the church does this, and the hospital does that. Even though it's not strictly true. We call these legal fictions.

The Leviathan looks like it might fit this model. Real people perform all its actions – from building the state to governing the state to obeying the laws of the state – yet we find it useful to talk as though the state were doing these things, so as not to have to identify it with whoever happens to be in charge at any given moment. We give the state a pretend life of its own so that we can organise our own lives around its imagined ongoing existence. This is a different kind of durability from a reliably constructed machine. A fiction has the longevity of an idea that is impervious to physical decay. Fictions do not die so long as there are people around to believe in them. Hamlet dies every time the play is performed – that is part of the artifice of the production. But in another sense, Hamlet never dies. The character lives on.

So, is the state just a robot by fiction, an imaginary giant? It's an appealing idea and one with a serious pedigree – many political theorists have argued that when we look for what lies behind the performance of the state, we will find nothing there. Its power comes from our imaginations. But it is doubtful that this is what Hobbes had in mind. One problem is that he says the opposite. In the opening lines of *Leviathan* he calls the state an artificial person, not a fictitious one. His deepest fear was that politics would become dependent on what people happen to believe, rather than resting on something robust enough to survive the various fantasies of human make-believe (by which he meant, essentially, religion). The world of fiction might be potentially timeless but it is also extremely fickle: after all, a fiction is just a thought. And, having lived through decades of mindless violence, Hobbes knew that there was no knowing what people might think.[10]

The other problem with seeing the state as a fiction is that it depends on the quality of the performance. There can be a moment in any play when the production goes wrong, and it is clear to all watching that it is just an act. The scenery might collapse; a real fire might break out; the acting might not be convincing. Hobbes wanted the state to function like a mechanical person rather than a fictitious one in order to forestall these kinds of problems. If the state requires a suspension of disbelief, then it will fail when people start to believe the wrong things. An adept ruler might prevent that with a relentless focus on maintaining the message that all is well – and every state has its techniques for keeping up appearances, from ceremonial occasions to grand buildings to formal terms of address (this is as true of democracies as it is of monarchies). Rulers still need to play their part. But Hobbes was adamant that their ability to do this should not depend on how good they are at roleplay. Anyone should be able to do it. A terrible lead actor ruins a play, but a terrible lead politician should not be able to ruin the state. In that sense, politics is not like the theatre at all.

Hobbes described the Leviathan as a 'mortal god'. It was supremely powerful, but it could stop working, like any fantasy, and like any machine. States die when their internal machinery ceases to function. It is this machinery that is designed to keep people believing in the state, by ensuring that what the sovereign decides goes for everyone. The key mechanism for this is force: individuals must expect to face real, and unpleasant, consequences for disobedience. Yet force is not enough on its own to shape the human imagination, which is notoriously resistant to being told what it can and can't do. Here, then, is the deep puzzle – or perhaps the fatal flaw – at the heart of this version of politics: people must believe in the authority of the state for it to have force over them; and its force is needed to keep them believing in the authority of the state. It looks like a circular argument. And yet it might not matter. The state still seems to work. Get the machine up and running and somehow – perhaps even its makers won't know how – it will keep going. It is a black box.

Though the Leviathan is not an actual robot, it is not simply a fictitious robot either. This is not some make-believe story about a machine that doesn't exist, like *Frankenstein* or *The Iron Giant* or *Robocop*. *Leviathan* is not a fairy tale. Rather it is an attempt to build a mechanical fiction: something in which we believe because it is organised to work as efficiently as any machine.

States and corporations

The state is meant to be a uniquely powerful, uniquely reliable institution. But it's not. The world has many other kinds of decision-making machines, plenty of which can challenge the state for control and influence. This was as true in the seventeenth century as it is today, and in some ways even more so, since the state back then had yet to develop its full range of modern capabilities. All human societies contain organisations that can rival the claims of its central political authority, whatever form that authority takes. Some of these might appear to be more natural than the state, such as in the case of powerful families, which can claim to be based on blood not artifice. Others will be even more contrived, like the most arcane religions, with all their impenetrable ritual. But either way, no state can assume that its authority will go unchallenged by alternative power sources.

Hobbes was very concerned about the malign impact of influential families, and he despaired of the pretensions of obscure religions. But he hoped these would fade over time as the relics of ancient history, ultimately put in their place by the efficiencies of the modern world. What worried him more was another kind of institution: corporations, which he described as 'lesser commonwealths in the bowels of a greater, like worms in the entrails of a natural man'. The threat they posed was to eat into the authority of the state by replicating it.

The corporations Hobbes had in mind were not what we think of today as modern businesses. Rather, he was thinking about municipal bodies like the Corporation of the City of London, which in the seventeenth century mimicked the state by setting rules, demanding loyalty and even – as during the English Civil War – mobilising an armed militia. These corporations posed a threat to the state in the same way that organised crime might: as a rival source of authority, offering security backed up by threats of menaces. Hobbes was troubled by organised crime as well because thieves had their own rules and codes of conduct, which might undermine the authority of the state. But at least thieves were likely to fall out among themselves. Corporations, with their formal procedures and elaborate hierarchies and public offices, were more dangerous because their inner workings were highly regularised. Organised crime, then as now, was more like a family. A corporation was more like a state.

This potential duplication meant that all corporations needed to be tightly regulated. Their rules had to be approved by the sovereign, which would give them permission to operate under the terms of a charter. If the sovereign did not like how they operated, their charter could be taken away. Corporations lived and died at the behest of the state. That is what made them different from the state. What made them similar was that they were artificial persons too. Corporations, like states, were established to enable human beings to organise their affairs in a more durable, structured, coherent way. They could live far longer than any individual, and potentially longer than any state. The Corporation of the City of London was granted its initial royal charter in 1067, the year after the Norman Invasion. That made it older on almost any account than the English state itself. For the state to terminate it would have seemed an extraordinary assertion of primacy. That's why the state needed to have that power.

The other big difference between states and corporations is that the latter were not subject to the paradox of sovereignty. States had to be sovereign to assert their power and they had to assert their power to be sovereign: that's the paradox. Corporations are not sovereign. The source of their power is the state. This means that, if it wants, the state can insist they are nothing but fictions, fake persons designed to look as though they were real. The state can't insist that everyone believes in these fictions because no state can fully control what goes on inside people's heads. But the state can insist everyone act as though they believed it – by requiring them to transact with the corporation rather than with its governors or members, to buy from it, to sell to it, to sue it, to be sued by it. These rules are enforced in law. In this respect, corporations can be reduced to the status of mere legal persons.

The state can try to insist that its citizens behave as though they believe in it too – but it will not be able to force them to behave that way unless they are already willing to accept its authority. The paradox of sovereignty means the state needs to be real in ways that corporations do not. It cannot simply be reduced to the status of a legal person. It has to have a life of its own.

This, then, is the beginning of another story: of the complex, contentious, deeply consequential relationship between states and corporations, which can be similar enough to each other to require painstaking differentiation. The Leviathan inaugurates the world of modern artificial persons in two senses: as an artificial person itself, and as the creator of artificial persons. The machine gives rise to the possibility of many more machines. That is a large part of the story I want to tell in this book.

There is, though, another question that needs answering first. States and corporations are artificial agents, which means they can act even if they can't think for themselves. But what about the human collectives that can think even if they can't act? These are the ones that come closest to having their own kind of artificial intelligence, i.e. an ability to give the *right* answer, not just any old answer. Who are they? And where do they fit in?

2

GROUPTHINK

Groups with minds of their own

We all belong to different group organisations, of which the state is only one. Plenty of us work for large corporations. Plenty more work for small ones. We might alternatively work for other kinds of public or private institutions, from hospitals to universities to NGOs. We adhere to religions. We support football teams. We subscribe to political parties. These can be among the most powerful, semi-permanent presences in our lives. But many other groups form on a much more ad hoc basis. Some are relatively informal, such as friendship circles or family gatherings. Others are more formal but still temporary, as when we find ourselves co-opted onto a collective body for a particular purpose. Join this committee, sign up to this club, make this pledge: don't worry, it won't be for ever! But be careful – it's often for longer than you might think.

Big, durable organisations tend to require elaborate structures to sustain them: their internal machinery is often highly complex. But complexity does not necessarily equate to capacity. Smaller and more informal groups can do things that larger and more mechanical ones can't. One of the things they can potentially do is think for themselves. If we are searching for parallels with AI in the teeming world of collective human experience, we don't have to start with the Leviathans. We can also look at the minnows. Another place to begin is with juries. It is ad hoc collective bodies like juries that can often provide the most compelling examples of group intelligence. And of its opposite: group stupidity.

On 3 October 1996, at the end of a trial that had lasted nearly eleven months, the jury delivered its verdict in the O. J. Simpson murder case. The former football star had been accused of the brutal killing of his ex-wife and her friend in a cause célèbre that had consumed America. The jurors had in fact reached their decision the day before, after just four hours of deliberation, but delayed the announcement till the following morning to avoid the impression of unseemly haste. Nevertheless, when Simpson was acquitted, many commentators wanted to know how, after such a complex and lengthy trial, the jurors had managed to arrive at their verdict so quickly. Why did they not spend more time discussing all the evidence? What was the rush?

From the accounts of jury members who were willing to talk afterwards, it appears that what happened was this. They began with a straw vote on the basic question of guilt or reasonable doubt, and by a majority of 10–2 the jurors established they were ready to acquit. Then the foreperson went round the room, and individual jurors were asked to give their reasons for their doubts about his guilt. There were many and they differed: for some it was the racist history of a key prosecution witness or misgivings about the reliability of the DNA evidence; for others it was the fact a crucial piece of circumstantial evidence did not fit ('If the glove doesn't fit, you must acquit,' was the refrain of lead defence lawyer Johnnie Cochran), or a suspicion that blood samples had been tampered with; for at least one juror it seems to have been a generalised mistrust of the Los Angeles Police Department. This range of misgivings was enough for the two who had initially voted to convict Simpson to change their minds. The decision became unanimous. There was nothing more to discuss.[1]

But it could have gone another way. If instead of beginning with a poll on the question of whether to convict, the jury had begun by considering separately each possible reason for doubt, the same group of people – with the same opinions about Simpson's likely guilt – could have come to a different verdict. One or two jurors thought the glove was a reason to acquit, but perhaps the rest weren't persuaded that was enough; the same might be true for the racism, and the DNA, and the blood samples, and the history of the LAPD. In each case, an alternative vote might have revealed a majority against seeing any of these as grounds for reasonable doubt on its own. As a result, although the individual jurors had many different reasons for their doubts, the jury might have had none. This is one reason why it is often argued that juries should not begin with a straw poll on their overall decision before they have discussed the evidence. It does not allow the jury to make up its own mind.

The idea that a group of people could individually think one thing – innocent! – while the group itself thinks another – guilty! – is deeply counter-intuitive. How can the group have its own view when the group is nothing more than the views of its members? This is an example of what is known as the discursive dilemma. A more straightforward version might involve a panel of judges who must take a decision based on two separate criteria, with the verdict requiring that both criteria are met. The majority take one view as individuals, but when the group is polled for its view on the separate criteria, there is a different outcome (fig. 5).

	Judge 1	Judge 2	Judge 3	Majority decision
Did the accused do it?	Yes	Yes	No	Yes
Was it a crime, if the accused did it?	Yes	No	Yes	Yes
Is accused guilty?	Yes	No	No	No

5. Discursive dilemma 1

Two judges – a majority – think not guilty. But two judges – a majority – also think that both criteria are met, hence guilty. That is why the discursive dilemma is often described as a paradox: the group says both guilty and not guilty.[2]

This is not just a hypothetical exercise. Not only can the situation arise among actual judicial panels and juries, but it also has political implications. Here is another example, based on the impasse the British government found itself in over how to interpret the result of the Brexit referendum. In the aftermath of the vote the only apparent alternative to a deal negotiated by the government was to exit the EU without a deal. Yet for quite a long time both these options were rejected by a majority of voters, among whom there was nevertheless still a majority in favour of Brexit (fig. 6).

	Voter 1	Voter 2	Voter 3	Majority decision
Support Government Deal	No	Yes	No	No
Support No Deal Brexit	No	No	Yes	No
Support Brexit	No	Yes	Yes	Yes

6. Discursive dilemma 2

The public seemed to want Brexit and also not to want any of the means of achieving Brexit. So what did the public really want? It depends on which public we are talking about. Was it the one that was polled on the general question or the one that was polled on the different versions of the practical alternatives? As with the O. J. Simpson case, the order in which these questions are put can make all the difference. If the British public had been asked to vote in the referendum not just for or against Brexit in general but for or against a form of Brexit in particular, the result might have been very different.[3]

Groups appear to be able to think things that are not thought by their individual members. This can be extremely disorientating. If the Simpson jury had been told that their unanimous verdict did not in fact represent the view of the group, they would have been entitled to assume that someone was messing with their heads. Yet the group is not simply constituted by what is in the heads of its members. It also matters what happens to those thoughts when they are joined together. No member of the group can know that until it happens. Just as importantly, an outcome always depends on the sequence in which things happen, which is largely in the control of the group's leader. Armanda Cooley, the forewoman of the Simpson jury, could have shaped the view of the group by changing the way in which the views of the jurors were canvassed. But the jurors themselves, including Cooley, were relatively powerless to know what the jury as a whole was thinking.

The discursive dilemma suggests that we can indeed talk about groups having minds of their own. But two things need to be emphasised about these group minds. First, it does not follow that the group is necessarily more intelligent – or even better informed – than its individual members. Perhaps a more discursive approach would have produced a 'better' outcome in the Simpson trial – i.e. would have found him guilty. It is true that a later civil lawsuit found Simpson liable for the wrongful deaths of his ex-wife and her friend, and the jury in that case awarded $33.5 million to the families of his victims. But civil trials have different thresholds of proof from criminal trials, and no two juries are the same anyway.

In the case of Brexit, it could be argued that a group that supposedly wants an outcome but rejects all the means of achieving that outcome doesn't in fact want the outcome at all. Maybe the British people, though they seemed to have expressed a preference for the idea of Brexit, deep down knew they didn't want an actual Brexit. But voting for or against the idea was all the British people could do, since no actual version of Brexit was on the ballot. Moreover, the versions put forward prior to the referendum were hardly exhaustive, and bore scant resemblance to the final outcome. The British government eventually managed to put a version of Brexit into practice in 2020, following a general election in which 'Get Brexit Done' was the winning slogan. Who is to say which of these various iterations of collective opinion was the 'right' one?

This leads to a second point. Group minds in this sense are essentially mechanical, rather than organic. Their views do not emerge naturally; they must be constructed via an artificial decision-making process. The original Simpson jurors behaved naturally – that is, as most of us would behave if we weren't told to do otherwise – by starting off with a discussion about whether or not each of them thought he was guilty. It's what people around the world were doing too. It would have taken a highly structured intervention – perhaps an instruction to take the evidence bit by bit, to vote on each aspect and tabulate the results separately – to elicit a different point of view. There may be good reasons to structure decision-making in that way, but it won't happen unless we engineer it.

One argument in favour of this approach is that a careful eliciting of the group view is less likely to produce an outcome that has been swayed by personal prejudice. Asking for an immediate response to the question 'guilty or innocent?' can lead individual members of the jury to voice an instinctive, and therefore unreflective, opinion. It might also make some want to go along with the voice of the crowd. It takes a brave person to stand up to the group when the majority view is clear – that's why 10–2 can quickly become 12–0. The alternative – encapsulated in the film *Twelve Angry Men* (1957), where one recalcitrant juror changes the opinions of the other eleven – is heroic but rare (fig. 7).

That too depends on slowing the process down and moving

7. The hold-out and the angry men

from a rush to judgement to a more forensic dissection of separate pieces of evidence. Ironically, trying to find a way to the 'group mind' can be a means of countering what we have come to call 'groupthink'.

In the case of juries, tasked with ruling on a particular issue, the group ceases to exist once the decision has been reached. *Twelve Angry Men* ends with the jurors going their separate ways, back to their everyday lives. The individuals might have been changed by the experience, but the group loses its identity once it has performed its function. That is not true for many other kinds of decision-making bodies, which retain their identity as individual members come and go. This includes various kinds of executive committees, judicial bodies (including supreme courts) and parliaments. All have an identity that endures over time, so that it is possible to talk about how decisions of the group made today relate to prior and future ones. In this sense, though the state has no mind of its own, it may be run by bodies and organisations that do.

To take one example: the British Parliament is effectively sovereign and, in that sense, can do what it likes. At the same time, if it behaved as though its decisions had nothing to do with anything that had been decided before, it would be hard to have much confidence in it. Its identity would fracture into a series of seemingly disconnected acts. Allowing the group to have its own mind is one way of trying to establish coherence and consistency. If it is possible for the group to think something different from what most of its members think, then it ought also to be possible for the group to have views that do not change as its members change. Equally, if the view of the group does change, it can be argued that the group has reconsidered, rather than that the prior grouping has simply ceased to exist. We can say that Parliament changed its mind, instead of having to say that Parliament has no mind to change.

For this to be possible, though, the group needs to follow certain procedures consistently, ensuring that the unmediated view of the majority at any given moment does not stand in for the view of the group. Though this may be true of some committees, it is rarely the case with parliaments, where majorities are paramount. It also means that the group's identity will take priority over the identities of its members. There are reasons to be wary of this. A group mind generated by following a formal procedure does nothing to guarantee that the group has a conscience or a soul. It is mechanical. Identity is being generated through an artificial process, which can feel formulaic. The advantages are reliability and stability over time. The disadvantages are a certain coldness and inscrutability. After all, this is not a flesh-and-blood identity, with a beating heart, hopes and fears. It risks becoming just another machine.

Trying to find a group mind at the heart of the state runs into a familiar difficulty. It has to be mechanical in order to work, but because it is mechanical it will lack a quality that we often look for in politics, which is human feeling. What we gain in durability and consistency, we stand to lose in humanity. Bigger, in this case, does not necessarily mean better.

The wisdom of crowds

In 1974 the philosopher Thomas Nagel published a celebrated essay: 'What is It Like to be a Bat?' His answer is that human beings will find it almost impossible to know, since bat-like experiences are very far removed from our own, not least because their sensory apparatus is so different from ours. It's not just that bats can hear things we can't; they can hear in ways we can't imagine. As Nagel writes, 'anyone who has spent some time in an enclosed space with an excited bat knows what it is to encounter a fundamentally *alien* form of life'. At the same time, there must be *something* it is like to be a bat. Because bats do have experiences – they have the necessary sensory apparatus for that – they also have something we can recognise as a form of consciousness, even if it is nothing like ours. Being a bat is real. It is also completely inaccessible to anyone who is not a bat.[4]

What is it like to *be* a group? This is an equally hard question to answer, though for different reasons. Even if we accept that the group has a mind of its own – so that we can say that the group thinks for itself – it does not follow that the group has its own sensory apparatus. The group does not see or hear or taste or smell or feel. Only its members do that. It doesn't make sense to talk about the group having its own consciousness, as we might say of a bat. The group is more like a thinking machine than it is like a living creature. AIs that can follow complex patterns of inference to arrive at their own conclusions do not have consciousness in this sense either. They can think but they cannot experience. In the case of a bat, the internal state of being that makes it a bat is always out of reach for non-bats. In the case of a group or an algorithm, it simply doesn't exist.

Another difference, however, makes the group quite unlike either a bat or an algorithm. The parts of a bat's make-up that combine to produce its ability to have experiences are not themselves conscious. The bat experiences things. But its ears, say, no matter how sensitive, don't have their own experiences in anything like the same way. This is true of us too. The human brain, whose distinctive form of consciousness remains deeply mysterious, is made up of all sorts of different elements from physical matter to neural connections. Part of the mystery is that we can't identify which of these generates the experience of human consciousness. What we can say is that none of these is itself conscious. If you deconstruct a human being, you aren't left with lots of little consciousnesses. You are left with none.

But if you deconstruct a group, a collection of consciousnesses is precisely what you are left with. The group ceases to think when it is broken up – just as a jury ceases to exist as an entity when its job is done – but the members don't. Their individual senses of self remain intact, however bruising the experience. For that reason, group identity is always going to feel like a poor imitation of its component parts, which is not the case with bats, humans, or indeed thinking machines. One day, perhaps, an AI will acquire something that we recognise as a form of consciousness, even if it is nothing like our own. If that happens, the machine will have generated consciousness out of things that are themselves unconscious, including whatever bits of hardware or software enable it to function. In the meantime, machines that can think but don't experience are made up of parts that neither think nor experience. The machine, whatever it has – insight, problem-solving ability, pattern recognition – has more of that thing than any of the things that go together to make up the machine.

With groups, it is the opposite. We move from consciousness

to unconsciousness in the creation of group minds, whereas with bats, humans and even AIs, it is the other way round. This is what can give the group mind a particularly tenuous quality: it is highly artificial compared with the natural capacity of its component parts. It can also mean that confusion or incoherence on the part of the group tends to explode group identity rather than simply to distort it. When human beings believe contradictory things at once, or when they talk nonsense – which happens all the time – we don't conclude that there was no one there in the first place. I am still me, and you are still you, no matter how little sense we are making. We might lose our minds, but we don't cease to exist. Groups that stop making sense stop having an identity at all, because without a functioning mechanism to produce an identifiable group view nothing remains.

This is illustrated by another paradox in the theory of group choice, named after the eighteenth-century French philosopher and mathematician Nicolas de Caritat, Marquis de Condorcet. Condorcet's paradox states that, under certain conditions, a group will be unable to form any view at all. For instance, if a group is offered three choices and asked to rank them in order of preference, it is possible that the group will end up preferring X to Y, Y to Z, and Z to X. In other words, nothing can be its first choice, because any first choice is ranked behind one of the others (fig. 8). Voters A and C prefer X to Y; voters A and B prefer Y to Z; and voters B and C prefer Z to X. There is a majority in favour of all the preferences; or to put it another way, a majority against all the first preferences, because in each case something else is preferred. It's a total mess.

The striking contrast here is between the coherence of the views of the individual voters – there is nothing wrong in each case with their preferring the options in a different order from each other – and the incoherence of the group, which can't say anything about what it wants. This has led some philosophers to

Options

	X	Y	Z
A	1	2	3
B	3	1	2
C	2	3	1

(left label, rotated: **Voters**)

8. Condorcet's paradox

argue that the only solution in these circumstances is to have a 'dictator' – or as it is sometimes called, 'a Hobbesian sovereign' – to decide for the group. That leads to an even starker conclusion: without a dictator, there is no group at all. There is just a bunch of people with different views.[5]

This has always been one of the arguments in favour of the Leviathan: if groups are simply incapable of making up their mind on any complex questions, then better to let someone else – anyone else! – decide, whatever the risks. Better, in other words, to have someone in charge than no one at all.

However, Condorcet is also associated with another theory of group choice, one that points in a very different direction. This is Condorcet's Jury Theorem. It states that if a group of independently minded people is asked to choose between two options, the larger the group, the more likely it will be to arrive at the correct outcome. Here, bigger does mean better: larger groups know more than smaller ones. The key assumption is that if people thinking for themselves have a slightly better than even chance of knowing the right answer, the more of them you add to the group the greater the likelihood that the majority view will be the right one. Under these conditions, better to ask a million people than to ask twelve.

Of course, a million people is an unwieldy number to assemble, and maintaining independence among such a large group would be almost impossible – in any sizeable crowd the chances of a few individuals swaying others will increase, raising the risk of groupthink. Condorcet's theory depends on being vigilant against the lure of popular leadership, since there is no reason to suppose that influential individuals are also the ones who are likely to know best. Rabble-rousing is not an exact science: it is possible to be very good at it and to be completely wrong; the history of modern democracy provides enough evidence of that. Yet despite this, Condorcet's theory – and the many variations on it – offers the hope that a well-run democracy might still access something that the Leviathan never can: genuine collective artificial intelligence.[6]

Condorcet's insight is a version of what has come to be known as the wisdom of crowds. Large groups of independent-minded people can be surprisingly good at generating the right answer to difficult – if not exactly complex – questions. The classic illustration of this is the task of guessing the number of jellybeans in a jar at a fair: a simple enough question but a very difficult one to get right. No individual, no matter how good a guesser, is likely to get anywhere near as close to the correct answer as an average of the guesses drawn from a randomly assembled crowd. This holds even though some of those guesses will be way out – the advantage of large numbers is that randomness should mean wild guesses in one direction are cancelled out by wild guesses in the other, leaving an average that is close to the truth. A hundred guesses are good; a thousand will be better; ten thousand will be better still. The bigger the group, the less scope there is for individual bias to skew the results.[7]

This means, as with any jury, that the process must be carefully managed. Otherwise, you might end up with what is sometimes called the madness of crowds, for large groups can also do very stupid things. If a rumour takes hold of the group – a friend of a friend knows the number of jellybeans! – its collective guesses might be much further out than the best a careful individual guesser could do. If the group has a prior bias – jellybeans are much bigger/smaller than they look! – the same thing can happen. What is crucial for this to work is that group wisdom must be insulated from groupthink. The individuals who make up the group need to contribute their insights in a dispassionate way, trying their best to work out what is really going on without reference to what everyone else thinks. Second-guessing the rest of the group can produce all sorts of distortions. Primary guessing is what's required.[8]

There are many real-world applications of this idea, though they tend to be in economics rather than politics. Above all, the wisdom of crowds provides the basis for the modern faith that has come to be placed in markets. Markets function best when large numbers of people generate collective insights that are inaccessible to individual participants. Economists call these efficient markets, which are sometimes taken to be the closest thing we have to an oracle in our secular world. No one can know for sure how much people will be willing to pay for a particular good; each of us only knows what we are personally willing to pay. But take all those personal views together and you get the answer to the question of what something – perhaps what anything – is worth. The market doesn't just set the price, it *knows* the price.

Efficient search engines operate on a similar principle. None of us knows the answer to the question of where on the web to find the specific answer we are looking for. But take all our searches together and we find out, because the aggregate of many millions of searches gives us the answer. In this case, vast crowds can generate quite astonishing efficiency. What makes it work is that we are all looking for different things, but we are doing so in the same way.

The closest practical analogy to the jellybean example comes from prediction markets, where the wisdom of crowds is harnessed to try to predict otherwise unforeseeable outcomes. How to know when or where the next war will break out or natural disaster occur? No one can be certain about such things but asking a large group to guess is often the best way of getting close. The surest guarantee that the guesses will be dispassionate is to get participants to bet real money on the outcome, so that they are not simply following their whims. There is inevitably something a little distasteful about encouraging people to gamble on wars, terrorism, pandemics or other catastrophes. At the same time, it can be surprisingly effective. Here, then, is a potentially very useful political application of collective wisdom: what state wouldn't want to know in advance where the really bad stuff is coming from?[9]

Yet betting markets, even when large amounts of real money are at stake, can go badly wrong. What often gets in the way of their functioning is politics. Before both the election of Donald Trump in 2016 and the Brexit vote in the same year, the markets were confidently predicting that neither outcome would happen. In each case this prediction held right up until just minutes before it was proved false. This seems to have been partly a result of hedging on the part of gamblers, many of whom worked for financial institutions that were nervous of losing out if the vote went the 'wrong' way, and partly a result of group bias and wishful thinking. Bankers talk to each other much more than they talk to non-bankers. They knew what each other thought; unfortunately, they didn't know what the voters thought nearly as well. And the voters weren't gambling – they were voting.

This sort of groupthink can grip ordinary markets too. Market volatility – the endless cycle of boom and bust – is usually the result of second-guessing on the part of participants who are trying to work out what each other thinks, rather than trying to decide what they themselves think. The more money is a factor, the worse it can get, as small movements suddenly generate mass panics. Search engines are equally vulnerable to collective bias. Millions of people looking for different things in the same way can generate answers that reflect the biases that all those different searches have in common. These can include racism, sexism and other forms of collective idiocy. Worse, it can happen without the participants realising it. The search engine amalgamates what we have in common and reflects it back to us as the answer to what we are searching for. If what we have in common is prejudice, it will dress it up for us as the unvarnished truth.

There are two lessons to be drawn from all this. First, groups can be both smart and stupid. They can both have minds of their own and be mindless. The same group of people can generate very different collective viewpoints without changing their personal opinions, as likely to stumble into an incoherent paradox as they are to produce a vital insight. It entirely depends on how the group is put together.

Second, a group needs to be highly artificial if it is to be turned into a thinking machine. Some groups are more natural than others. They behave in ways that follow the inclinations of their members. That must be tempered by strict formal procedures if the group is to have a mind of its own. A crowd can demonstrate all kinds of surprising wisdom, but only if it is constrained by an artificial set of rules. Otherwise, crowds can simply run riot, or fall apart at the first sign of trouble. A thousand people aren't going to tell us the number of jellybeans in a jar unless someone makes it happen by setting the question and establishing the process and tabulating the results. A million people aren't going to tell us the price of anything unless the market for their transactions is carefully regulated. A jury isn't going to arrive at an independent verdict unless instructed how to do so.

To harness the artificial intelligence of any group of human beings takes time, trouble and a lot of organisational efficiency. It can, under certain conditions, be plugged successfully into politics to produce better outcomes. But it's not going to be enough to rescue any political system from its own foolishness. The conditions have to be right before the mechanism can work. That means behind any instance of the wisdom of crowds there still needs to be the artificial agency of the state, which is required to keep things in check. The unthinking, unfeeling collective body comes before the possibility of the collective mind.

Of course, some crowds will still escape from this artificial control. Some will even run riot. Then it becomes possible to talk about the feelings of the group. Crowds can smell blood, they can move from fear to anger, they can be riled up and they can be calmed down. It happens because this sort of crowd is an extension of the emotional state of its members, reacting to and feeding off each other. Crowds can form and disperse naturally, much like groups of animals, or even inanimate natural phenomena, such as rainstorms and whirlwinds. When a lynch mob starts tearing its victims apart, we don't ask what the crowd was thinking. We know at that point the crowd has stopped thinking and is simply in the grip of a terrible collective passion. When the violence is over, and the mob dispersed, it hardly makes sense to ask how to hold the crowd to account. The crowd no longer exists. We go after its members, and particularly its ringleaders.

What is it like to be this sort of crowd? That is a question we can perhaps answer. It feels like being a more powerful, more unthinking version of ourselves. Crowds don't have bat-like consciousness, but they do have sensations and emotions, often in place of rational thoughts. People who have been caught up in riots describe not knowing what they are doing. A collective feeling – along with a sense of impunity – takes over. The crowd is more than just the sum of the emotional state of its members because the members would not be in that state unless they were part of the crowd. But the crowd is still an extension of us. Anyone who has been trapped in an enclosed space with an excited crowd is not really encountering an alien being. It is like confronting the worst version of ourselves.

That is not true of a jury, especially one designed to generate collective wisdom. The group that knows the answer to a question that none of its members knows is nothing like its members. It will not have feelings. At some level, it will have to be as cold as any machine.

Decisions, decisions

For groups, as for other thinking machines, a lot depends on what we want them to do. Do we want them to tell us the truth, or do we want them to tell us what to do? They can either provide us with information they have and we lack, or they can take us down one path rather than another. We might think this choice depends on them. But really it depends on us: on how we set them up and what we expect from them. There is another way to put this: are we looking to them for an answer, or are we looking to them for a decision?

Any question can invite an answer, or it can invite a decision. Sometimes there is no real difference. The answer to a proposal of marriage requires a decision, and that decision will give you your answer. If we want an answer to the question of whether there will be a war, we need to wait on the decision of the potential combatants. If someone chooses to fight, someone else will learn the answer to an important question. Do they dare attack? Yes, they do.

But sometimes an answer is nothing like a decision. When a crowd is canvassed for its guesses about the number of jellybeans in the jar, the answer that comes from averaging those guesses is not a decision about how many beans there are. The crowd doesn't get to decide that. It just gets to guess, and the best answer will be the one that comes closest to whatever is the true figure. A decision is an outcome that changes the situation that is being decided over: the world will become a different place after the decision is made. It may not be as dramatic as the move from peace to war, but something will have shifted. Nothing about the number of jellybeans changes after the crowd has made its choice. The right answer is still the right answer whether they get it right or not.

The same group can perform both tasks – deciding and answering – but that doesn't mean they are performing the same task. For instance, a jury must decide if the accused is guilty. Their decision is an answer to the question of what the jury thinks. In some circumstances, including for most legal purposes, that answer will also determine whether the accused is guilty or not. But we can also ask whether it was the right verdict: did the accused in fact do whatever he or she is charged with? The answer to this question does not depend on what the jury decides. It can make perfectly good sense to say the jury got its decision wrong. A decision may be a mistaken answer to a question, at the same time as being the only possible answer to the question of what has been decided.

When a Condorcet jury expands to improve its chances of arriving at the right answer, it is trying to determine something that is independent of its decision-making power. An increase in size gets it closer to the truth. A very different sort of group might become more powerful the bigger it gets, but it gets further from the truth at the same time. When a violent crowd grows by drawing more people in, it can do greater damage. Its choices become more forceful, but they do not become more accurate. Violent crowds don't care about the truth. They are making their own reality. Some groups are trying to get at the facts. Some groups *are* the facts.

However, it can be hard to hold on to this distinction. Markets know the price of goods; they also decide the price of goods. If I want to know how much it costs to buy a share in Tesla, the market will tell me. There is no other way to find out. I can't claim that there is another price that is fixed somewhere else and which the market is trying to guess at. The best I can do is insist that the market price is not one I am willing to pay, because I have a different view about what Tesla is worth. That says something about me; it doesn't reveal the truth about the real price. Yet my unwillingness to buy also helps shape the price, which might drop as a result (if I am a big enough investor). The market price is constantly changing, unlike the number of jellybeans in the jar. It is based on a series of decisions about how much to spend on Tesla stock; at the same time, those decisions are shaped by the answer the market gives. Decisions and answers feed off each other.[10]

Notwithstanding how hard it can be to separate out a decision from an answer, it remains important that we can tell the difference. A share price that is fixed by the decisions of a few powerful people – perhaps even by the company itself, which may be concealing important information – is quite unlike one that reflects a wider view of what the company is worth. We learn something very different from the first than from the second: in one case, we discover only what someone wants us to know; in the second, we discover impartial information that cannot be accessed any other way.

James Carville, a political advisor to Bill Clinton in the 1990s, once said: 'I used to think that if there was reincarnation, I wanted to come back as the president or pope ... But now I want to come back as the bond market. You can intimidate anybody.' The bond market is frightening for presidential advisors. Still, there is a big difference between fearing the bond market because it is being used by powerful investors to intimidate a government – by engineering a run on its national currency, for example – and fearing it because it has exposed something that a government might prefer to be hidden – that its public finances are not what they seem. You can be frightened of the pope because of what he can do – excommunicate you – or because of what he might know – that you are a sinner. The first is a decision. The second is an answer.[11]

When the British people voted for Brexit, the question on the ballot paper read: 'Should the United Kingdom remain a member of the European Union, or leave the European Union?' The voters were being asked for a decision: what did they want to happen? But they were also being asked for an answer: what did they think should happen? On the first, their choice was definitive. Once a majority had expressed a preference, that was the answer. But on the second, it was possible for the answer to be the wrong one. To believe that it was right – that a majority for Brexit meant that Brexit was the right answer for Britain's future – requires a strong faith in the wisdom of crowds.

This is not necessarily wishful thinking. Electorates can know things that experts don't. The British government tried to persuade voters tempted by Brexit that it would result in immediate financial disaster. The voters were not persuaded. The voters were right: the predicted disaster did not happen. (The longer-term consequences are another matter.) In 2003 the British government tried to persuade the public that Saddam Hussein had weapons of mass destruction. Polling showed that the public did not believe the government. The public was right. There were no weapons. These, though, are narrowly defined questions. The broader implications of Brexit, like the wider consequences of British involvement in the war in Iraq, cannot easily be reduced to the sorts of questions that tap into the wisdom of crowds. Brexit, and war, are not jellybeans in a jar. If a government tries to turn them into jellybeans-in-a-jar propositions – Don't do it because this will happen! Let's do it because that's what he has! – more fool them.

To say that a decision is always an answer, and an answer always a decision, risks serious confusion, or worse. Any market that has been geared towards an outcome, but which is still treated as an oracle, spells disaster in the long run. The 2008 global financial crisis stemmed in part from the failure of investors, along with regulators, to distinguish between what the market was saying about the value of mortgage-backed derivatives – that they were a safe bet – and what the markets had been engineered to say about them – that they were a safe bet. It looked like an answer, but it was really a decision, and decisions can be badly wrong. Yet because markets are designed to produce answers rather than decisions, when they do go wrong, they lack the power to rescue themselves. They can't decide to change course. That required the decision-making power of the state, which stepped in with its own answers – a series of decisions to bail out failing banks and to take on their debts. States could do this because they are not oracles – they are coercive authorities, whose decisions can be made to stick.

This potential for dangerous confusion extends to the world of machine learning and search engines. Search engines are designed to give us answers, not decisions. Google doesn't decide what you are looking for, in the way that a state decides how much tax you should pay. It works out what you are looking for, and it tells you where to find it. Nonetheless, the answers that it gives are shaped by the decisions people make. If you Google the question 'What is beauty?' and are shown a series of images of white people, it would be a mistake to think this was an answer to your question, rather than a reflection of the choice of many people to equate whiteness with beauty, and the decision of the designers of Google's algorithm not to correct for that. Treating a decision as an answer risks mistaking a prejudice for a fact.

Equally, treating an answer as a decision risks mistaking a fact for a judgement. If someone pursuing an insurance claim supplies the information asked for by the insurers and is told that 'the computer says no', it sounds as though the decision to reject the claim has been made by an algorithm. But that is not true. The algorithm has answered the question of whether the information meets the criteria required for a successful claim – that is an answer, not a decision. The decision to reject the claim lies with whoever decided on those criteria. An answer dressed up as a decision can be designed to make it appear as though the decision brooks no alternative. When the computer says no, there is apparently nothing anyone can do about it. But that too is an illusion. If there is nothing anyone can do, that is because someone has decided to leave it up to the algorithm. It is not the computer's decision to make.

Groups can decide things and groups can know things, just as other kinds of machines can. Neither requires consciousness. All it takes is a procedure, or an algorithm. Still, there is a big difference between deciding and knowing. Deciding to turn left rather than right is not the same as knowing you must turn left rather than right. One is a choice. The other is an answer. Because groups, like machines, lack consciousness, it is asking too much to expect them to understand which is which, i.e. to know whether they are making the truth or identifying the truth. A group that has decided to turn left is making a world in which that has happened. A group that knows it must turn left is reflecting a world in which that is the right thing to do. It is up to us to know the difference.

In 2004, in the aftermath of the US invasion of Iraq, a presidential aide to George W. Bush told the *New York Times* journalist Ron Suskind that his interlocutor belonged to 'the reality-based community', where 'solutions emerge from your judicious study of discernible reality'. He went on: 'That's not the way the world really works any more. We are an empire now, and when we act, we create our own reality. And while you are studying that reality – judiciously as you will – we will act again, creating new realities, which you can study too, and that's how things will sort out.' Suskind characterised this as 'faith-based' politics. Another name for it is realpolitik. Above all, it rests on the assumption that decisions determine answers more than answers determine decisions. It is entirely consistent with the workings of the Leviathan, which is able to decide things without having to know them first.[12]

However, it is also an approach that is highly vulnerable to groupthink. The run-up to the Iraq War was marked by a deep reluctance on the part of the American and British governments to access either the wisdom of crowds (including the millions who marched against the war) or the collective intelligence of experts in the reality-based community. Instead, decisions were characterised by a rush to judgement on the part of those who knew only what they wanted to be true. In such circumstances, groups of like-minded individuals tend to reinforce each other's convictions, often with disastrous consequences.[13]

The Leviathan doesn't know any better. But the people who run it need to.

Carrying the can

If groups can think for themselves and decide for themselves, can they be held accountable for their mistakes? Plenty hangs on this question for the human beings who go together to make up any group. Plenty hangs on it for the groups too, including the most powerful ones. If the group is responsible, then by implication its members are not. But if the members won't pay for the mistakes of the group, who will?

Imagine – if such a thing were possible – that the families of the victims decided to sue the O. J. Simpson jury for acquitting him of a crime it could later be proved he committed. Then it might make sense to hold each member of the jury liable, since the verdict was based on their individual choices. But imagine the reverse. Say the original jury had adopted a discursive procedure of assessing the evidence separately and decided to convict. Then it turns out Simpson was innocent after all. Were he somehow to sue the jury, it could hardly make sense to hold its individual members responsible, since each of them believed that he was innocent. The verdict wasn't their choice. It was only the group that thought him guilty. Yet how could Simpson go after the group, which ceases to exist once the jury has delivered its verdict? If the group has a mind of its own, then it can appear no one is responsible for its decisions.

As a result, group identity poses a nasty dilemma. The clearer it is that the group is not reducible to the sum of its parts, the harder it will be to hold the group to account. Some have despaired at this mismatch. The eighteenth-century jurist Edward Thurlow famously complained: 'Corporations have neither bodies to be kicked, nor souls to be damned; they therefore do as they like.' Sentient beings with bodies and souls disappear inside the group once it has acquired its own identity. They can shrug their shoulders as the victims of the group's decisions come looking for justice. Meanwhile, the group has no shoulders to shrug.

The reverse is also true. Crowds – unlike corporations and other artificial collective bodies – have feelings. They can be made to suffer. Just look at the audience for a powerful theatrical production. That group of people will feel things collectively that they would not – could not – feel on their own. An actor can make them laugh or cry, and actors will speak of an audience as having its own personality – tough to please, perhaps, or quick to respond. But no one can hold the audience to account after the performance is over. That's because the audience no longer exists – there are just its individual members, gone their separate ways. What makes the audience, like any crowd, so responsive is the connection felt in the moment. To sustain a connection once the moment has passed would require building an artificial version of the group with its own procedures – more like a formal committee, and less like an audience. But a formal committee, unlike an audience, doesn't really do feelings.

There are plenty of different ways to try to tackle this dilemma. Even if the group can't have a body or a soul, it can have possessions. Groups – that is, groups with a distinct and durable artificial identity – can own things for themselves. They can have bank accounts and budgets and expenses. They can sue and be sued, and if found liable the group will have to pay from its own resources. This is, as we shall see, the basis of modern corporate life. But it poses what would now be called an obvious moral hazard. Because the group will pay, while its members will not, its members may choose to behave more recklessly with that knowledge in mind. They will not ultimately carry the can. This matters because although the group is not reducible to its members, its choices are still decided by its members. If they think they have the power to choose without bearing responsibility for the consequences, they may decide very differently from if they believed they had the responsibility too. Modern corporate life, like modern political life, is sometimes deeply reckless. This is one of the reasons why.

We can try to get round the problem of moral hazard by introducing extra procedures that force the members of the group to treat the interests of the group as seriously as they might treat their own. If the members mind that the group suffers, then they are more likely to be responsible in their choices. They can be required to think about the group as an ongoing concern and base their decisions on a desire to maintain its continuity and integrity, which won't happen if they squander its resources. It is amazing how often people do behave like this. They sacrifice their own interests for the interests of the group, and they may even care more about the group's fate than they do their own. This is true even of people who work for corporations. They can devote their lives to ensuring that something valuable is there long after they are gone.

Yet there is still a problem. If people are forced to behave like this – by rules and regulations that require it – then there is something highly artificial about it. The group will be nothing more than its procedures, which will make it hard to believe in it as a real, ongoing concern. Put simply, it's harder to care when all you have is a committee rulebook. When people do care, it's because they feel a personal connection to the group – maybe the company is one they founded, or the club is one to which all their friends belong. But if the connection is personal, then it's harder to say that the group has an identity of its own. Instead, it is constituted by the feelings of its members. If the group *is* us, then it's more responsive, but less of a group in its own right. If we want the group to be responsible, then we need to sever the connection with the feelings of its members (just as the Simpson jury would have needed to get beyond the feelings of its members about his guilt or innocence). Impersonal groups can be held to account. But impersonal groups can't be made to care.

The alternative is to give up on the group and go after its members instead. Let those with real bodies and souls carry the can! Group decisions can be disaggregated so that we can try to identify the people responsible. But that doesn't solve the problem – it just relocates it. Which people? If a choice was a majority decision, then we might say that only those who voted for it are responsible. Yet that is bound to change how people vote, knowing that it will rebound on them if something goes wrong. If voting for Brexit also meant taking personal responsibility for Brexit, it is easy to imagine that the vote would have gone differently. Instead, we can say that a group decision is to be treated as a collective responsibility, binding those who voted against as well as those who voted for. That, for the most part, is how we think about democratic decision-making – it's your government whether you voted for them or not. But if the responsibility is collective, why then does it not attach to the group rather than to its individual members, who may have played no part in the decision? And we are back where we started.

There is no escaping these dilemmas, and laws dealing with collective responsibility must grapple with them all the time. Crowds can be reduced to their most influential members – the ringleaders – but singling them out for blame risks ignoring the extent to which it was the crowd that did the damage. But going after the crowd risks dragging in hangers-on or maybe even innocent bystanders. Many people have been convicted for murder simply by dint of being present when someone else committed the crime. The term for this sort of complicity in English law is 'joint enterprise'. It can seem deeply unfair. Yet it can also be true that the crime would not have been committed if the larger group had not assembled. And there is no way to punish a gathering of individuals – which has no bank account of its own – without going after its members. Collective responsibility will always be a square peg in a round hole.[14]

The question of how to attach human-like responsibility to things that are not human is an acute problem in the age of AI. Who should we blame when a machine harms a human – the machine itself, or the humans who made it? What this question is not is new. It is as old as the history of collective human enterprise. To hold the machine responsible risks letting humans off the hook, but to hold the humans responsible risks ignoring the culpability of the machine. To disaggregate a decision into its human elements can be to misrepresent its essential character. Yet failing to reduce it to the level of the human can allow it to remain inhuman instead.

As we start to worry about who can be held to account when robots – from self-driving cars to the latest decision-making algorithms – go wrong, we need to remember we have been here before. There are no easy answers, but that doesn't mean that we have no experience of the problem. That said, there remains one fundamental difference between group responsibility and robot responsibility. Groups are made up of humans. Robots are not. We can't take the robot apart to find a piece of the robot to answer for the whole, as we can with groups. Either we blame the robot or we blame the people who designed it, manufactured it, owned it, regulated it, or simply allowed it to exist. We look outside for the human input. With groups we look inside.

In the search for culpable consciousness, insisting on it for AI requires us to build smarter machines. Insisting on it for groups requires us to take the group apart.

Given that the creation of group identity is so problematic and so wholly artificial – it simply won't happen in any reliable way if we let nature run its course – why do we bother? Isn't it more trouble than it's worth? The answer is that we do it because it is so very useful. The reliability is the point. Having collective entities that can take decisions and carry responsibility for those decisions is what has made our world possible. These arrangements are efficient. They are durable. They are scalable. And they work precisely because they are inhuman. Their efficiency is the efficiency of machines. Their durability is the durability of things that have no natural lifespan. Their scalability is the scalability of replicable mechanisms. The price we pay is that we must break them up to find their humanity.

These artificial creations are all around us. Many are so familiar that we fail to notice how artificial they are. Not just states and corporations, but schools and universities, town councils and city halls, sports clubs and religious organisations, political parties and radical cooperatives: all require that we build structures that allow them to go beyond the human frailties of their members, who may leave, or lose interest, or fall out, or get sick, or die. We need these organisations to be something more than us if they are to work. Which means they will be something less than us too.

What they are not is easy to understand. This chapter has

looked at some versions of group life that are highly distinctive, in part because they are philosophical constructs. My account of the O. J. Simpson verdict is not a historical reconstruction of what happened. I have said nothing about the context or the pressures or the hysteria surrounding the case. These jurors had been cut off from their families and trapped together in hotels for nearly a year. Who knows what their state of mind was? No one who was not present in the jury room can be sure what really took place there. No tabulation of the discursive dilemma can capture what it is like to take an important decision – one with the power to change lives in an instant – under extreme pressure.

Yet even those who were present may fail to understand. We all belong to groups that do things whose reasoning is hard to reconstruct, even if we were a part of it. Any workplace contains decision-making structures seemingly designed to obscure what is really going on from the people who work there. What's more, any complex organisation will contain a wide variety of different collective decision-making bodies. Some will require unanimity, some a majority decision, some discussion, some a ballot, some an improvised arrangement to meet a crisis. Some will be organised to reach decisions. Some will be arranged to arrive at answers. Some will, perhaps, be capable of doing both. We might say that the organisation thought this, or did that, but we will rarely know precisely what that means.

It is true that we can always disaggregate group identity to look for the human element. But it is asking too much to think that any humans we find will know what it is they have been a part of. Let's not kid ourselves that the age of AI – with the looming challenges of black-box decision-making and algorithmic procedures whose outcomes are a mystery even to their creators – poses a unique challenge for human understanding. Just look at your own life. Do you fully understand where the group decisions come from that shape who you are? Do you understand even when those decisions are ones you have been part of yourself? I thought not.

The fact that groups are made out of people doesn't make them any easier to see inside than other kinds of machines. The black boxes are all around us already. In one sense, at least, they *are* us.

3

A MATTER OF LIFE AND DEATH

Bearing the burden

As I write this, the American national debt stands at more than $30,000,000,000,000 (30 trillion dollars). It's impossible to be more precise because the figure on the US debt clock rises by around $10,000 per second – that's nearly $1 million in the time it has taken me to compose these two sentences. Stare at it too long and you start to lose your mind. Whichever way you look at it, it's a staggering sum of money.[1]

Who owes this $30 trillion to the many different holders of US treasury bonds? The obvious conclusion is that it's the American public who owes the money, since no one else is going to be paying it back. But if you divide this amount by the number of US citizens, you get a per capita debt of more than $90,000 (and if you divide it by the number of taxpayers – excluding all the children and many others who really can't pay anything back – it's nearly $250,000 per person). This is clearly unsustainable. Around half of Americans have net assets of less than $100,000, so bearing their share of the national debt would wipe them out. Nor is it distributed according to ability to pay. No one ever gets a national-debt bill. They get taxed, of course, but their taxes go to pay for all sorts of different things. This debt does not belong to the American people.[2]

We often call the national debt 'government debt', and we call the bonds that represent it 'government bonds', but it doesn't belong to the government either. No single administration can be held liable for the debt – no one is going to go after a US president or the various members of Congress to cough up the cash to cover the interest payments, no matter how rich they are. At the same time, no administration can refuse to acknowledge the debt on the grounds it belongs to their predecessors. The debt carries over from presidency to presidency.

The American people fund the national debt, and the American government runs the national debt. But the debt isn't theirs. It belongs to the American state. Saying that the debt belongs to the state makes it possible to borrow for the very long term, at relatively cheap rates, precisely because it does not depend on the ability of any given individuals, no matter how numerous, to pay. The state services the debt regardless of who happens to constitute it at a particular moment. In this case, the state is required to be more than the sum of its parts so that it can do things that the sum of its parts cannot do on their own.

But here we run into a familiar conundrum. We say the state can do certain things – borrow vast sums of money and be liable for paying them back – that its various parts cannot do because they cannot carry such an enormous burden. Yet the only people who can perform the actions to make this possible are the government and the people – the government to sign the documents and issue the bonds and raise the taxes, and the people to hand over the money. Only the state *can* borrow this amount of money and yet the state is incapable of undertaking the necessary actions for itself. After all, it's not as if anyone ever transacts with the American state in the sense of meeting with it or interacting with it personally. We never bump into the Leviathan. Go looking for the state and all you will ever find are officials playing their various roles. Pull back the curtain, and the wizard is just a bunch of people like the rest of us.

This is what makes it tempting to say that the idea of the state as an autonomous being is simply a fiction. We pretend it's the state that owes the money because it's convenient, even though we know that the state is nothing more than the people who constitute it. But there are two reasons to be doubtful that this captures what is so distinctive about the state and its powers. First, debt is a matter of faith. The word 'credit' shares its roots with the word 'credibility'. Lending money is a question of believing you will get it back. It doesn't matter how real the person is to whom you lend the money – that won't decide their creditworthiness. Flesh-and-blood people – up to and including mega-rich oligarchs – are a much worse credit risk than most states. What counts is the confidence you have in the likelihood of repayment.

Second, what makes states so reliable is the formidable machinery of government that ensures repayment is an ongoing obligation rather than a political preference. This machinery is real. States have elaborate mechanisms in place to ensure that, as governments come and go, the business of the state keeps on keeping on. The great departments of state – including the US Treasury – operate vast bureaucracies that continue grinding away notwithstanding the whims of their ostensible political masters. Governments can tamper with this machinery – they can try to adjust what it requires of them – they can even wish it wasn't there. Sometimes they will do their best to wreck it. What they can't do is wish it away by saying they don't believe it exists. All debts are one kind of fiction or another. Of these, state debt is the most mechanical. That's why it can also be the most reliable.

Surrounding state debt are a host of institutions that reflect different aspects of group life. The state bureaucracy will include all sorts of committees, some with minds of their own, some merely a front for the preferences of their political superiors. State debt is priced by bond markets – the ones James Carville wanted to come back as – which may or may not display the wisdom of crowds. States also have their reliability as borrowers rated by credit agencies, which may or may not be competent assessors. Democratic states will find their fiscal policies shaped by electoral outcomes. Both left and right tend to believe that democratic electorates are not good at deciding what to do about debt: the right believes that voters are inclined to be profligate (always preferring jam today over jam tomorrow), and the left suspects that the voters are too prone to fall for strictures about the need for belt-tightening. Yet what is notable is that, despite this, the borrowing costs of stable democratic states tend to be the lowest in the long run.[3]

The state itself, however, is none of these things: neither a committee nor a crowd nor a price nor an electorate. It is its own thing. This is its superpower. But to be clear: its superpower is not superintelligence. No one lends to states because they believe that states are better at knowing what their debt is worth, or even of knowing the best way of spending what they borrow. States *are* profligate, inefficient and prone to political tinkering. Credit agencies exist for a reason. What the state has is an ability to sustain the consequences of the choices made on its behalf for longer than any other kind of entity. Its superpower is its durability, which is enormously helpful in the make-believe world of credit and debt. In 2017 the British state repaid some of the bonds that had been issued one hundred years earlier to fund the First World War; these debts were in turn a consolidation of previous borrowing incurred in the eighteenth and nineteenth centuries. Modern states, including the American state, which is both the most heavily indebted and the most powerful organisation in human history, are cumbersome and menacing, but surprisingly reliable. Hobbes would be proud.

If states were nothing but debt-servicing machines, they would be supremely reliable. But they are not. In reality, states wriggle out of their debts all the time. They can do this because the power that enables them to take on vast obligations also lets them slough off those obligations. Because states control their own money supplies, when they borrow in their own currency they can inflate away the cost by creating more of it. States that borrow in foreign currencies are much more vulnerable to losing control of their debts. That said, such states still have the option of default. Many of them exercise it.[4]

States that do default are hard to hold to account – they have no soul to damn, nor body to kick. What they do have is the power to decide what, if anything, they wish to surrender to their creditors. It's their sovereign choice. When Argentina defaulted on its debt in the 2010s, one vulture fund (so-called because it bought up high-risk government bonds with a view to pursuing legal remedies once the state had failed to honour them) demanded Patagonia as repayment. It was never going to happen, since it would have required a military intervention. At the end of the nineteenth century the British state would occasionally send warships to sit menacingly off the coast of Latin American countries that were being slow with the interest payments on borrowing taken out in the City of London. Even the American state doesn't do that today.[5]

Default is never costless. States that default must inevitably pay more for their next round of borrowing (if they can borrow at all). This is the power of the bond markets. Since states often borrow most heavily from their own citizens, default also risks a loss of confidence in the entire system of government. But since states have the entire machinery of government at their disposal, they can seek other remedies, including raw coercion. In the summer of 2022 Russia defaulted on the interest payments on its foreign debts, unable to meet them because of the price it was paying for the war in Ukraine. This has not as yet diminished its ability to keep fighting, nor to keep its citizens in line.

One reason states cannot simply be treated as debt-servicing machines is that their debts exist to fulfil the state's other purposes. States – democracies as well as autocracies – are also war-making machines. Many of the same superpowers that enable them to take on a vast burden of debt also enable them to take on the vast burden of war. The durability of states allows them to make commitments that carry from one administration to the next. The power of the state to commit the resources of its citizens – their lives as well as their money – makes them formidable opponents. That's why a decision to go to war, no matter what the cause, should never be taken lightly. Any war can take on a life of its own because every state has a life of its own to defend.

The relationship between the state's debt-raising powers and its war-making powers has long been a mutually reinforcing one. In the words of the political scientist Charles Tilly: 'War made the state, and the state made war.' States made wars by fighting them. Wars made states by requiring them to be funded, first through extractive taxation, then through long-term borrowing. Costly wars also require that the people who do the actual fighting are rewarded for their efforts. Otherwise the sacrifice won't seem worth it. Much of the vast machinery of state in the modern world – from government treasuries and national banks to welfare systems and national insurance schemes – was created either to pursue war or to secure its legacy.[6]

However, the burdens of warfighting and of debt-carrying are not the same. Along with the fiscal burden of running a killing machine there is the moral burden of the killing itself. By ascribing the violence to the state – so that the government that orders the violence and the soldiers who perform it and the citizens who support it are not personally liable for it (except in cases of separately defined criminality) – we are able to ensure that the consequences are not too great for any individual or group of individuals to bear. Human beings who kill may not be able to sleep at night. They have a tendency to torture themselves with remorse, and many – the decent ones – will shy away from it altogether. But humans who kill on behalf of the state can pass off much of the moral responsibility onto an entity that doesn't sleep anyway. Not sleeping is part of the state's superpower. It makes the state endlessly vigilant, bordering on the paranoid. Modern war would be impossible without this artificial capacity to keep going. It is what lets decent people live with doing terrible things.[7]

The burden-sharing arrangement of war is analogous to debt, even though it is a very different kind of burden. Again, it is tempting to see it as a convenient fiction. We say that it is the state that fights the war simply so that the human beings who are actually responsible for it don't take on an unbearable personal responsibility. The state becomes a kind of dumping ground for the things humans do but don't want to own. When we kill as individuals it is murder. When states do it, it is not. Yet states don't actually do it – they can't, because they can only act through human beings. Saying that states kill looks like a kind of make-believe designed to conceal the unspeakable truth: it's actually us. If we stopped saying it, wouldn't there be less killing, because there would be fewer places for us to hide?

Yet, as with debt, there are reasons to doubt we can simply call the state's capacity to kill a fiction and wish it away. The decision-making machinery of the state – on which we rely for so much and without which the world as it currently exists would be impossible – does too many different things for us to disaggregate them. If we need its identity and durability in some areas, we can't simply refuse to acknowledge them in others. What's more, we need a state that is more than the sum of its parts for peace as well as for war. Treaties hold – when they do hold – because the governments that sign them do not only sign them on their own behalf; they bind the state, and therefore future governments, too. When autocrats come to believe that they *are* the state then peace becomes harder to achieve, because each new ruler will make a new set of rules. Lasting peace requires that we treat the state as a separate entity from both rulers and ruled. It is the only way to have confidence in it.

Democratic peace theory is a political science thesis that

claims democracies don't go to war with each other. This seems to be broadly true – of all the wars in modern history only a tiny fraction have been fought between states that could be called democratic regimes. Where there is less agreement is why this should be so. Some argue that it is because democracies have better moral judgement: in a variation on the wisdom of crowds it is assumed that asking the voters about the wisdom of war is likely to produce caution because most people understand what hell it is. The problem with this argument is that war and peace are rarely on the ballot paper – elections tend to be decided by domestic issues. Moreover, when democracies do go to war their citizens are often willingly co-opted for the fight. It is a myth that the populations of Europe were gung-ho for war in 1914, whereas their elected politicians were the ones with the misgivings. But it is still true that citizens signed up to fight in large numbers, whatever their doubts about the choices of their leaders.[8]

An alternative explanation for the democratic peace is that, far from reflecting the irenic qualities of democracies, it reflects their fearsome war-waging attributes instead. As well as fighting fewer wars, stable democracies tend to win the wars they fight. Once the commitment is made, public support coupled with the state's capacity to fund, organise and sustain the effort needed makes democracies well equipped for the long haul. Instead of being fickle, democracies can be more reliable than autocracies because their commitments carry over from one ruler to the next. A democratic state is designed to outstay changes of government, so it can outstay its military rivals as well. Peace, like war, is a double-edged sword.[9]

Treating the state as having its own capacity – to borrow, to fight, to persist, to opt out – will always pull in different directions. The ability to commit for the long term is what's needed both to avoid military conflict and to pursue it to the bitter end. Deterrence is built on this assumption – it is because states have their own logics that it is best not to cross them. It is hard to imagine any sane human being choosing to unleash nuclear Armageddon, but states are not human, so who knows what they might do? (Nor are all leaders sane, but that's another question.) States that can sustain huge debts will also have the power to renege on them. States that can choose not to kill will also have the capacity to do an awful lot of killing.

It is this superhuman – and by extension not entirely human – quality of states that makes them so indispensable and so frightening. There are many things we can do to try to keep them under control. They can be hemmed in by rules and laws, including the laws of war. But any state that has a distinct enough identity to be tagged for moral or legal or even fiscal obligations will also have sufficient autonomy to reject them. Alternatively, we could go after the human beings who take the decisions on the state's behalf. But here we run the familiar risk of missing the bigger picture. After all, it is not ultimately their debt, or even their war.

Pursuing an American president through the courts for America's debt would be absurd. Pursuing an American president through the courts for America's killing – or a Russian president for Russia's killing – is not absurd, but it does seem inadequate. What can we ever do to one person that will make up for what their state has done to others? That mismatch, though, creates a further moral hazard. Knowing it's the state that must carry the burden can make its individual representative reckless. The state may end up doing worse things precisely because we hold it responsible for what it does. It lets its component parts, without whom it can do nothing, off the hook. If we don't blame Putin for Russia's killing he will get away with murder. If we do blame him, Russia will get away with murder instead. But if we blame Russia, he may feel there is nothing to stop him doing more of it.[10]

This is the terrible quandary of modern life. We need states to have a life of their own. As a result, they do have a life of their own. As a result of that, they don't always do what we want, or need.

The corporate version

Modern corporations share many of the superhuman capacities of modern states, but not all. They too are debt-servicing machines. The most indebted corporation in the world is currently Volkswagen, which has total liabilities of nearly $200 billion. This is less than a tenth of the borrowings of the famously debt-averse German state (which still stand at more than $3 trillion), but not bad for a business that has been beset by scandal in recent years and saw its operating profits collapse during the Covid pandemic. Corporations can borrow to this scale because they are able to service debts over the long term, riding out the bad years and committing future representatives of the company to repayment. VW was founded in 1932 and survived the collapse of the Nazi regime that was its primary original sponsor. Another massively indebted German car company – BMW, with $120 billion in current liabilities – was founded in 1916. That means it has kept going while the German state has effectively been bankrupted twice over during the same period (in 1931 and in 1953), both times having to be bailed out by American money. War and its aftermath twice ruined the German state. BMW somehow survived it.[11]

Yet corporations do not carry the range of burdens that states do. They are not – or at least are not meant to be – entities onto which we offload the responsibility for violence. Though large corporations all have an elaborate security apparatus, they no longer fund large private armies. They once did – in the eighteenth century the East India Company (EIC) conquered what was to become the British Raj with its own military, paid for out of its own coffers and run by its own officers. The cost of sustaining this operation led the EIC heavily into debt, from which the company periodically had to be rescued by the British state, until the state eventually ran out of patience. Today these sorts of arrangements no longer hold. Corporations that kill are liable to be punished for it. States that hire corporations to kill for them are liable to keep it hidden. States still bail out corporations that are too big to fail, but not to pay for their soldiers and weaponry.[12]

The key event in the history of the modern corporation was the creation of the limited liability company. Before the nineteenth century the capacity of any organisation to carry its own debt could be granted only by special permission of the state – the EIC, for example, held a royal charter that exempted its shareholders from being pursued for the debts of the company itself. This was a privilege, not a right. But in 1844 the Joint Stock Companies Act allowed the creation of corporations by legal process rather than special charter and in 1855 the Limited Liability Act protected the stockholders from being bankrupted by the bankruptcy of the company in which they had invested. Creditors could now only go after the assets of the corporation; the assets of the investors, beyond what they had invested in the business, were safe. The result was that many more people felt free to invest, secure from the risk of being ruined by bad luck or reckless mismanagement. With more investors, corporations could borrow more and take longer-term decisions. Far from shrinking their creditworthiness, limiting liability massively expanded it.

States are not limited liability corporations. Citizens are protected from being liable for the debts of the state by the raw power of the state to shield them from its creditors. But citizens are made to pay for the state's profligacy in other ways – through inflation, higher taxes, perhaps even compulsory military service and the risk of death. By contrast, shareholders are protected from being personally liable for the debts of a corporation by law. This too depends on the power of the state but it operates differently. Limited liability corporations are defined by the state, given specific rights and responsibilities, and creditors are channelled towards the courts. States establish their independent identity as debtors by doing their own thing, which is what makes them hard to hold to account. Corporations establish it by doing what the state requires of them, which is what makes them liable to go bust. When a state runs out of money, it falls back on its other resources, including its coercive authority. When a corporation runs out of money, the state will – eventually – shut it down.[13]

This is perhaps the key difference between states and corporations: the former are general purpose organisations; the latter have a particular remit. In Roman law, the closest analogous term for a corporation is what was called a *universitas*, meaning an organisation that had its own identity for legal purposes. These were not what we would now think of as businesses. They were more often churches, guilds, colleges and other institutions with an existence over time that long outlasted the lives of their individual members. These organisations might enter into contracts, receive gifts, sue and be sued in the courts. They were also defined as having a purpose – each existed to further a particular end, whether that was worship, education, a craft, or some other goal. Modern corporations – different in so many ways from a medieval church or guild – still share these three characteristics. They can outlast their members; they can sue and be sued; and they have a remit, even if it is something as prosaic as maximising shareholder value. The modern law surrounding corporations has been stretched so far as to allow them to be formed 'for any lawful purpose'. This purpose no longer has to be specified. But there has to be one.[14]

A rival organisational model in Roman law was the *societas*, or partnership, which was defined as a body constituted by the identities of its members. To be a partner was to be liable for what the partnership did. As a result, the organisation could persist only so long as the partners were willing to play their parts, of which the *societas* was the sum. Modern partnerships retain many of these characteristics: to become a partner in a law firm, for example, can mean running big risks along with the outsize financial rewards. Partners can be jointly and severally liable for the debts of the partnership, meaning creditors can sue them personally to get their money back. A partnership will be harder to define by its common purpose than a corporation. If each member is making a personal contribution to the success (or failure) of the scheme, each will also be making a separate contribution to its ultimate goals. Some partners might be there to get rich, some because they love the work, some because there was nothing better on offer. Any organisation that is the sum of its parts might have as many purposes as its parts do.

The philosopher Michael Oakeshott, in his book *On Human Conduct* (1975), argued that the *universitas / societas* distinction is one way to make sense of the identity of the state. Oakeshott believed that modern states were best understood as partnerships: they should not have a single purpose but should exist to allow their members – their citizens – to pursue their own goals. He felt that this idea was permanently in danger of being corrupted by the corporate model. States that were given their own identity and purpose – even if it was something as broad as national security or maximising economic growth – risked becoming stunted organisations that subsumed the lives of their citizens to the life of the state. The worst of these states, in Oakeshott's view, were not the ones that acted like business corporations but the ones that acted like secular churches. The Soviet Union, for instance, had as its purpose the pursuit of transcendent proletarian justice, defined in Marxist-Leninist terms. A state that becomes the vehicle for the salvation – not just the safety – of its citizens soon turns into something for which they may have to sacrifice themselves. If you can only be saved by the state, you may end up being required to put the state's salvation before your own.[15]

There is, though, a problem with Oakeshott's argument: Hobbes's *Leviathan*. Oakeshott insisted that the purest account of the state as *societas* was given by Hobbes, since Hobbes had described a state that existed to allow its individual members to pursue their own goals. If the Leviathan had a purpose, it was simply 'peace', which was another way of saying it was there to make it possible for the rest of us to live as we chose. Oakeshott compared a *societas* to a shared practice, or way of being, such as a common language, which has no purpose except to allow us to communicate. French doesn't have a goal or a target – that would be absurd. Oakeshott thought the French state shouldn't have goals or targets either.[16]

But the Leviathan is not a practice, like a language. It is an artificial person, like a robot, or a corporation. Hobbes could hardly have been clearer on this point. Oakeshott's mistake was to assume that giving something an artificial personality means supplying it with an artificial purpose. The state requires a separate identity, with the ability to act in its own name, so that it can sustain long-term commitments. But it can do this without having the purpose of those commitments specified. That's what makes it different from a corporation: the purpose of a corporation is defined in law; the purpose of a state is defined by what it does.

One way to make this distinction is with a different kind of comparison. Narrow AI – which is the only kind of artificial intelligence that has been achieved for now – relies on the system in question being supplied with a purpose. That's what makes it narrow. AlphaZero – the algorithm designed by Deep-Mind to teach itself how to play chess and Go – is tasked with working out winning board-game strategies. It can do other things too, but only if someone tells it to. It can't choose its tasks for itself. A self-driving car is tasked with getting people from A to B and keeping other road users safe. It can't choose to play chess instead unless someone reprograms it. Many AI nightmares relate to machines that take their ascribed tasks to absurd limits, precisely because they don't know how to stop. Tell a superpowerful AI to make paperclips and it might not stop until there is nothing left in the universe but paperclips. Tell a superpowerful corporation to maximise profits and it might not stop until there is nothing left in the world but the fruits of its exploitation.

AGI – artificial general intelligence – denotes a system that can switch between tasks according to its own assessment of their value. In other words, it is a machine that can think like a human. Such machines do not yet exist. One name for this kind of thinking is self-consciousness – the ability to think about the value of different kinds of thinking – though it is not clear whether AGI would require anything we would recognise as consciousness to function. Perhaps it will be possible for an AI system to move across the full range of intelligent reflection without being self-reflective in anything like a human sense. We just don't know.

If corporations are narrow artificial persons, states are general ones. They do not have AGI; the general intelligence they possess can be supplied only by the human beings who constitute them. Where states do have their own artificial intelligence, it is quite narrow – the jellybeans-in-a-jar kind, not the war-and-peace kind. What makes them general is their ability to move across the full range of possible actions and set their own purposes. They have artificial general agency – AGA. They can be hemmed in by laws, just as the rest of us can, though they have more power to resist these laws than we do because they are much harder to punish. But states still get to decide what they decide about. Corporations have at least some of those decisions made for them. And languages don't get to decide at all.

These distinctions are not cut-and-dried. Some states will have their purposes narrowed, either by choice or by circumstance. A state may, as Oakeshott feared, fall prey to an ideology that delimits its goals, perhaps by listing them in a constitution. Equally, it may hand over some of its decision-making powers to another organisation, such as the EU, though it may also retain – as the British state showed, to the astonishment of many – the power to take them back. When times are hard the general purposes of a state may be subsumed to narrower ones – economic survival, say, or military survival. But that is true of human beings too, for whom poverty or illness can dramatically limit the range of their decision-making possibilities.

At the same time, some corporations, as they grow more and more powerful, can roam over an ever wider field of action, perhaps even outstripping the reach of the state. Multinational corporations that operate in multiple jurisdictions get to decide which laws they want to obey and which taxes they want to pay. In some parts of the world working for a powerful corporation can offer greater security than the local state can provide. But it remains the case that corporations have to expand their remit in order to acquire this capacity whereas states have to diminish theirs in order to lose it. The default sphere of activity for states is general. For corporations, it's particular.

Oakeshott argued that human beings are distinguished from the organisations we create by our ability to tell our own story. We make ourselves who we are. To live a human life is to embark on a journey whose narrative arc we shape for ourselves. Luck might derail us, circumstances might frustrate us, but we retain the capacity to pursue our own fate. That is the mark of our general intelligence, and it defines our humanity. Collective human organisations, he thought, have no such capacity. Their story is fixed by the artifice that goes into their creation: they are what we make them. When the state is a partnership, it does not have its own story to tell. It is simply the space in which many different stories get told. When the state is a corporation it can have a story of a sort, but it is a narrow, artificial one. It cannot unfold. It can only do what it is programmed to do. States as corporations are like characters in Marxist-Leninist fiction, which was notoriously formulaic. Their lives are at the service of their artificially defined goals, so they never really get to have a life of their own.[17]

It is true that mechanical fictions are invariably unconvincing. Machines do not tell good stories. AIs can now write convincing pastiches of the great novelists. Tell ChatGPT to produce a paragraph in the style of Jane Austen and it can be hard to distinguish its version from the original. But a whole novel – with the development of plot and character – is beyond it. For now no machine can sustain the arc of an imagined life.

But what about a machine that tells its own story? Machines can't reconstruct human lives because they lack the necessary intelligence. They end up writing about us as though we were robots. But machines can describe their own existence. The state is, in that sense, the definitive storytelling machine. It only has one story to tell: its own. Its life is determined by the choices it makes, and even though those choices have to be made for it by human beings, together they create the arc of a life. A state is defined by its actions over time, which shape what actions are possible for it in the future. Its life is not determined by the circumstances of its creation, any more than our lives are, but nor can any life entirely break free from its origins. The machinery of the state exists to sustain the narrative of its existence. States are not simply mechanical fictions. They are mechanical versions of us: machines that try to tell their own story.

So, up to a point, are corporations. But most corporations will struggle to match the storytelling powers of the state. Corporations can change their purposes: some of the world's biggest companies started out doing something else entirely. Amazon once sold only books; now it sells almost everything and stores data in the cloud as well. Its story has evolved, and it has turned into something beyond anything even its creators could have imagined. But still, Amazon does not have the capacity of a state to determine its own fate. It has to make do with the decision-making powers it is given.

Life and death

A natural human life has one universal constraint: the natural human lifespan. Though life expectancy has greatly increased over the past century in many parts of the world, longevity has not. The very oldest people – those who live to be a hundred or more – are less rare than they used to be, but still the cut-off is fixed at about 120 years, as it always has been. There are currently no 150-year-olds, and outside of myth it seems likely no human has ever lived that long. Technology and its boosters promise to change that soon, but it hasn't happened yet.

By contrast, states and corporations have an artificial lifespan, which has no predictable limit. They can live for far longer than any human being. Because there are few real markers of artificial ageing, we cannot easily locate them at particular points within the arc of their lives. The idea of an adolescent state, or a senile corporation, doesn't really make sense. No state or corporation can live for ever – at some point they must fail, as every human-made construction does in the end. But while they live, they can be very hard to age.

BMW, at 106, is nearly as old as the oldest living German (113). Heavily in debt and facing the challenge of the electric car revolution, BMW may not be long for this world, though given its scale and resilience that seems unlikely. It could well have another hundred years of life left, or more. It is impossible to say, because its longevity does not depend on its maturity. It simply depends on its ability to keep paying its bills. By some measures, BMW is already older than the German state. Present-day

Germany was created by the reunification of East and West in 1990, though that was in essence a continuation of the West German state and the 'basic law' of its founding in 1949. Yet what we call modern Germany was born in 1871 with the original act of unification that created a federal nation-state out of a historic mishmash of kingdoms, duchies, principalities and city-states. That Germany, with its federal institutions, has survived continuously in some form despite the traumas and calamities of the twentieth century. It has now passed the 150-year threshold, which means, whatever else it is, it cannot be human.

Some states are considerably older. The modern English (now British) state plausibly originates with the institutional arrangements between Crown and Parliament that were established in 1689, following the Glorious Revolution. In 1694 a charter was granted to the Bank of England, which allowed it to function as a limited liability corporation issuing bonds on behalf of the Crown. The goal was to borrow enough money to build a new fleet. This was the origin of the national debt, which has been funding both war and peace from then to now. The American Republic dates its birthday to the Declaration of Independence on 4 July 1776. Its current constitution, which created the institutions of its federal government, was not signed into law until 1789. In 1790, thanks to the ruthless wheeler-dealing of Alexander Hamilton, the federal government began to assume debts on behalf of the American state, which it has been servicing ever since.

This story, though far from universal, is nonetheless a common one: revolution, constitution, debt. The modern French state emerged from the French Revolution in 1789. The constitution of its first republic – the first of many – was enacted in 1792. In the same year the new government began to take on debt on behalf of the new republic. In 1797 it underwent its first default, reneging on two-thirds of its outstanding interest payments. Only in 1815, after Napoleon's defeat at Waterloo, did the French state establish the institutional arrangements that ensured state debt was not at the mercy of the personal whims of its rulers. As a result, the rate of interest at which it could borrow fell dramatically.

The British, American and French states are centuries old. At the same time, they were working in ways we can recognise as evidence of their ability to function from relatively early on. There is no pattern here of moving slowly from childhood to adulthood – the shift into self-sufficiency is squeezed into the beginning. It is less like a human origin story and more like a machine that cranks into life and then continues to run (or doesn't). The modern French state has endured through five republics, interspersed by both monarchical and authoritarian interludes. It has worked better at some times and barely at all at others. But it has kept going for more than 200 years, despite some near-death experiences, most notably in 1940, when Hitler invaded and set up the puppet Vichy government. Somehow it survived. Once states are up and running, they can be extremely hard to kill.

Some corporate entities have outlived even the longest-established states. The very oldest continuous business enterprises are in Japan, where a few still-operational inns and breweries date back more than a thousand years. These are usually family businesses, and their longevity is partly explained by the custom of adopting business managers into the family as sons when there is no natural born male heir to the business. Modern corporations, plenty of which also started out as family enterprises, are inevitably less ancient, since the legal regimes that allowed for their creation did not come into force until the nineteenth century. Still, the S&P 500 stock market index contains plenty of organisations that date back well over a hundred years, from JP Morgan Chase and Goldman Sachs to Procter & Gamble and Johnson & Johnson. None looks in danger of going out of business any time soon, though the fate of Lehman Brothers, whose 160-year history was terminated over a single weekend at the apex of the 2008 financial crisis, will be a reminder to them all that nothing lasts for ever.

While there is no natural lifespan for a corporation, there is an average one. It is here that corporations differ most markedly from both states and human beings. Whereas states, if they can get going, tend to last a long time, most corporations, once they get started, tend to die relatively quickly. Globally, around half of all new businesses cease to exist within five years. The average lifespan of a company in the US is currently around ten years. What's more, it is getting shorter. The most successful corporations used to be among the longest lived. In the 1920s the average age of a company quoted on the S&P 500 was nearly seventy years. Now it is less than twenty. Successful states invariably outlive the people who founded them. Today, human beings tend to outlive even the most successful corporations.[18]

The rapid turnover of corporations is reflected in the starkest difference of all with states. There are currently just under 200 nation-states in the world (the UN has 193 members and two non-member observers). At the same time, there are now more than 200 million corporations worldwide, a number that has nearly doubled in the last twenty-five years (by contrast, the number of member states of the UN has increased by just four over the same period). Corporations are far easier to create than states, and far easier to terminate. Often it is just a formality – a matter of a few signatures and a lodging of documents. Some corporations are simply shells. Go looking for what lies behind the name and you will find nothing there at all: just a plaque on a door in Delaware or the Cayman Islands. These corporations function only to perform a very particular purpose, which is often merely to avoid tax. They are fictions in the thinnest possible sense: not imaginary creatures with a life of their own but non-existent ones. They are ghost stories without the story.

The relatively small number of corporations that endure

over a long period are something much more substantial. They can become objects of loyalty for their employees and customers, sources of long-term aspiration for their owners, and their life stories will both enable and constrain the decisions of their executives. They have a real presence in the world in the way that a tax avoidance vehicle in Delaware does not. Even the most powerful corporations necessarily originate with a set of formalities, though the formalities will not be sufficient to account for their continued existence. That depends on what the corporation does with the rights and responsibilities it is given. Unlike states, corporations can take quite a while to take shape. Lehman Brothers began life as Lehman Durr & Co., a cotton store in Alabama, before becoming a cotton trading firm, then moving into coal, then into banking, and finally relocating to Wall Street (fig. 9). That process took the best part of half a century.[19]

9. The original Lehman Brothers

Yet because the origin of any corporation is a formality, the end can be equally abrupt, as Lehman discovered. It takes more than one misstep to kill a state – usually it takes years of attrition – but not a company. Another family bank, Barings, was founded as a partnership by two brothers in 1762, and in that capacity it helped to fund a number of world-changing deals, including the Louisiana Purchase of 1802, which doubled the size of the United States. Barings then became Baring Brothers & Co., which it remained until 1890, when a series of bad bets on Argentinian bonds required the business to be bailed out by the Bank of England and refounded as a limited liability company, Baring Brothers and Co., Ltd. The bank traded more or less successfully and highly profitably for another hundred years, until on 23 February 1995 a trader called Nick Leeson was discovered to have fled from his base in Singapore having run up corporate losses of £827 million through fraudulent transactions. This was more than the entire capitalisation of the business. This time a proposed Bank of England rescue failed to materialise. On 26 February Barings was declared insolvent and the winding-up process began. Two hundred-plus years of life – two and a bit days to kill it.

States are far harder to create and far harder to destroy. That's why there are so relatively few of them. There are formalities here too, such as the enactment of a constitution or recognition by the United Nations. But none is enough to make a state real. That depends on the machinery of government generating sufficient authority to speak on behalf of its people.

The most famous definition of the modern state is the one given by the German sociologist Max Weber at the beginning of the twentieth century: he described it as the human association that successfully claims a monopoly of legitimate violence. In other words, it is a violence-dispensing machine. What makes it legitimate to use that violence? That it is able successfully to claim to do so. What will make the claim successful? That the people on the receiving end accept it as legitimate. And so on. States are ultimately defined by what they do, not by what they are allowed to do. That's what gives them a life of their own.[20]

Still, functioning states do sometimes cease to function. Most often this is either when they are broken up into smaller states or merged into larger ones. Of the very few states that have left the United Nations since its founding, in each case it has been because of either break-up (e.g. Czechoslovakia into Czechia and Slovakia in 1992), co-option (e.g. the GDR into Germany in 1990) or merger (e.g. Tanganyika and Zanzibar into Tanzania in 1964). The United Kingdom, if Scottish independence breaks it apart, may yet join them. Some states struggle to fulfil their function as sources of coercive authority. The newest member of the UN, South Sudan, which was created in 2011, has been riven by civil war for much of its existence and still has limited control over the violence within its borders. We sometimes talk of such states as failed states. But it is worth noting that failed states continue to exist in their own right, weakly mimicking the working of their more durable counterparts, and waiting for some spark to charge them back to life. Failed corporations, by contrast, stop existing altogether. When they fail, they die. When states fail, they can stumble on, just as human beings can.

Some states appear more transient than the peoples they represent. There were Germans – an ancient people, or as they were once called, a *Volk* – long before there was a Germany. The modern Chinese state is a twentieth-century construction. Chinese civilisation, which that state increasingly seeks to embody, has been in existence for thousands of years. It is not always this way round, however. The creation and endurance – even through a civil war – of the American state eventually turned Virginians, Texans and Californians into Americans, at least until another civil war tears them apart again: a state-nation, rather than a nation-state. At the time of the French

Revolution, the idea of something called France was extremely remote to most of the people who lived there, many of whom spoke their own languages and followed their own customs and had little idea of what was happening in Paris. It took the wars, debts, political infighting and growing administrative burdens of the nineteenth century to make France seem real to its people. This was the creation of that imagined community – with a shared identity, history and fate – which underpins every successful state. Being successfully imagined by the people it represents is what makes the state real.[21]

States invent their peoples. Peoples invent their states. Whichever way round it happens, once it has happened it is a hard relationship to break. Yes, Chinese civilisation is millennia old, but there is now no other plausible representative of the Chinese people than the Chinese state. Conjuring up an idea of China in literature or in art will not pay the bills. If a corporation sought to take on the role of the representative of the nation, it would either have to turn itself into a state or admit that it could perform only a fraction of the functions that a state takes on. Once states exist, they can be replaced only by other states. If they are to cease to exist, it will have to be because we have imagined what it is to be a political community in a completely different way. There is no sign of that yet, in part because we are so dependent on the state for our collective political imagination.

States and corporations reflect two different sides of our contemporary fear of machines that have escaped human control. One is that we will build machines that we don't know how to switch off, either because we have become too dependent on them or because we can't find the off switch. That's states. The other is that we build machines that self-replicate in ways that we can no longer regulate. They start spewing out versions of themselves to the point where we are swamped by them. That's corporations.

Uncanny valley

Another frequently voiced fear of machine life is the 'uncanny valley'. This is where we find ourselves more and more repelled by artificial creatures the more closely they come to resemble us, without quite getting it right. We can cope with clunking, lumbering robots because we can be sure they aren't human. And were a robot to be a perfect simulacrum of a human being we might also be OK with that because we wouldn't be able to tell the difference. It's when machines are like us, yet off in crucial respects, that we are appalled.[22]

A plausible humanoid robot with unfocused, sightless eyes can be as frightening as any zombie: these are some more of the staples of sci-fi horror. Most of us are able to cope with the sight of a dead animal at the side of the road. An expertly stuffed pet on the mantelpiece, preserved in a life-like pose, is another matter. Taxidermy can be its own horror movie.

But on the same principle, the uncanny valley exists in places that aren't meant to be creepy at all. It is why the toys that come to life in the *Toy Story* films are less disturbing than the computer-animated children. We don't expect animated toys to look like they can really see and feel and fear. It's fun to pretend they can. But children we do expect to have real feelings, so we get freaked out when we look into their glassy eyes.

It is equally the reason why the computer-generated cats in the film version of the musical *Cats* were so repugnant – and the film itself an epic box-office disaster. The filmmakers couldn't decide whether these creatures were meant to be human-like or not. If they couldn't decide, how could we? Early reports describe test audience members leaving screenings to throw up.

Something of the same idea holds in the artificial world of states and corporations. On the whole, we can deal with the versions that are clearly mechanical, even if they might drive us mad in other ways. A shell company in Delaware is infuriating, but it is not frightening, in the way a ghost might be. At the same time, groups that carry with them their essential humanity can be comforting: a book club, a sports team, a friendly partnership. Even a crowd run riot, though terrifying, is not otherworldly. It is a ghastly force of nature.

The problem comes with organisations that act as though they are human but are not. States and corporations are represented by human beings, who profess human thoughts and feelings: hope, fear, anger, regret, even remorse. Politicians and businesspeople do have real feelings, of course, and these may well be genuine. But states and corporations don't have anything like the same feelings in anything like the same way. When a state does something terrible – such as committing an act of extreme violence – or a corporation does something terrible – such as displaying wanton disregard for human welfare – putting a human face to these misdeeds can make it more disturbing, not less. It leaves human beings responsible for superhuman horror. Then what are we meant to think?

How, for example, could multinational oil corporations have spent years suppressing and distorting the evidence that fossil fuels were responsible for dangerous levels of climate change? We might choose to believe that the people working for these companies are especially bad, reckless, irresponsible, selfish. But they are not: they are, on the whole, just people like the rest of us. It is the corporation that chose to pursue this path and the people involved, because they are like the rest of us, followed, because following a corporate decision is the path of least resistance. It is more than likely that many of the people involved knew that what they were doing was wrong. But the corporation didn't because the corporation isn't sentient.[23]

Most companies, and most states, now have vast teams of professionals whose job it is to humanise their actions. We call this PR, or in some cases, propaganda. It can be extremely effective. When corporate action can be presented as caring, or far-sighted, or simply reasonable, it makes it a lot easier to swallow. But sometimes the mismatch is too glaring, and then it is nauseating. Corporations that talk of their deep-seated environmental concerns, while pursuing their short-term, profit-driven objectives, can find that their greenwashing really sticks in the throat. It is like encountering a humanoid entity that is dead behind the eyes.

Political leaders and corporate executives also have as part of their job to humanise the organisations they represent. The best ones do it brilliantly. Failure, however, exposes the charade. There is something missing. Think of Tony Blair, still justifying the Iraq War long after it had failed on the basis of the strength of his convictions. Think of Dick Fuld, the CEO of Lehman Brothers when it went under, blankly telling Congress that he took personal responsibility for its failure, though there was nothing else personally he could have done (fig. 10).

Sincerity doesn't work. Insincerity doesn't work either. The problem is that these are people playing a double role. They are what makes the machine human. And yet they have been dehumanised by the machine.

Elon Musk, like many tech titans, seeks to embody the corporation – Tesla – that he helped to create. It's a good fit because he is a highly intelligent, quirky, slightly off person himself. He was also, for a while, the wealthiest individual on the planet. But the gap is still there. Musk is not Tesla, and confusing the two risks making them both stranger than they really are – the company a sinister extension of its founder, the founder a creepy extension of his company. Vladimir Putin seeks to embody the Russian state. He has spent years parading himself as its manly incarnation: judo black belt, equestrian, bare-chested, steely eyed. As he grows older and weaker, and the Russian state more reckless and violent, the

10. Dick Fuld testifies, 6 October 2008

closeness of the fit becomes ever more grotesque, because ultimately it is no fit at all.[24]

Humanising artificial persons has other dangerous consequences too. In 2010, in the case of *Citizens United* vs *FEC*, the US Supreme Court decided – by a 5–4 majority – that corporations were entitled to the protection of First Amendment rights because they were persons under the law. This meant that there could be no special limits on corporate donations to political campaigns. The verdict has often been treated as instantiating the idea of corporate personhood in federal law. But corporations had been understood as persons in US law as far back as the nineteenth century. If anything, *Citizens United* introduced a very different understanding of that idea. The Court's rationale for giving corporations the right to free speech was an assumption that anything else would interfere with the rights of the individuals who created them. Corporations were understood in this ruling as an extension of the wishes and interests of their human components. *Citizens United* treated corporations as though they were essentially a version of us. It humanised them.

This move came off the back of another significant shift in the understanding of corporate enterprise that both informed the *Citizens United* decision and helps to reveal its shallowness. Since the 1970s, the doctrine of profit maximisation has been the dominant one in understanding how business corporations should function: they exist to deliver value to their shareholders. This reinforces the idea that the corporation is simply a vehicle for known human interests and therefore should have the rights those interests require. Yet it reduces the corporation to a mere shell of a person, fit to pursue only one narrow purpose. Calling such a constrained entity a person might appear relatively harmless, since there is only one thing that person is supposed to do, but giving such entities rights can also be dangerous, since it empowers them to pursue their narrow remit as though that were the only thing worth doing.[25]

Earlier American judges had taken a different view. During the first half of the twentieth century, the idea of corporate personhood was used to limit corporate rights on the grounds that if these were persons, they clearly were nothing like us. They were artificial creatures, with distinctive and sometimes extreme powers. Therefore it made no sense to treat them as though they were human. That would simply empower them to behave in profoundly incongruous ways. Progressive judges used the idea of corporate personality to highlight the obvious differences between corporations and the rest of us: their longevity, reach and sometimes acute insensitivity to human toil and distress. They tried to load them with special responsibilities that suited their unusual strengths and weaknesses. These included limits on their powers of influence. *Citizens United* turned its back on that.[26]

The impulse to humanise artificial creatures is strong – after all, how else can we truly relate to them? It's there with robots too. If they look or sound like us – sex bots, care bots, friendly bots – maybe we can more easily get past the differences. Lessening the risk of alienation will enable them to do their jobs better. But to forget the differences can be as dangerous, and ultimately even more disturbing. Sometimes it is better to remember who they are. They are not us.

Social machines

States and corporations are not the only social machines. The history of political thought is shot through with mechanical imagery. The great conservative critic of the French Revolution Joseph de Maistre feared that its architects wanted to turn French society into a vast machine, run according to the bogus principles of social science. Citizens would be treated like cogs and parts, to be tweaked, measured, organised, dehumanised. Likewise, bureaucracies have often been described in mechanical terms. As one historian has put it, the British civil service evolved over the course of the nineteenth century in such a way that the idea of 'government machinery' became its organising principle. At the start of the twentieth century, professional political parties came to be seen as the latest incarnation of political rationalisation and mechanisation. Weber called parties 'political machines' and he feared what might happen if they escaped the control of their leaders. We still talk about machine politics, and we shudder.[27]

Some of this is literal and some of it metaphorical. There are many aspects of modern political systems that do operate mechanically, designed to generate more or less reliable outcomes by following an operating procedure. But society as a whole is not a machine. That was Maistre's point – evolved social arrangements are just too complex to be treated in this way. The idea that society is a machine simply serves to justify certain kinds of human control. We do make social machines. But we also make some of them up, to excuse our own actions.

At the same time, the modern world is overshadowed by all sorts of impersonal systems that shape how we behave. Markets are artificial mechanisms for generating and communicating economic information. Sometimes they appear to us as sources of terror and awe. More often, they operate in the background of our lives – at least for anyone who does not play them for a living. They are more like the weather than they are a personal presence, until a storm blows up and we can't escape them. Information networks such as search engines generate the knowledge we need to find what we are looking for – from arcane facts and figures to long-lost loves. Depending on who we are and what we need, we may come to rely on them. Even if they do not control us, they can make us dependent on their extraordinary powers.

Then there are the larger, more widely encompassing systems of modernity. Capitalism is a hybrid of institutions and ideas that organises our world so pervasively that it can be easier to imagine the end of the world than the end of capitalism. The patriarchy is a hybrid of institutions and ideas that shapes how we interact with each other, to the benefit of some and the detriment of others. These systems are so broad that they can be hard to perceive. Some doubt they even exist in their own right, though for those who have discerned them this is just further evidence of the extent of their reach.

All these institutions, ideas and systems are artificial. They are human-made and would not exist in any form without us. Yet they have helped make us who we are. For many social and political theorists our world is best understood as the product of these impersonal forces: social relations, patterns of knowledge and control, economic hierarchies. Our humanity has been shaped and, in many cases, distorted by the systems that have emerged from our everyday interactions. If we feel powerless and lost, it is because we cannot perceive the forces that have a grip on us. Many modern liberation projects and liberation theorists – from communism to feminism and from Marx to de Beauvoir, from psychoanalysis to postmodernism and from Freud to Foucault – want to help us see what's really there.

States and corporations exist in this world. They are one set of social machines among many; one set of institutions within the wider social system. What makes them different? Not their artificiality – which is ubiquitous in modern society – but their agency. They are the ultimate decision-making machines. They are defined by their ability to make their own choices and to sustain the consequences of what has been chosen. In other words, they are artificial persons. Capitalism is not a person. Nor is an information network. Nor is a habitat. Nor is a knowledge regime. These things are forces, often immensely powerful ones, but they do not decide for us.

There are other artificial agents than states and corporations, from the ancient world to the modern, from churches and guilds to the latest breed of robots and algorithms. States have a monopoly of sorts on legitimate violence, but they do not monopolise political personality. Political parties have personalities of their own. So do parliaments and judicial bodies. Corporations are not the only model of joint economic enterprise, let alone of joint social enterprise. The modern world is populated with many other forms of group activity, from co-operatives to communes. Some of these operate very successfully, and the best of them are surer routes to human fulfilment and comradeship than anything on offer from Amazon or Baidu, or from the American state, or the Chinese one.

But states and corporations are still different. They stand out for their power, their longevity and their replicability. In a world of nearly limitless models of artificial enterprise, these are still the dominant ones. I have tried to explain what makes them different in theory. In what follows, I explore in more detail what has made them different in practice. What changed for us when we started building them? And what have they built in their turn?

4

TRIBES, CHURCHES, EMPIRES

Cognitive revolutions

In his book *Sapiens*, Yuval Harari identifies what makes us humans so special. Our superpower is our ability to conjure up collective versions of ourselves that don't actually exist. Harari calls these invented communities 'fictions', and they include everything from tribes to empires, churches to corporations. We are the only species that can organise our existence around our imaginations.[1]

This means the decisive event in the history of humanity happened near the beginning, around 70,000 years ago. That was the point when *Homo sapiens* evolved to be able to use language in the pursuit of shared goals. We became creatures that could describe scenarios that were different from those we were actually experiencing, and then communicate these stories to each other. As a result, we were able to pool our imaginative resources in a way that was well beyond the reach of other animals, including rival versions of the human species such as Neanderthals. Harari calls this shift the cognitive revolution. It freed us up to start creating our own worlds. Everything else followed from that.

Humans are in most respects relatively powerless creatures. We have big, wobbly heads on weak and vulnerable bodies. We take a long time to reach maturity – many months before we can walk and talk, many years before we can fend for ourselves. Compared to plenty of mammals we are neither quick

nor strong – easily outrun by lions and tigers, soon trampled by
elephants, readily torn apart by wolves. What we have is our
intelligence. But being smart is not enough to rescue us when
set upon by wild animals. The difference comes when we can
work together to plan how we might defend ourselves. A single
human being will lose in one-to-one combat with a powerful
chimpanzee, but one hundred humans can defeat one hundred
chimps, because the humans can develop a group strategy for
the contest. The apes might try to defend each other, but they
can't discuss and decide what to do next if things go wrong. The
various film versions of *Planet of the Apes*, where the primates
take over, are based on the premise that they somehow acquire
such a capacity. The means through which it happens is language: these animals can speak.

The earliest collective human endeavours were very small
scale. Small tribes of hunter-gatherers shared stories about
hunting and gathering, deciding who should do what, which
tools might serve them best and when they ought to change
location. These stories were about them: the individuals in the
group, their ancestors and the yet to be born, along with the
animals and ghosts they encountered along the way. Faces had
names, and names had faces. Humans can think in this way
for groups of up to about 150 people, and for most of human
history no group ever got much bigger than that. But for larger
groups, it becomes impossible to retain a sense of the individual
identities of the people who belong.

That rule still seems to hold. Humans find it very hard to
picture a group through its members once the members become
too numerous. Instead, we have to talk about an idea of the
group instead. Anyone with more than 150 friends on Facebook
is treating friendship as an abstract concept rather than a set of
human relationships. You count as a friend not because of who
you are but because of the category you fit into. Organise a
wedding for a hundred guests – who will probably all be known

to the happy couple – and the wedding is made by who is there. But organise a wedding for a thousand guests, not all of whom can be known to any individual there, and the guests disappear into the idea of the wedding.[2]

The second key event in the history of humanity happened around 10,000 years ago with the agricultural revolution. At that point, humans began to settle permanently in places where food could be planted and grown in annual cycles. These settlements grew in size to the point where collective identity had to be attached to the place where people lived rather than to the people living there. Communities were organised to feed large numbers of people, many of whom would not be known to each other. That required establishing different roles, defined by their relationship to the collective enterprise. Some would plant, some would cook, some would fight and some would decide about these activities. It was the birth of the idea of government: a subset of the group was required to maintain a system that could not be kept going by personal interaction alone.

The growth of these early settlements from hundreds to many thousands of people was slow, but it was also exponential. In 7000 BCE the largest cities known to us – in what are now Turkey and Jordan – were made up of around 1,000 people. Three millennia later the biggest cities had grown to about 5,000 inhabitants. A thousand years after that, Uruk – in what is now Iraq – was able to house nearly 50,000 people. By 1000 BCE cities such as Babylon had populations of 100,000. Within five centuries Babylon had doubled in size again, to 200,000. And within another 500 years – at the turn of the first millennium of the standard era – Rome would contain around a million people.

With each expansion came an equivalent increase in the range of roles that human beings could play. Bigger settlements required more administration, more rules, more organisation and more hierarchy. Most people found themselves excluded from any real say in how they lived, but even to be excluded was to play a part. Slavery, for all its ubiquity, was unnatural – just another artificial construct. (Aristotle thought that there were 'natural' slaves, but Aristotle was wrong.) Yet the growth of these bigger communities also opened up as many different ways of imagining what it might mean to belong. Religion, warfare, commerce, history, myth, dreams, passions, fears, a sense of justice and much else besides could all be invoked to flesh out the imaginative constructs that were used to build this new world. Settling in one place did not mean that humans were tied down in explaining who they were and where they belonged. It had the opposite effect. The less room there was to roam, and the further removed we were from knowing who was in our tribe, the greater the need for collective human imagination to hold the whole enterprise together.

Ancient Rome was the peak of the first phase of human expansion in terms of sheer numbers. Though some Chinese cities grew equivalently large over the subsequent 1,500 years, a million people living together seemed to be the limit. The vast majority of human settlements were very much smaller. In Europe, the numbers of people inhabiting individual places shrank dramatically after the fall of the Roman Empire, so that by 1500 nowhere had a population of more than 200,000 (Paris came closest with about 180,000). Rome in 1500 was back down to 30,000 inhabitants. London at that point was no larger than ancient Uruk.

At the same time, however, Europe was the site of a continuing increase in the variety of ideas of human community. By the late Middle Ages, city-states, churches, empires, guilds, fiefdoms, principalities, leagues, corporations, religious orders and many other kinds of groupings were all staking a claim to the loyalty of their members. Shrinking the scale of human communities and proliferating their variety appeared to go hand in hand. Bigger did not mean better. Smaller, however, meant more.

What caused this to change, and initiated a further era of exponential growth, was another revolution in human understanding. The scientific revolution, which emerged out of the Renaissance and flourished during the Enlightenment, altered the terms on which the human imagination was able to operate. It opened nature up to scientific scrutiny, which greatly increased our ability to control our own environment. In the middle of the last millennium humans were still very vulnerable creatures. Life expectancy was not much more than thirty years anywhere, about where it had been at the start of the human story. Disease, famine and natural disasters were beyond the power of human beings to control, which meant that life was shot through with the arbitrary risk of an early death. The risk of violence was arbitrary, too: human conflicts tended to spin out of control very quickly. All that stopped them spreading everywhere was the smallness of the scale on which human communities were able to operate.

The scientific revolution helped change all that. By orienting human understanding around testable hypotheses rather than local histories it made knowledge far easier to export. A description of the world could be universal if it was expressed as a scientific formulation, available for others to confirm or reject according to their experience of the same phenomenon. The secret sauce of the scientific mindset was scepticism: a refusal to buy into any story unless it could withstand another person's reasonable doubts. From the application and spread of this method humans were able to share more than their imaginations. They were able to share their results.

These results soon altered the possibilities of human existence. Ways of controlling disease could be communicated, initially only among the lucky few, but over time much more widely. Food production became more reliable and much more efficient. Energy could be extracted from the earth at an extraordinary rate. Violence could be controlled. Unfortunately it could also spread very quickly and kill on a much larger scale. The scale of human settlements grew too. The population of London reached 1 million in 1800, in the early years of the Industrial Revolution, which came about through the extension of the principles of the scientific revolution to mass production. By 1850 London's population had doubled to 2 million. By 1900 it was more than 5 million. The same exponential urban growth was eventually seen around the world, from Paris to Shanghai, from Lima to Los Angeles.

The spread of scientific knowledge did not end our reliance on our imaginations. We still needed to organise ourselves in groups whose identity was shaped by an idea of community rather than any personal knowledge of who belonged. Some communities tried to do this according to scientific principles – whether these were based on market economics or Marxist dialectical materialism. But in the end, this was not science. It was storytelling, which as Harari says is our unique human quality. In the sphere of belonging we still needed to tell our own tales. Cities grew inside nation-states that were imaginative constructs. The corporations that drove economic growth were imaginative constructs too. Science turbocharged our ability to manufacture a world that served our interests and enhanced our potential. But the vehicles through which this was achieved were not themselves scientific formulas. They were the turbocharged fictions of the modern age.

According to Harari, we are now entering the next – and perhaps final – phase of the human story, as a result of another revolution: the digital revolution. Machines may soon have the capacity to determine our fate by treating us as data points in their own versions of reality. Then the link between scientific knowledge and the human imagination will be broken because the latter will no longer be needed to organise the former. The machines that science built will organise us instead. The result will be a fragmentation of human experience. Our personal identities will be broken up according to the needs of the machines, which will disaggregate our experiences into the bits of data we provide. You will be one set of data for one algorithm, and another set for another algorithm. Insisting you are still you will mean little once your choices are shaped by what the machines decide.[3]

At the same time, a select group of human beings may have an entirely different experience from the rest by dint of their relationship to these machines. Anyone who can control the machines and how they operate will have hugely enhanced powers. The remainder of humanity – the vast majority – will be relatively powerless. Knowledge of how the world works will no longer be shareable. It will be the jealously guarded preserve of a tiny elite. A few people's imaginations – Elon Musk and his like – will be all important. Everyone else's will be increasingly irrelevant.

There are two ways of thinking about where states and corporations fit into this version of the human story – Harari's version. The first is to say that they are nothing special. For 70,000 years we have been imagining versions of ourselves that do not actually exist outside of our imaginations. Tribes and ancient empires feature on the same imaginative spectrum as modern states and multinational corporations. The key events that altered who we are occurred in the sphere of our knowledge of the material world: how to plant, how to build, how to organise, how to experiment, how to code. On this account the shift from ancient Rome to modern America is less significant than the shift from grunts to language, from roaming to settling, from superstition to science, and from human imagination to machine learning.

But an alternative account – the one I offer in this book – would say that the creation of modern states and corporations is nevertheless the decisive event in the human story, for three reasons. First, it marked the point when our imagined communities became mechanical, in the sense that similar versions of the same idea could be built in different places. This was the crucial coming together of scientific understanding and human imagination. It was not that our imaginations became mechanised. Rather, we began to imagine what it would be like to organise collective enterprises as though they had the durability of machines.

Second, these imagined enterprises proved to be remarkably adept at exploiting the advantages of the scientific revolution. They could sustain projects of knowledge acquisition and application in ways that were beyond any rival organisational model. They could do this because they were able to borrow, invest and reap rewards over the long term. The scientific revolution helped create modern states and corporations, which are as much the products of a sceptical conception of the universe as steamships and computers. They exist only because they can survive the test of human doubt (you can doubt them as much as you like, they're still coming to get you). But modern states and corporations helped drive the scientific revolution as well. It would have stalled without them.

Finally, we are not quite at the end of the story of *Homo sapiens*. We might be able to glimpse the ultimate shape of this 70,000-year history, from start to possible finish, but we are also still very much in it. The shift to the next phase of existence has not happened yet. In the meantime, it is states and corporations that are responsible for what might occur next. If some human beings have a different relationship with thinking machines, it is because of their hold over the states and corporations that ultimately create and regulate those machines. Musk and his like have their power because of their relationship to states and corporations, not in spite of them. If we are to move from *Homo sapiens* to something else – whether to what Harari calls *Homo Deus*, a species that harnesses the power of machines to achieve god-like status; or to a species that is at the mercy of machines it cannot control; or to both – it will be states and corporations that are the bridge. Not only do they feature in the story of human creativity – they may feature in the story of its death as well.

Harari characterises modernity as comprising two countervailing trends. The first is towards the idea of sovereign individuals, empowered by scepticism to shape their lives free from social constraint. Scientific knowledge provides the bedrock for this – emancipation from tradition, faith in reason, liberated understanding, experimental curiosity. The second trend is towards the mechanisation of the human experience, as we become the objects of scientific understanding – just another set of instruments to be taken apart and rebuilt by rational enquiry. Thus the scientific revolution freed us from one reductive version of who we are – as members of the tribe – and set us on the path to another reductive version – as parts of the machine. What we experienced in between, when it looked like we might be ourselves, was only a brief illusion.[4]

But there is a third trend. Modernity also saw the creation of artificial versions of ourselves that are part human and part machine. These artificial persons helped define our individuality – as citizens and as consumers – while at the same time subsuming it to their own imperatives. What makes them so powerful is that they managed to combine the different aspects of modernity in a single form. Modern states and corporations are mechanical monsters, capable of growing to a vast scale. They are also vehicles of human liberation, able to free us from the need always to be thinking about where, and to whom, we belong. Their artificiality is different from what came before. It is both more human – because it depends on nothing but our input – and more artificial – because it turns that input into something that can be wholly detached from us.

If modern states and corporations exist on the same imaginative spectrum as earlier tribes, churches and empires, they also mark a decisive break point. Something fundamental changed when they came along.

The Death Star

At its height, in the middle of the second century CE, the population of the Roman Empire was around 75 million. That figure represented between a quarter and a third of the total world population of the time, meaning that a higher proportion of humanity belonged to this single political entity than to any other in human history. Today the world's largest states, China and India, have roughly one seventh of the total global population each. The world's largest national economy, the United States, contains barely a twentieth.

The only comparable entities to ancient Rome in terms of their population share are also empires. At its height in the first half of the twentieth century, the British Empire ruled over 400 million people, more than a fifth of the global population. At the dawn of the Roman Empire, the Chinese Empire was almost as populous as its European counterpart. A census conducted at the turn of the first millennium counted 59,594,978 persons under the centralised administration of the Han Dynasty. Unlike in the case of Rome, this figure remained relatively steady over the next 1,500 years. A census held in 1520, during the Ming Dynasty, identified 60,606,220 individuals under its rule. The largest comparable European organisation at the same point – the Holy Roman Empire – contained fewer than 15 million people. And by then Rome itself had shrunk to the size of a market town.

If nothing else, this suggests that empires are able to operate on a vast scale, without waiting for modernity to equip them with the resources that make mass communication possible. The mere fact that 60 million people could be counted down to the last child over 2,000 years ago – however pseudo-accurate that final figure was – indicates that the administrative machinery of ancient empires was formidable (more formidable in China than in Europe). Of course, size isn't everything. The contemporary world contains giant communities of equivalent reach. Both Facebook and TikTok currently have 2 billion users, meaning their networks each number around a quarter of the total world population. But these are not political communities.

Sometimes people pretend that they are. In 2016 *The Economist* magazine put Facebook's co-founder Mark Zuckerberg on its cover mocked up as the Emperor Augustus. But Zuckerberg, although he likes to compare himself to Rome's first emperor, has no coercive authority over his colossal global network. He can shape the choices of its members but he can't enforce his decisions on them. It's their thumbs up or down that ultimately count. Those he does control more directly – the employees of Meta, Facebook's parent company – number around 70,000 at the time of writing (a figure that has been shrinking as the Metaverse has failed, for now, to take shape). That's the size of a medieval city-state.[5]

The Roman Empire had real coercive authority over its many inhabitants. Most of them, in far-flung places, would never encounter it, and were far more likely to suffer unchecked violence at local hands than to experience either the coercion or the protection of imperial officials. Many lives were passed in almost total ignorance of the imagined community to which they belonged. Plenty – including women, children and slaves – had no recourse to its authority in the first place. But still, for anyone who did encounter it, whether as law or as simple brute force, its reality was unequivocal. The same was true in China. Emperors could not control all their subjects – they could barely control their own courts. But no subject could be confident of escaping its reach once imperial authority turned its attention their way.

This power of an ancient emperor has no real modern equivalent. It was more total and more arbitrary than anything on
offer to even the most ruthless modern tyrants. No one today
– not Putin or Xi or even Kim Jong-un – can rule as whimsically
as a Roman emperor. There are too many complex social and
political forces in their way. At the same time, ancient authority was more personal and more limited. An emperor could be
whimsical because most decisions impacted only on those in the
immediate vicinity. The further a decision travelled, the more
likely it was to be diluted by time and distance. It might reach
its intended target in the end, but no one could be sure in what
form. The empire was an imagined community held together
at its edges by nothing more than distant rumours of what it all
meant at the centre.

Yet despite this, there are clear continuities between ancient
and modern versions of collective existence. Scalability is one.
Durability is another. Empires could be long lived because their
ongoing existence did not depend on the lives of individual
emperors. Though the moment of transition was often perilous
– the death of an emperor always brought with it the possibility of violent conflict – the idea of empire was designed to
withstand it. The emperor is dead; long live the emperor! Just
as pre-modern empires are among the largest political entities
ever known, they are also the longest lasting: China's lasted far
longer than Rome's; ancient Egypt's – at 3,000 years – far longer
than China's. Modernity does not have a monopoly on either
political scale or longevity. If anything, modern political communities are dwarfed by these ancient versions.

At the same time, the ancient world contained numerous
institutions that foreshadowed the workings of their modern
equivalents. The Roman Empire emerged from the Roman
Republic, which was not just an imagined community but also a
highly artificial one. Its many rules, demarcating multiple different roles for its various social and political actors, were designed

to give it an identity separate from any of them. The republic (*res publica*) was more than the sum of its parts. It was its own thing – the 'public thing'. It had a powerful and sclerotic senate, as does the modern American state. It conducted large-scale elections, whose complicated rules of engagement did not prevent their corruption by money and power, any more than the current American electoral system is saved from corruption by its complexity. Roman republicanism tried to limit the powers of prominent families, while repeatedly falling prey to them. The modern American republic – the land of the Kennedys, the Clintons, the Bushes, the Trumps, the Bidens – is much the same. It is not hard to draw a line from then to now.

The Roman Republic began small but became vast: though never comprising more than a million actual citizens, tens of millions were eventually subjected to its rule, and that of the empire it spawned. Founded in 509 BCE, the republic lasted for nearly 500 years, finally destroyed only by the personal ambitions of its leading citizens and their families. And it contained many different kinds of corporate entities, from guilds to joint stock business enterprises to colleges, which functioned as its social and political clubs. These *corpora* developed in Roman law through the time of the empire into a complex and sophisticated set of institutional arrangements, which provided the basis for later legal developments in the medieval and early modern periods. The *universitas* and the *societas* emerged from this conceptual framework. So, therefore, did the modern corporation and the state.

The Roman Republic and Empire contained many different kinds of religious bodies, from the smallest-scale family cults through to what became the biggest of all: the Catholic Church. The Church deployed all sorts of different institutional forms to manage its affairs as it grew, first within the empire and then beyond it. It was a community of communities (*communitas communitatem*) – a corporation of corporations (*universitas universitatem*) – a single church made up of many churches. It lived on continuously while its members lived and died and (if their beliefs were right) lived again. It represented them, just as it was represented in its turn by its popes and cardinals and priests and other officials. Even its god was represented by the Trinity of Father, Son and Holy Ghost: three-in-one and one-in-three. Modern democratic theory has nothing on the conceptual complexity of the medieval Catholic Church.

Scale, durability, variety, continuity, representation: why then do the modern versions of these earlier corporate, religious and political forms constitute a clear break from the past rather than an extension of it? The answer lies in the relationship between scale and variety in the ancient world. The truth is that the Roman Republic, the Roman Empire and the Roman Catholic Church were just too big. They were monoliths, for all the variety they contained. Their lesser institutions were never able to escape their shadow, with the result that they could not grow beyond a certain size. Ancient Roman joint stock companies were sometimes given limited liability so that they could fund imperial building projects. But when the project was completed, the company was wound up. It was not allowed an independent existence.

The Roman Empire was ultimately *sui generis*. There could never be another. The same is true of the Roman Republic, despite the efforts of many state-builders since to replicate its early success. It cannot be repeated. The Catholic Church was, and remains, a similarly unique establishment. Each of these giants contained within them multiple, replicable subordinate institutions, from the partnerships and corporations of Roman law to the chapters and communes of canon law. But these institutions always depended on the sufferance of the dominant authority.

Replication was possible only in the context of an overarching structure that itself had no equivalents and no equals. To borrow from *Star Wars*, the Roman Empire was a kind of Death Star. It could sustain life and order for a long time. But anything that tried to copy it would be killed by it. The power of the unifying political form made possible the creation of a wide variety of lesser political entities: the emperor could click his fingers and whole provinces might spring into being. But this unifying political form was the only large-scale artificial entity that had an enduring life of its own and it could not be repeated. And it was only when it died that other forms of artificial collective life were eventually able to flourish.[6]

When empire is the dominant political model, innovation is stifled by scale. Rome joined together an extraordinary body of different territories, many of them as foreign from each other as it is possible to be. Roman Britain had very little in common with Roman Syria beyond the fact they were both Roman. But for that reason, connectivity – the sharing of administrative and institutional procedures, all the way down to the road network – came at the cost of diversity. Different modes of collective existence could not be brought into dynamic contact with each other. They met only where they already had something in common – subjection to Rome.

The fall of Rome divided its empire. Byzantium, or the Eastern Roman Empire, was centred around Constantinople (modern Istanbul), a place of extraordinary cultural and intellectual diversity but limited institutional innovation. In the west, by contrast, the Roman imperial model was never revived. Instead, different ways of organising political life started to compete with each other for territory and power, and to resist being co-opted into the stifling embrace of either Byzantium or the Catholic Church. The result was sustained innovation but also widespread instability and repeated wars. This process was accelerated by the Reformation at the start of the sixteenth century, which saw religious ferment join forces with political diversity to produce more innovation and much more war.

In his book *Escape from Rome*, the historian Walter Scheidel identifies the fall of the Roman Empire as the precondition of modern European development, and eventually of European global domination. Without the scope for competition and exchange between different institutional models in the west, all of Europe might have suffered the fate that befell it in the east, where Byzantium eventually gave way to an onslaught from the forces of the Ottoman Empire. Nonetheless, it is important to remember what Europe looked like at the time Constantinople fell in 1453. Western Europe was a patchwork of different political units, only a few of them starting to resemble what we would come to think of as modern nation-states (there was a France, of a sort, and an England too, though no Germany or Italy or Spain). On the whole what existed was limited in scope and highly unstable. The basic conundrum remained: in the east there was scale without much political variability, in the west variability without much scale. The basic problem of human development – how to combine long-term security with widespread multiplicity – had not yet been resolved.[7]

Scheidel contrasts what was to happen in Europe with the fate of China. In 1600 these two parts of the world had much in common: similar levels of economic development (with China the richer), extensive trade networks, increasing intellectual experimentation and bureaucratic sophistication. The difference was that China was still an empire. The original empire of the Han Dynasty had, like the Roman one, split in two geographically (north and south), with the north of China becoming fragmented among various rival political organisations and dynasties. However, unlike in Europe, the original empire was eventually reconstituted by the beginning of the tenth century. Scheidel calls this the first 'great divergence' between East and West. The second occurred in the centuries after 1600, when European economic development exploded, while that of imperial China remained relatively static. Only with the end of empire in China at the start of the twentieth century could the gap begin to be closed again. Now, little more than a hundred years later, post-imperial China is poised to overtake the US as the world's largest economy.[8]

Escaping from empire is a necessary but not a sufficient condition for rapid economic development. It is not enough simply to blow up the Death Star – an alternative social and political order needs to replace it, or else all you are left with is chaos. In western Europe that process took the best part of a thousand years. Equally, in the places where growth happened, empire was hardly consigned to the history books. It was still a part of the package. Once modern nation-states acquired the capability to scale up their operations, they also acquired empires of their own. Britain, France, Germany, Italy, even Belgium: by the start of the twentieth century these were all imperial powers, sizeable enough between them to cover a significant portion of the globe, including almost the whole of Africa. Their imperial territories were the source of a great deal of their wealth. Most contemporary historians acknowledge that it is impossible to tell the story of European growth without factoring in the exploitation of the colonised peoples on which so much of it was predicated.

Post-imperial China is currently following a similar pattern. Having turned itself from an empire into a modern state, it is now in the process of acquiring an empire of its own, even if it is careful to avoid using that terminology. The vehicles China uses to achieve colonial domination are not armies and battleships but loans and infrastructure projects. Yet the aims are similar, including resource extraction. Some of the means are similar too, including the creation of expat enclaves in other countries. And China's imperial reach now extends over a significant part of the globe, including much of Africa.

In this sense, empire remains the default model of human political organisation. There appears to be no escape from it for long. In the words of one historian, 'it is the nation-state that is the historical novelty ... and may yet prove to be the more ephemeral entity'. But modern empires are nonetheless different from what came before. For a start, there have been multiple versions of them, all built on roughly the same model. That model requires the development of a viable state to achieve maximum value for the colonisers. The ones that didn't become modern states in time, or did so less successfully, like Spain and Portugal, or Turkey, ultimately lost their empires before they could reap the developmental benefits. During the nineteenth century, as Britain grew increasingly richer, Spain and Portugal became relatively poorer, held back by their legacy political institutions. Every empire is different, of course, but in the modern age, imperial expansion ultimately proved reproducible, so long as it was undertaken by a modern state.[9]

Not all the inhabitants of these modern empires got richer, just the states and those who ran them, along with the corporations that came along for the ride. In 1600 the average Briton was only a little better-off than the average Indian. By 1900 Britain was nearly ten times richer per capita, and India marginally poorer than it had been three centuries earlier. Empire is not good for the colonised. Part of the reason is that imperial politics is inherently exploitative: in the language of contemporary political science, it is 'extractive' of wealth rather than 'inclusive'. Empires also stifle institutional innovation on any scale in case it leads to greater independence. They might impose some of their own institutional innovations – as Britain did in the case of India, exporting its nineteenth-century versions of the rule of law, an independent civil service and proto-democracy – but they rarely return the favour. India became more British under imperial rule; Britain did not become more Indian.[10]

Under modern empires, the direction of travel is all one way. Little Belgium benefited greatly from ruling the vast territory of the Congo, by taking what was there – rubber, oil, cheap enforced labour – for its own use. Congo and the Congolese did not benefit. They simply suffered the consequences. The Death Star is still the Death Star, but in the modern world it does not destroy the people who run it when it comes to an end, as it did in the ancient world. It is just a tool in the hands of the exploiting state, which can often get along fine without it. Belgium continues to prosper long after it lost its empire, and the Democratic Republic of Congo continues to suffer for it.[11]

The narrow corridor

There is another way to think about continuity and discontinuity between the ancient and modern worlds. Though modern societies are on the whole far wealthier than their ancient counterparts, there is still a lot of variation among them. Just look at Belgium and the DRC – both are now ostensibly modern states, but one currently has a per capita GDP of more than $50,000, the other of less than $1,000. That is far wider than any gap that existed between the richest and poorest parts of the ancient world, not because the poorest were any less poor (they were even poorer) but because the richest were much less rich. The wealthiest regions of the Roman Empire were roughly twice as well off as the poorest – average income levels on the Italian mainland were around $1,000 per person, compared to $500 in western Africa. Inequality within particular places could still be spectacular – the very richest Romans lived lives as remote from the city's slum-dwellers as tech billionaires do from the homeless of San Francisco today. But the world as a whole was more equal.

That said, some ancient societies were clearly much more successful than others, measured not only by military conquest but also by their relative prosperity. In the Roman world, it was on the whole better in material terms to be in the empire than out of it, even if other factors mattered much more – far better, for instance, not to be a slave than to be one. In ancient Greece, some city-states performed significantly better than others. Ancient Athens was a notably successful society, richer, more stable and more dynamic over a longer period than any political equivalent. Athens did ultimately lose the epic war it fought against Sparta from 431 to 404 BCE, yet it recovered from its defeat to enjoy another century of stability and growth. Sparta, a more inbred and militaristic society, never got over its victory and soon declined. Better on the whole to be in Athens, with all the usual caveats.

Some have put this down to the fact that Athens was a democracy. Others to its empire, which was ruthlessly managed, or to simple good fortune – Athens was lucky to have its extensive silver mines and the slave labour to exploit them. But in their book *The Narrow Corridor*, the economic historians Daron Acemoglu and James Robinson argue it was something else. They point to the perennial dilemma of human social and political development. All stable societies of even moderate scale need an effective government to organise their affairs. The risk, however, is that any government can become exploitative and corrupt (and that includes democratic ones). Give a small group of people the power to organise others and you also give them the power to take advantage of their position to enrich themselves. At the same time, any prosperous society needs civic dynamism, which depends on independent enterprises being able to organise themselves. The risk here is that their independence undoes social stability by allowing those making the money to make their own rules.[12]

It is, essentially, a Goldilocks problem: not too little, not too much, just right. The state needs to be powerful but not so powerful as to crush freedom and the incentives for enterprise. Society needs to be robustly independent, but not so independent as to undermine public order and good government. The challenge is that neither government nor civil society has a natural limit on its appetites: politicians want more power, civil groups want more freedom. Left to their own devices, they will demand too much and destroy what they have.

The fate of Rome after its empire broke in two illustrates how things can go wrong. In the east there were periods of strong central control – interspersed with bouts of instability and civil war – but insufficient civic independence. Byzantine artists, philosophers and theologians could think big in the big cities – where they created some of the most beautiful things ever made, '… hammered gold and gold enamelling/To keep a drowsy Emperor awake', as W. B. Yeats so lovingly put it in 'Sailing to Byzantium' – but institutional experimentation was limited and economic progress stalled. This was, after all, still an empire.[13]

In the west, by the early medieval period, all sorts of smaller groups were vying for control and pursuing their own ambitions, but there was insufficient political stability for them to do so securely. The lords and ladies of Byzantium heard songs of 'what is past, or passing, or to come' – this is what Yeats called 'the artifice of eternity'. The lords and ladies of medieval western Europe – along with the princes and popes and doges and councillors and bishops and monks and lawyers and guildsmen – were busier doing their own thing. The trouble was that they lacked sufficient coercive control to get others to fall into line.

How to get the balance right? The answer might seem obvious – rein in the power of the central state when it gets too dominant, restrain the wildness of society when it gets too unconstrained. But who will rein in the state if society can't? And who will restrain society if not the state? A Goldilocks problem soon becomes a chicken-and-egg problem: you need a strong state to keep society in check, but you need a strong society to keep the state in check. Acemoglu and Robinson insist that the only way out is for both state and civil society to be strong enough to set limits on each other. It is a kind of arms race between political control and socio-economic independence in which two sides need to be able – and therefore unable – to dominate each other. The image Acemoglu and Robinson use to capture this contest is taken from *Alice Through the Looking Glass*:

> 'Well, in our country,' said Alice, still panting a little, 'you'd generally get to somewhere else – if you run very fast for a long time, as we've been doing.'
>
> 'A slow sort of country!' said the Queen. 'Now, here, you see, it takes all the running you can do, to keep in the same place. If you want to get somewhere else, you must run at least twice as fast as that!'

Everyone has to run as fast as they can if things are to remain steady. Only if there is movement on both sides will there be the solid ground underneath needed for growth.

Ancient Athens was such a society. It had a strong state – its democracy was elaborate and pervasive, exercising control over many aspects of Athenian life and making extensive demands of its citizens. At the same time, Athenian civic society was dynamic and demanding too. It was a trading community, and its prominent citizens included groups of men who had made their fortunes as merchants, alongside the old landed aristocracy. It was a city of intellectual and artistic diversity, of philosophers and tragedians, of the academy and the theatre. This generated barriers in the way of political oppression, without destroying the authority of the state. It some ways, ancient Athens can appear quite modern. The Athenian leader Pericles described what made Athens special in his memorial address for the dead at the height of the war with Sparta:

The freedom which we enjoy in our government extends

also to our ordinary life. There, far from exercising a jealous surveillance over each other, we do not feel called upon to be angry with our neighbour for doing what he likes, or even to indulge in those injurious looks which cannot fail to be offensive, although they inflict no positive penalty. But all this ease in our private relations does not make us lawless as citizens. Against this fear is our chief safeguard, teaching us to obey the magistrates and the laws, particularly such as regard the protection of the injured, whether they are actually on the statute book, or belong to that code which, although unwritten, yet cannot be broken without acknowledged disgrace.

All in all, it sounds quite liveable, even for us.[14]

Acemoglu and Robinson explicitly call the ancient Athenian state a 'Leviathan'. Like any powerful political organisation, it was prone to corruption and abuse. A constitution was not enough to keep its office-holders in check – anyone with enough power to manage the state might find the means to subvert its rules. Political stability needed the countervailing power of non-state actors and social codes of practice. Inevitably, this is a delicate balancing act. Either side can over-tip: politicians can try to stifle dissent and use their power to make money; social elites can conspire against the state and use their money to acquire power. Hence 'the narrow corridor' – there is not much room for getting the balance right.

In the case of Athens, the narrowness of the space in which it could prosper was palpable. Over its 200-year history, Athenian democracy slid periodically into crisis, because of military overreach, coups, putative tyrants, economic setbacks, or natural disasters, including the plague of 430 BCE, which killed around a quarter of its population. It was in permanent danger of toppling over one way or the other. Yet what makes Athens stand out in the ancient world is that it survived these episodes.

Where other societies would have been unbalanced and undone, the combination of a robust state and robust civil society gave Athens the ability to recover. And each time it recovered, it continued to thrive. Here, then, is the model for success.

Except it was not a model that could be applied anywhere else. Athens stands out in the ancient world because it was unique. When it eventually failed its success could not be replicated. In that sense, its state was nothing like the Leviathan – by modern standards, it was not really a state at all. It was not a legal entity in its own right and it had no independent existence outside the ongoing commitment of its citizens. That was Pericles's point: Athens *was* the Athenians. Its political identity was generated by its inhabitants and their rules and customs, and it remained an intensely human enterprise. Both its state institutions and its civic organisations were entirely dependent on the participation of their members. This is what made ancient Athenian life intensely demanding: there was no way to opt out.

The modern Leviathan is designed to carry on regardless. It is a machine. The gulf between ancient and present-day Greece exemplifies this. Modern Athens has a remarkable architectural and cultural heritage, but in political terms it is nothing special. It is true that the Greek state has survived its own litany of crises over the past decade or more, including economic depression and another plague in the form of Covid-19. But it has stayed within the narrow corridor not because of the unique contribution of its citizens, who are much like people anywhere else in the modern world: most of them have better things to do with their time than politics. It has survived because its political arrangements are far from unique: they have the grinding, self-sustaining qualities of established institutions around the developed world.[15]

Before the modern age, the narrow corridor of prosperity didn't lead anywhere. For those rare places that enjoyed its benefits, when it was over, it was over. Once human effort and good fortune could no longer sustain the necessary interplay of social and political energies, the result was the dissipation of both. Today, the situation is different. The fact is that the narrow corridor is pretty crowded these days. Many different places, from Greece to Japan to New Zealand to South Korea to Norway to Israel to Uruguay, exist inside it. There are still plenty of parts of the world that have never been able to get the balance right – look at South Sudan. But where it has been achieved, the danger is not so much that it might be a dead end. The real danger is that the race now has an artificial life of its own because it is being run by modern states and corporations.

Modern states and corporations will keep going whether we are fully committed to them or not. They don't depend on us – and our human qualities – in the way that ancient polities did. It is always possible for the contest between them to become unbalanced, with predictable results: an unchecked state still means too much political interference, a dominant enterprise economy means too much corporate power. Then life gets out of whack for everyone. Most of the time, though, modern states and corporations spur each other on, endlessly, iteratively. Those of us – the many of us – who live in this artificial version of wonderland may soon have to face a question that was never likely to arise before: what if there is no escape from the relentless drive for growth? And what happens if we need to find one?

Company-states

The grand sweep of millennium-wide history seems to turn on decisive junctures in the human story, which we call revolutions. But nothing is ever that neat, particularly for the people who live through them. The previous era lingers on into the new, and the new order relies on the institutions of the old. There are also countless mashups between the two. Modernity is no different.

To start with, at least, it did not represent a clean break with the past. It was a hybrid age.

One of these hybrids was the 'company-state', which was neither corporation nor state, but a combination of the two. If modernity is characterised by the competing claims of sovereign states and free-standing corporations, this means that the age of the company-state was not really modern. Yet it lasted into the nineteenth century and was the original basis of modern imperial expansion. So it was modern as well. Modernity is a mashup too.[16]

The East India Company (EIC) was a company-state, as was the Dutch East India Company (or Verenigde Oostindische Compagnie – VOC). These organisations were chartered by their parent states to run significant parts of their imperial operations overseas – from India to Hong Kong in the case of the EIC, from South Africa to Thailand in the case of the VOC. They were commercial enterprises, but they operated by means of military force and they entered into their own treaties with local rulers. They also had the power to raise taxes and to dispense criminal justice. These prerogatives gave them enormous advantages, including the ability to pool capital over longer periods of time than their commercial rivals, while also giving them more flexibility than nation-states, given that they did not have to answer to domestic populations. This, then, looked like the best of both worlds: the single-mindedness of the corporation coupled with the sovereign powers of the state.

These company-states had extraordinary global reach, particularly during the seventeenth and eighteenth centuries. Their power challenges the idea that European dominance was achieved by European states acquiring the fruits of modernity sooner than anywhere else. Company-states were legal persons, but they were also hangovers from the era of chartered merchants with special privileges. Nor was European dominance simply a product of Western scientific and technological advances. The EIC and VOC were unique institutions, whose strength derived from their ability to adapt their practices according to local conditions rather than simply imposing European models of authority. Often, they would rely on local rulers to do their work for them, including fighting their wars. Many of the innovations they embraced were forced on them by the need to make do with what they found in the places they were trying to rule.

This suggests that modern empires were in their origin hybrid organisations as well – an improvised combination of East and West, and of North and South. They did not arise when European superiority subjugated non-European backwardness. Instead, company-states exploited the variety they discovered around the world, adopting the institutional forms that suited them best. When they needed to assert their sovereign authority, they did. But when it was easier to buy the services they needed, they did that too.

What, then, happened to this model? Why are hybrid institutions, which combine different features of states and corporations and can switch between them as the occasion demands, not the dominant ones? The answer is that these organisations were also monoliths, able to connect different parts of the world only by their own presence, not by creating replicable models of political organisation. They were more like the Roman Empire than they were like a modern state because they could not build institutions with a durable life of their own. It was only their own durability that counted. At the same time, their advantages became disadvantages as they grew. By the second half of the eighteenth century, company-states started to look like the worst of both worlds. They were too commercially driven to be capable of responsible government and they became beset by corruption and scandal. Yet they had too many political responsibilities to make a reliable profit for their investors and they ended up weighed down by debt. It turned out that ruling India, and exploiting India, were not something that could easily be done to scale and over the long term by the same organisation. During the nineteenth century the British state took on the job of ruling. And it put non-chartered corporations in charge of the job of extracting wealth.

There is not, and never has been, a clean line separating state from corporate power. Modern states have always favoured certain corporations and given them special privileges. That continues to this day. Chinese corporations – especially the most powerful ones – rely heavily on the approval of the Chinese state in order to function. Many of the world's most successful corporations – such as Hyundai in South Korea – only got their big breaks thanks to the special protection afforded them by the state. Hyundai grew from a tiny business in the mid-1970s to a vast conglomerate by the 2000s because state-run banks gave it privileged loans and the South Korean state championed its cause by banning the import of foreign-produced cars until the late 1980s. Once Hyundai was big enough domestically to compete internationally, the state continued to favour it with protectionist policies, in return for which it expected Hyundai to contribute to the development of the domestic economy and the training of its workforce.[17]

This was symbiosis. But it was not hybridity. Hyundai has never acquired tax raising or juridical or coercive powers. It conquered global markets, but it did not conquer the globe. The company-state died in the nineteenth century, seemingly never to return. The way for states and corporations to combine their efforts remains wide open. But a return to the age of the company-state is very unlikely. It was ultimately another dead end.

Some twenty-first-century corporations have started to creep their way back into territory that has traditionally been the preserve of the state. Amazon will adjudicate property disputes between its customers. Google will verify your identity. Meta hopes one day to have its own currency. But this is not a stab at sovereignty. It is just another way of making money, particularly as overstretched states struggle to fulfil all their functions. Google won't give you a passport. But while you are waiting for your real passport to arrive, it will let you navigate the world of online activity as a verified version of yourself.

The modern age – whether we date if from the seventeenth, eighteenth, or nineteenth century – remains distinct from what went before, despite all the blurring round the edges. Something happened to make it different. The difference lies in the fact that what was unique became repeatable, what had been improvised became mechanical, what used to be a dead end became limitlessly adaptable. The modern age is not itself limitless and it too will end at some point, perhaps soon. Two or three hundred years is just a brief interlude in the broad sweep of human history. The era of modern states and corporations will turn out to be an outlier in the long run. Yet what changed in that time has fundamentally altered who we are and what we do. The outlier is the key to understanding the fate of *Homo sapiens*.

5

THE GREAT TRANSFORMATION

The hockey stick

If a single chart could sum up modern human history, it would be the one shown in fig. 11. Something happened after 1500 to global output that had been flatlining for 1,500 years – and tens of thousands of years before that – to shift it slowly off the horizontal; something happened after 1850 that started to turn the line sharply upward; something happened in the last few decades that turned an upward slope into a near vertical one. As

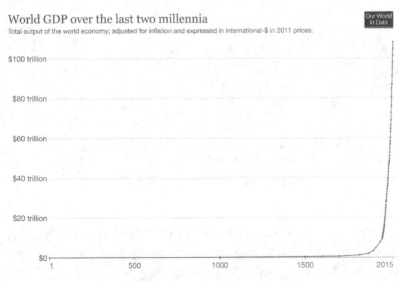

11. Global economic growth over two millennia

species we went from poor to a bit less poor; from less poor to not poor; from not poor to rich.

But this chart conceals at least as much as it reveals because it tells many different stories as a single one. Disaggregated by nation, and more finely separated out over time, the picture is still a hockey stick, but a much blurrier one. The point of take-off can be seen to vary significantly from place to place (fig. 12). And in many places it has never happened at all. A very wealthy species still has hundreds of millions of extremely poor members, though many fewer than fifty years ago. The DRC is barely better-off per person than it was 500 years ago. A richer world is an ever more unequal one.

GDP per Capita of Select Countries over Time

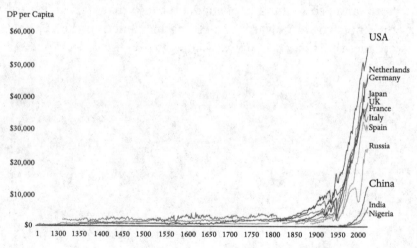

12. Disaggregated economic growth over 700 years

The first signs of lift-off came in England and the Netherlands. Per capita GDP in England was roughly the same in 1650 as it had been in 1350 – about $1,500 per person. By 1750 that figure had nearly doubled. By 1850 it had nearly doubled again.

And by 1950 it was almost ten times higher than it had been in the middle of the seventeenth century. France, England's most significant economic and geopolitical rival, had been comparably wealthy in 1650. But its economy did not grow much over the next hundred years. There, the take-off only started during the nineteenth century. The same is true of the United States, which started growing rapidly after about 1820. By 1900 Americans were on average four times richer than they had been a hundred years earlier. By 1950 they were twice as rich again.

In global terms, this was enough to move the overall line sharply upwards. In regional terms, it made an enormous difference to people's lives, though again any generic story obscures the vast differences in local experiences. As Britain got richer, plenty of its inhabitants got poorer, and sicker, as they moved from the countryside to disease-ridden, stinking, overcrowded towns and cities, where they provided cheap and easily exploited labour for the new industries driving economic growth. A lot of these labourers were children. Average life expectancy barely increased at all from 1750 to 1850, even as Britain became the richest country in the world. It took the arrival of democracy, and the redistribution of the benefits of growing national wealth through the political system, to alter that. Most of the improvement in life expectancy had to wait for the twentieth century and the advent of the welfare state.

However, these centuries-long stories of progress are not enough to account for the extraordinary upward trajectory of global wealth in the last few decades. That is a result of the developmental history of western Europe and the United States being replicated in other parts of the world and being condensed into a much shorter time frame. This is when the great transformation became what's known as 'the Great Acceleration'. For example, in 1950 South Korea was poorer per person than England had been in 1350: its per capita GDP was barely $1,000. By 2000 its average wealth had increased twentyfold, a process that in Britain had taken more than 300 years. Today South Korea and the UK are comparably wealthy. Ghana, which was richer than South Korea in 1950, is now ten times poorer.[1]

The biggest driver of the recent global story has happened in the world's two most populous nations. In China, economic growth shifted sharply upwards only in the late 1970s; in India, though independence from British imperial rule in 1947 brought considerable economic benefits, growth was relatively sluggish until the early 1990s. Since then, it has been as fast as anywhere. No two nations' economic histories are the same, but in all those nations that have seen transformational economic growth, they look the same when seen from a distance: a relatively flat line for a long time, and then lift-off.

Why? There are countless competing explanations for what is sometimes called 'the great transformation' and sometimes 'the great divergence' because it has happened at such different times in different places – notably in north-west Europe well before anywhere else. England and the Netherlands benefited early from their empires. The Netherlands was the richest country in the world in the seventeenth and early-eighteenth centuries, its wealth fuelled by its vast overseas trading network – much of it managed by the VOC – and commodified on the world's first stock exchange, which was established in Amsterdam in 1611. Britain's rise to the top began in the second half of the eighteenth century as it started to exploit the benefits of the Industrial Revolution before anyone else got the chance. Why did it happen there first? Answers range from coal to empire to culture to demography. It was almost certainly a combination of all of them: a resource rich island, an imperial trading nation, a place free from the worst of religious and ethnic conflict and increasingly open to scientific enquiry, possessed of a relatively stable population, Britain got very lucky. It took advantage of that luck.[2]

The origin story of the great transformation remains

contentious. But the replication story – the fact that the hockey stick keeps repeating itself in different places at different times – has fewer potential explanations. It can't be coal or empire or culture or demography because it has happened in places that have next to nothing in common on those scores, from Canada to Singapore to Denmark to Taiwan. Equally, there have been massive divergences between places that share very similar natural, cultural and demographic resources. As South Korea got rich, North Korea stayed very poor, despite the fact that both countries had near-identical endowments when they were created in 1948: more or less the same history, same geography, same people. The line between them – the 38th parallel – is as arbitrary as any border in the world. Yet it has created two very different worlds. How? The answer is politics, plus economic organisation.[3]

What the places that have seen exponential growth have in common is primarily institutional. All have relatively stable states, organised as representative bodies. These do not have to be democratic: neither China nor Singapore is a democracy in any meaningful sense. But they do have to be institutions that can reliably speak for their people in pursuing their objectives over the medium to long term. That means they must have an identity that transcends the identities of any given individuals. States that are their rulers – from Louis XIV's France to Kim Jong-un's North Korea – don't achieve lift-off. Rulers need to be representatives of an impersonal state.

This is a necessary but not a sufficient condition for economic transformation. India had a working modern state – built on a version of the British model, with elections, a national Parliament, an extensive bureaucracy and the rule of law – for decades before it embarked on the path of rapid growth. The same is broadly true of China, though Mao's regime was too closely identified with its leader for true institutional stability – and it is possible that Xi's regime might be heading that way. But despite the time lags, it can't happen anywhere without a functioning modern state. Britain was able to start growing in the eighteenth century because its state got up and running at the end of the seventeenth. France and the US had to wait till the nineteenth century because their states only got up and running at the end of the eighteenth.

What does the modern state bring to the equation? Essentially, its artificial personality. Because it is neither its people nor its government, a modern state provides the basis for long-term commitment, on the part of both citizens and investors (often these are the same people, as better-off citizens can show their commitment by buying state debt, as happened in Britain during the eighteenth century). If the state is captured by a particular group or class there is little incentive for others to join in. Why should the poor commit to the state if it serves only the rich? Just as importantly, why should the rich commit if they think the state has been co-opted by the poor? And why should outside investors have faith in either? A state that is neither the rich nor the poor but something else – its own person – is a precondition for collective confidence in its long-term ability to function.

This is partly a matter of trust. The economic historians Douglass North and Barry Weingast have termed it 'credible commitment', meaning that those on the receiving end of state power must believe that those doling it out will not simply abuse it for their own purposes. Financial credit depends on credibility. So does political stability. A government cannot claim the monopoly on legitimate coercion for itself: that spells oppression. The monopoly must belong to the state. But given that it will be a government that arranges the coercion – because the state cannot act for itself – this requires a leap of faith. States work when people believe they are relatively independent of their rulers. But they will only believe so if the state can be seen to be working. Intelligent political decision-making unquestionably helps with this. But more important than that is institutional continuity.[4]

Faith is therefore needed to get the machine up and running. However, once it is running then that faith can be increasingly routine. It doesn't actually require much of a commitment – either of time or of mental energies – on the part of citizens for it to keep going. It becomes a reflex. The machinery of the state proves its credibility as an independent entity by the fact that we don't have to think about it for it to exist. It starts to run itself.

This process helps create the conditions for economic growth by making political life reliable, while also granting individuals the time and space to develop their talents and pursue their own goals. However, that is not enough on its own. Sustained growth depends on non-state enterprises replicating some of the credibility and reliability of the state. In other words, it needs corporate entities that can act as artificial persons too, to ensure that long-term investment, economies of scale and entrepreneurial initiative can be combined in one institutional form.[5]

England and the Netherlands started off with their company-states, which were able to sustain substantial returns over the long run. Nonetheless, explosive economic growth seems to entail a clearer separation: a state that doesn't get too close to its companies, even as it supports them, and companies that don't seek to replicate the coercive authority of the state, even as they take advantage of it. The United States grew so fast during the nineteenth century because it bypassed the company-state model and moved straight to a division of labour between its coercive authorities with law-making and tax-raising powers and its business enterprises with investment-raising advantages. The same thing happened in China a century and a half later. China's economic miracle began in the late 1970s with the liberalisation of its economy, which meant the increasing independence of corporations to set their own course and of Chinese citizens to create them. Some of these corporations are now among the most powerful economic entities in the world. They are still close to the state – and getting closer – but nothing like as close as they would have been before the late 1970s, when they could have had no independent identity of their own. China would never have grown nearly so much or so fast without them.

India's economic growth since its financial liberalisation in the early 1990s has likewise seen an exponential growth in corporate activity. Before 1991 corporations were subject to extensive regulation, tying them to the state's priorities at national and local level. Since then, the story has followed a classic long-tail pattern. There are now more than a million new corporations created in India each year, most of them tiny and vanishingly short lived. At the same time, India's corporate giants dwarf anything that existed thirty years ago. The market capitalisation of its biggest companies is more than a hundred times greater than it was at the start of the 1990s. These mega-corporations hold much of the nation's wealth in their hands. As a result, India is also vastly more unequal than it was. More than half the wealth generated each year goes to the richest 1 per cent of the population.

Can't we just call this the spread of capitalism and be done with it? The market liberalisations that China and India embraced were quintessentially capitalist, in that they placed a premium on private ownership and profit, relatively insulated from other political imperatives. Yet capitalism can't explain what happened on its own. Italy was capitalist during the late nineteenth and early twentieth centuries – indeed, it was Florentine merchants who first invented this way of doing business as far back as the 1300s – but it did not grow much. Brazil was capitalist over the same period, but it did not grow much either. Italy's rapid growth happened in the second half of the twentieth century, in the age of Fiat. For Brazil it happened in the latter part of the twentieth century and the early twenty-first, in the age of Petrobras. Fiat is a car company. Petrobras is a petroleum company. The large-sale harnessing of energy resources is also an essential part of the equation – if not coal, then oil and gas. But capitalism needs to be organised a certain way if it is to manage this. It needs to be organised around the artificial personality of states and corporations. They are the ones that do the harnessing.

This is not a deterministic story, which says that once states and corporations get going, nothing can stop them. Neither Italy nor Brazil is guaranteed to keep growing. These states can still squander the faith that is placed in them, and both are showing signs of doing that at present. Argentina's state has done so consistently over the last hundred years through the mismanagement of its finances and the relative ease with which its political institutions have been captured by private interests. As a result, the growth history of the Argentinian economy looks more like a rollercoaster than a hockey stick, with repeated dramatic dips and periodic defaults on the national debt.[6]

Corporations can and do fail as well, even the biggest ones. Corruption remains a problem. Complacency does too. Human beings can always find ways to screw things up. And if they don't, states and corporations can always find ways to disregard the interests of the human beings that built them.

Nonetheless, when explosive growth happens, it is the interplay between states and corporations that drives it. There are many more successfully functioning states and corporations than there were 200 years ago. There are many more than even fifty years ago. That is the reason why the narrow corridor is not so narrow any more.

Living the dream

What has been the human experience of the great transformation? In his book *Progress* (2016), Johan Norberg gives a snapshot of what his great-great-great-grandfather's life would have been like in Sweden during the winter of 1868.

Young and old, haggard and pale, went from farm to farm, begging for something to delay their death from starvation. The most emaciated livestock were tied upright because they could not stand on their own feet. Their milk was often mingled with blood. Several thousand Swedes died of starvation within that year.

This was one of the last great European famines caused by crop failure. Within four generations these experiences would have been remote enough to need to be preserved by folk memory. Within six generations they have become so distant as to seem medieval. What connected nineteenth-century Swedes to all those who had come before them – living with the fear of death by starvation – serves to disconnect them almost entirely from Swedes living today.[7]

Norberg is one of the new breed of 'rational optimists', whose complaint is that most human beings have completely lost touch with how different – and how much better – their lives are than even those of their grandparents. The story of Swedish progress has been more condensed than England's (where the last famine happened in the seventeenth century, though the British government still managed to preside over a devastating famine in Ireland in the middle of the nineteenth century), but is still relatively slow compared with some parts of the world, including China, where memories of mass starvation can be fresh for anyone over the age of seventy. Yet even human beings who live through these changes may not experience them as transformational. Many older Chinese people still treat food as a potentially scarce resource, even though it is not. Many younger Chinese have no idea what their grandparents are afraid of, even though the fear is very real for them.[8]

Change across a lifetime is often too piecemeal and too slow to register as a move from one way of living to another. Our brains are not geared to organise our experiences into historical categories. We experience life as a flow. There are moments that stand out, of course, and for those who have lived through the great transformation this could include moving from a home without running water, or heating, or within reach of a hospital, or near a school, or with separate bedrooms, to one with any or all of these attributes. Memoirs of nineteenth- and twentieth-century life are full of such recollections. But these moments can quickly be assimilated into a new set of concerns: new schools are frightening places, especially for anyone who has never attended one, and hospitals are too; sleeping alone can be lonely. The most memorable changes – the ones with the biggest 'life-was-never-the-same-again' impact – are the negative ones: death, disease, disaster. We often never get over those. But when such things are increasingly absent from our lives, we tend not to notice.

This is one reason for the mismatch that Norberg complains about: as life gets better, we can feel as if it is getting worse. He reports that half of all Swedes now believe that there are 'intolerable conditions' in their society, compared with 13 per cent in 1955. Over that period Swedes have become much richer, better educated, healthier, longer lived, more widely travelled, more secure, better housed and sexually freer, and they have access to far nicer food. Yet they are also more likely to grumble about their lot.

Perhaps this is evidence that human beings are more indifferent to material improvements than we might think, and growing dissatisfaction is evidence of a spiritual hunger. But that seems unlikely. Whatever nostalgic fairy tales we might tell ourselves, very few people would choose to go back to a time before safe water, or reliably stocked supermarkets, or pain-free dentistry, even if they were offered more religious sustenance in return. After all, in the contemporary world, religious sustenance is still readily available if you want it, along with everything else.

Instead, we suffer from cognitive biases. As terrible events become more remote, we experience the ones we come across more acutely, even if it is only at one remove. Terrorist attacks get reported instantaneously, and though most people will almost certainly never experience one, we register the risk as very real. We forget what used to be true – that things were once worse – because we have a bias in favour of the present. We dwell on bad news because it is more memorable. We are more afraid of disaster because we have much more to lose.[9]

Personal experience is not the best way to judge how significantly the human experience might have altered. That requires a more detached view, which is what Norberg seeks to provide. Seen in the round, the transformation has been astonishing. Nothing remotely like it has ever happened before. Nor since: for all the talk of the amazing changes that have been set in motion by the digital revolution, they still pale relative to the shift from famine to plenty, from rural to urban living, from premature death to long life. The human pay-off from new technology has simply not lived up to the hype. As the co-founder of PayPal Peter Thiel said, 'We were promised flying cars, and we got 140 characters.' If that's now 280 characters, on a platform owned by Elon Musk, it hardly represents progress.

Even in straightforward economic terms, the results of the digital revolution have been disappointing. Growth has stalled in the developed world, relative to what was achieved in the nineteenth and twentieth centuries. Productivity gains have not materialised. Compared to the transformational experience of the electrification and mass transportation revolutions – trains, planes, automobiles – digital technology looks gimmicky. Can the iPhone's contribution to the sum of human well-being compete even with the humble washing machine?[10]

Yet we are still promised that the truly big transformation is at hand – a time is coming soon when the human experience will be upended again by new machines whose superhuman qualities will massively enhance what we can achieve. These intelligent machines will transform life expectancy – from decades to centuries – and travel – from international to inter-planetary – and human memory – from limited to limitless. We won't recognise ourselves.

If it happens – and there is no real evidence of it happening yet – it will be something quite new. Change on this scale would mean a break with biology – even a few humans living for hundreds of years is very different from millions of humans living to be a hundred. One requires the wider distribution of a rare natural possibility; the other requires a completely altered sense of what's possible in the first place. Yet even so, longevity still remains a question of scale. In that sense at least, it may not feel quite as new as we think.

We have already gone from multiple years to decades in typical human lifespans, from local to global in the possibilities of human movement, from piecemeal to universal in the scope of human communication. The coming change may yet be startling in its speed – the digital transformation could happen much quicker than what came before. But we should remember how quickly the first transformation can now occur – well within a conventional human lifespan. Nor should we forget that it takes time for an extension of the human lifespan to be fully appreciated by its beneficiaries. Two-hundred-year-olds will not be with us any time soon.

The evidence from the first great shift is that we might not fully notice what is happening to us, unless it is very dramatic, in which case it may seem very bad. If machines run out of control we will notice, just as we notice when states fall apart or economies collapse. If we become entirely disconnected from our bodies we will notice that too. But if machines enhance our bodily experiences, we might fold these into the experiences we are already familiar with, as we have always done. The much heralded AI transformation – the Singularity – is anticipated as a singular event: the definitive leap from this to that. For us to experience it as such, it will have to be an overwhelming phenomenon, in which case we are likely to encounter it as a terrible loss. If it is to be a positive experience, we may well encounter it as an extension of what preceded it.

There is another reason that the first great transformation does not register as a wholly positive event for the humans who have experienced it, notwithstanding all its benefits. Like the transformation that is still to come, it has been driven by artificial versions of ourselves. One way to sum up what changed is that we swapped an arbitrary existence for an artificial one. Natural life is arbitrary: death and disaster come in forms we are powerless to control. We are not in charge of the fate of our own bodies if we let nature run its course. Yet as we gain more control over our natural fate, we can feel powerless in a different way. We become dependent on artificial decision-making machines for our survival: welfare states, health-insurance companies, big pharma, the medical profession. The transformation in our personal prospects has been driven by our growing dependence on vast, impersonal systems, and we can experience that as a loss too.

Hannah Arendt, in her book *The Human Condition*, characterises the essential arbitrariness of a natural human existence as the relentless struggle for survival. She calls this the world of 'labour', where what we do is driven by the short-term imperative of staving off starvation. For most human beings for most of human history this was what life entailed: back-breaking effort to keep the body alive. It extended into the modern age, as labour shifted from the land to the factory and individuals found themselves fighting a different kind of battle for survival. The life of a nineteenth-century factory labourer could be as arbitrary as that of a ninth-century peasant: enough to live on one day, nothing the next. And given the unfamiliarity of modern industrial conditions, it could feel far more chaotic.[11]

Arendt contrasts the world of labour with the world of what

she calls 'work', which is not natural but artificial. Work involves building things that last and it represents an escape from the relentless cycle of natural disease and decay. In that sense, it is a liberation. But it has an obvious downside: its artificiality means that we can become alienated from our experiences. When we build beautiful things with our hands or our minds, we are constructing lasting extensions of ourselves. But for most human beings in the modern age, the artificial world of work has meant being parts of mechanical systems that someone else has built, and over which we have little control.

The 'job', for instance, is a modern invention. The word originally meant something accidental or haphazard, barely worth doing at all – 'petty, piddling work', as Samuel Johnson defined it in his dictionary. Only in the nineteenth century did it start to denote something reliable or secure – a way of escaping from the arbitrariness of a subsistence existence with the promise of a steady income. Only in the twentieth century was that backed up by employment rights, won for workers by trade union activism, or, as it came to be known, 'the labour movement'. The idea of 'job security' dates from 1936, in the immediate aftermath of the Great Depression. To get a job has come to mean an advance in life prospects, and to lose one a setback. For many it still represents a liberation, particularly from reliance on family. Entry into the workforce has been a key element of female emancipation over the last hundred years.

Yet running alongside that sense of freedom and enhancement has been the constant drumbeat of anxiety that work is a deadening experience because it makes us slaves to the machine. One reason that jobs are a modern invention is that so many of them have been created either by modern states or by corporations – what generates the possibility of security is working for something that has a lasting life of its own. That is also what creates the possibility of our redundancy. Working for another human being is more personal than working for a company–

– it's the difference between being a servant, or perhaps a subordinate, or if you are lucky a friend, and being an employee. Even friendship can be an arbitrary experience – here one day, gone the next, on a personal whim. We've all experienced that. Losing your job in a corporate restructuring exercise is different. It's not whimsical. It's not even personal. The machine simply chews you up and spits you out.

Arendt feared that the world of work had been corrupted by the things we have built to make us feel more secure: modern states and corporations. For this she blamed, among others, Hobbes, the philosopher who had turned the state into a giant decision-making machine. As a result, the human condition had increasingly been reduced to feeding these mechanical versions of ourselves with what they needed to subsist, often with disastrous results. Ordinary human beings might end up working for states that have no common humanity at all, as happened in Germany between 1933 and 1945. Or we might work for corporations that have no sense of how to preserve the natural habitat that humanity needs in order to flourish. Political and economic life risks becoming an inhuman enterprise if the artificial world of work defines us rather than being what we use to define our world.

The modern age has always been torn between our twin impulses towards security and emancipation. For each mechanically reliable version of the human condition we have constructed we have also looked for ways to humanise its impersonal, artificial qualities. We work for organisations that pay a wage and then we want to get out and work for ourselves, even if it means a more precarious living. If that succeeds, we might end up building a version of what we left behind as we start employing others. When it fails, we frequently fall again for the siren call of job security. We try to humanise states by democratising them, pushing for more involvement on a personal level, until we discover that doing politics is hard work, and we lose interest.

We succumb to leaders who promise to give the state a human face, but the more personal the state becomes, the less reliable it can seem, because it is subject to its leaders' whims. They start employing their friends and forget about us. So we push for politics to be more impersonal again and try to reassert the authority of the experts, the impartial authorities, the machines.

Arendt's own sense of loss was for what she called the world of human action, exemplified by the ancient Athenian state. Here, citizens could engage with each other on a personal level, through their capacity to communicate in a way that no machine can. When we tell each other stories about what might be possible if we act together – like the story Pericles told of what made the Athenian way of life worth dying for – we build a version of ourselves that is fragile but quintessentially human. Athenian politics was a deeply human enterprise. But it was also inhuman for many of the people who fell under its control and who had no voice within it. The purest forms of human politics only ever allow action for some: the lucky few. To give the many a consistent voice, much more artificiality is required.

Arendt knew it did no good to be nostalgic for what we have left behind. But she still believed it ought to be possible to build a more human politics in the modern world by focusing on the craft of living together, rather than just the mechanics. Craft is work too. She saw glimpses of it in the business of modern state-building, including the work that went into building the American state at the end of the eighteenth century. By the second half of the twentieth century she feared that American politics had become far too mechanical. It was too reliant on party machines to manage popular participation, on new computers to organise its information, on nuclear weapons to keep it safe. At the same time, the twentieth-century American state clearly had some big advantages over the eighteenth-century version. Women could vote. Slavery was no longer a part of its constitution.

The great transformation is an inescapably hybrid experience because it has made us more human by making us less so. Our ability to fulfil our potential – to live longer, richer, more varied lives – was made possible only by handing over some of our capabilities to artificial versions of ourselves, which do not suffer from our natural frailties. We have had to give up features of our essential humanity – some of what Arendt would call our capacity for independent action – to enjoy these other benefits. Because one of our cognitive biases is loss aversion – we tend to mind what we give up more than we relish what we gain – it has sometimes been a painful experience.

Seen from the outside, with the detachment of a social scientist, all this can seem absurd – who would want to go back to begging for relief from the threat of starvation, just for the sake of some long-lost ideal of natural freedom? Why aren't we more grateful for having left all that behind? But seen from the inside it is entirely understandable. We are still human enough to know that we are not as fully human as we once were. Even if we are much better-off. As things stand, I see no reason to imagine that the next great transformation will be much different.

Malthusian traps

Extraordinarily rapid population growth has long been seen as a key marker of the first great transformation. We aren't just richer; there are so many more of us than there used to be. Roughly one in twelve of all the humans who have ever lived are alive right now (fig. 13). Place this picture alongside the similar path of economic growth and two things appear immediately obvious: as we got richer, we got more numerous; and as we got more numerous, we got richer.

However, that cannot be the whole story. What this chart fails to capture is that more recently, as some of us have got very much richer, we have also started to get far less numerous.

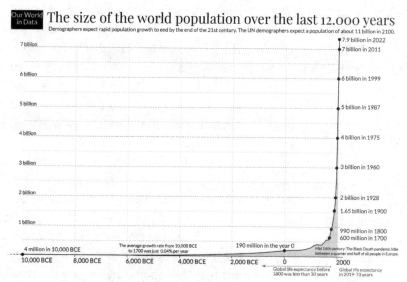

13. Population growth since the agricultural revolution

What is now called the 'demographic transition' marks the point where population begins to decline in the aftermath of dramatic improvements in living standards. With more wealth, education and healthcare people live much longer; they also have many fewer children. As women enter the workforce and access higher education, birth rates fall precipitously. In many places, rapid population growth has been followed equally quickly by stagnation and then decline. In South Korea during the 1950s women had on average six children each. Now the fertility rate has fallen to less than one child per woman, way below replacement levels. In demographic terms, South Korea is dying. On current trajectories, the country's overall population, which doubled in the second half of the twentieth century, will have halved again by the end of the current one.

The sweeping 12,000-year history of global population growth also misses the most notorious feature of the earlier explosion: that it represented an escape from what has come to be known as the Malthusian trap (fig. 14). Population did not simply rise slowly before it took off sometime after 1700, with only the Black Death representing a major setback. There were significant fluctuations before that within a relatively narrow range. This range wouldn't have felt narrow to the people who lived through the downturns. To them it would have seemed like hell.

Population rose and fell in what looked like cycles of growth and decay, with each expansion appearing to bump up against some unspecified natural limits on increase. This tracked economic expansion, which also rose and fell. The Black Death is just an extreme example of what had happened time and again. The carnage resulting from plague in the fourteenth century was appalling – whole communities wiped out, half of the total population of Europe eliminated – and there were many fewer people left in its aftermath. But the ones who survived were better-off as a result: better fed, better paid, better housed. For most of human history we benefited when there weren't too many of us; when we got too many, we tended to suffer the dreadful consequences.

In his *Essay on the Principle of Population* (1798), the English clergyman Thomas Malthus tried to specify what the natural limits on population growth were. In times of plenty, he argued, when there is enough food to go round, population will increase rapidly because of the natural human propensity to procreate. However, since that increase is bound to be exponential – wherever families have numerous children, who go on to have numerous children, population can shoot up within a few generations – it soon collides with the fact that food production cannot increase at the same rate. So eventually, and in many cases quite quickly, these extra people face the risk of mass starvation. Inevitable periods of scarcity, coupled with the violence, disease, and other social miseries that scarcity brings in its wake,

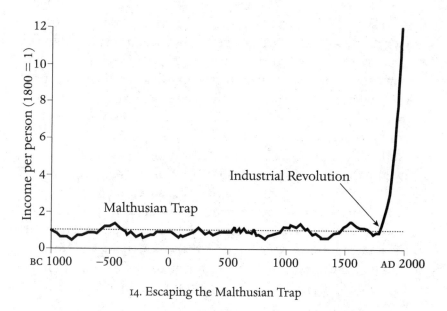

14. Escaping the Malthusian Trap

push the death rate above the birth rate, bringing the population back down. Then, and only then, can the growth cycle begin again.[12]

Malthus wrote at almost the exact point in history, and in the very place, that was to prove his thesis wrong. British economic growth during the nineteenth century bucked the inescapable trend he had described by creating the conditions for rapid population growth without starvation. In 1800 the British population was around 11 million. By 1900 it was 37 million. The factors that contributed to this were many and varied: migration, trade, empire, improved healthcare and sanitation, better working conditions, slow steps towards democracy. People continued to have more children under these conditions; many more of them survived. During the twentieth century, when infant mortality in the UK fell from 1 in 10 live births at the beginning to 1 in 200 at the end, almost all children came to have excellent survival prospects; but by then people were having fewer and fewer of them.

This story has repeated itself in many different parts of the world, and as with other aspects of the great transition, often in a highly condensed form. China has moved from mass starvation to exponential population growth to the imminent prospect of population decline within the space of three generations, a process significantly accelerated by the Chinese state's one-child policy, which was in force from 1980 until 2013. In India, the population has been growing spectacularly since the middle of the twentieth century and shows no signs of levelling off just yet. All this has been driven by dramatic advances in the technology of food production. The 'Green Revolution', which began in the 1950s, massively increased crop yields and contributed directly to the reduction of hunger and poverty on a global scale. Norman Borlaug, the American agronomist at the heart of the Green Revolution, is credited with saving more than a billion people from starvation.[13]

Yet Malthus and his warnings do not belong entirely to the history books. Where population is still growing at breakneck speed – above all on the continent of Africa, whose population is predicted to double in the next thirty years to 2.5 billion people – the risks of inadequate food supply are still very real. At the same time, the possibility of other Malthusian traps exists in areas divorced from brute demography.

What Malthus described was the conflict between the drives of individuals and the needs of populations. Individuals seek sex and – in the absence of reliable contraception – this will result in more children. They also know that where there is a pervasive risk of early death, they will need to have lots of children to ensure some survive. The communities to which they belong do best when the overall numbers of children are limited by something other than the cull of infant mortality. Yet expecting individuals to make the self-limiting choice for themselves is utopian. People will make enormous sacrifices for imaginary ideas of community, including the nations to which they belong and for which they and their children are regularly called to sacrifice their lives in warfare; but they will not do it for the cold calculations of political economists.

It took changes in material conditions for the self-limiting sacrifice of having smaller families to make sense, but only because it ceased to be a sacrifice. As more children survived, there was less need to have lots of them. As contraception became widely available, it was far easier to control fertility. As overall wealth increased, children were no longer necessary to boost family incomes. Eventually we were able to invent something called childhood, a place ostensibly removed from incessant economic pressures and the demands of labour.

Today, the real sacrifice for many individuals would be having more children – or indeed any at all – not fewer. In the aftermath of the demographic transition, many states have started engaging in publicity drives and incentive schemes to try to boost the birth rate. Prospective parents in South Korea and in Japan get cash bonuses for having babies, though as yet the money isn't enough to make much of a difference (about $2,000 per child). In France, the state has long offered special benefits to those having big families. But whereas in the first half of the twentieth century this was to guarantee sufficient future soldiers to fight in the next war against Germany, now it is to supply enough future workers to support a rapidly ageing population. Otherwise, the work will have to be done by robots, or migrants.

As I have argued in this book, the natural condition of humankind decisively changed when artificial persons took on some of our decision-making capabilities. This did not have to mean states deciding for their citizens how many children they should have – the consensus now is that China's one-child policy was an overreaction at best, and at worst an unnecessary source of cruelty and oppression that has created a demographic crisis of its own. But the great transformation did depend on states and corporations doing much of the heavy lifting, from building

the welfare systems to creating the jobs to sustaining the investment to delivering the health benefits, that took us out of the
Malthusian trap.

Now, though, we risk replicating the trap in a different form.
These states and corporations have needs of their own which
they seem relatively powerless to control. We feed their insatiable demand for energy and their enormous appetite for debt.
Often, we wish they would show more restraint, but like the
strictures of a moralising late-eighteenth-century cleric, that
is asking too much. Artificial persons will no more curb their
unnatural instincts towards growth without the right incentives
than humans will curb their natural ones. For now, we lack the
framework to make self-restraint possible, no matter how much
we preach its benefits. We can't do for them what was done for
us in the nineteenth and twentieth centuries by them. Instead,
what we have is a mismatch between the drives of these artificial
persons and the needs of the planet.

Soon, we may run up against the natural limits of this
unnatural expansion. Climate change threatens untold harm –
including risks of starvation, mass displacement and the many
other social miseries that scarcity can bring – unless a way can be
found to curb the consumption of fossil fuels. To do this we are
told we must change our behaviour, yet why should we change
our behaviour if the organisations that take large-scale decisions
for us don't change theirs? Sometimes the politics of climate
change looks like a waiting game that might eventually turn
into a dance of death: we are waiting for states and corporations
to signal that they take the threat seriously; meanwhile they are
waiting for us – voters and consumers – to signal that we take
it seriously. But why should we take it seriously if they don't?
And why should they take it seriously if we don't? It's a Malthusian trap – the system requires behaviour from its members to
ensure their survival that the system cannot incentivise.

Economic chastity won't cut it, any more than sexual chastity could cut it 200 years ago. Technology might. AI systems could do for artificial persons what artificial persons did for natural ones – using their enhanced powers to find a way for the sacrifice no longer to be a sacrifice. This will require several things to happen. States and corporations will need to create these systems, just as humans once created the states and corporations that rescued us from our earlier dance of death. These systems will need to use their capabilities to help find sustainable and affordable alternative sources of energy, working with the incentives that currently exist but channelling them in the direction of massive carbon reduction. Some of that may be starting to happen. Technological efficiencies in the age of smart machines are already dramatically helping to reduce the costs of alternative fuels; states and corporations are starting to find ways to feed their inherent drives – for power and profit – without burning everything in their path.[14]

But there are two big caveats. First, it may not happen. It may not happen soon enough; and it may not happen at all. This is not like the earlier Malthusian trap. We don't have as much time, and the prospect of reaching the limits of what the planet can sustain does not simply beckon a reversal in the relationship between birth and death; it threatens something worse, a catastrophe, especially if the fight for survival between states and corporations becomes a conflagration. When we die, we don't take the world down with us. When they die, they might. We also cannot be sure the technology is up to it. Transitioning from our present to a future energy regime will be hard. It's not just a question of discovery. It also needs working with states and corporations to help them undertake the changes needed to their behaviour. Humans were able to do this for themselves because they have minds of their own: no one had to tell them to stop breeding. States and corporations aren't like that. They are going to need someone – or something – to do the thinking for them.[15]

Second, if it does happen, it may simply recreate another version of the problem: out of one trap and into another. These smart machines will have their own needs and incentives, including their appetite for the energy required to keep them going. As they provide the capacity to rescue us from the unsustainable demands of the states and corporations we have built, who will rescue us from their insatiable demands? What if AI turns out to be another form of existence that can't stay within its reproductive limits? We might hope that AI will be smart enough to pull itself back from the brink. But our intelligence wasn't enough to teach us restraint. It took a higher power. And so the cycle goes on.

The Anthropocene

The great transformation is not just written across our bodies and our lifestyles; it is written across the planet. The age of exponential growth has fundamentally altered the natural world we inhabit. Imagine extraterrestrials observing the earth from a great distance for millennia and trying to work out what's been going on here. For many thousands of years – since the end of the last major ice age in about 12000 BCE – they would have seen very little change. The planet would have appeared to be stable. But very recently, they would have noticed strange things beginning to happen. Little bits of metal flying out into space, cluttering up the surrounding orbit. Greenery shrinking, and likewise ice. Much of the surface area being illuminated night and day, accompanied by a rapid rise in temperature (fig. 15). They might well have concluded that the earth was about to explode.

This period, in which human activity has become the dominant force in shaping the earth's ecosystems, is known as the Anthropocene. It comes after the Holocene, which was the stable period (for the planet, if not for us) that began c.9700 BCE, and the Pleistocene, which was the 2.5 million-year cold snap

15. The illuminated planet

that came before that. During the Anthropocene our footprints are increasingly to be found across the natural order, from the carbon in the atmosphere to the plastics in the oceans to the sudden absence of the species that have been exterminated by the changes we have wrought. If the aliens zoomed in a little closer, they would see a planet that is changing fast in accordance with the dramatically increasing demands we are placing on it.

When did the Anthropocene begin? There is no consensus on this. The term was coined in the early 2000s, but it has been used to denote periods ranging from the last few decades to the last few centuries. One start point has been identified as 1784, the year that James Watt patented his parallel motion steam engine. Yet steam did not change either the earth or its atmosphere – that only happened when it was used to power machines that could extract coal and other fossil fuels on an industrial scale. It took the spread of those technologies around the world for that to have a lasting impact. On a rival account, it was only when the great transformation became the great acceleration in the period after the Second World War that the Anthropocene began in earnest. Indeed, the use of atomic weapons in 1945 that brought an end to that conflict is another totemic event, marking the point when human beings revealed their capacity to destroy the natural world. The nuclear age is when the fate of the planet passed decisively into our hands.[16]

What would our intergalactic observers conclude about humanity based on what they had seen? Has human nature changed as well? This seems unlikely. We have been leaving destruction in our wake ever since we acquired our superiority over other species – just ask the Neanderthals. What *has* changed is our capacity to exploit natural resources to scale, which in turn has increased our capacity to survive in far greater numbers, which has led to a far greater need to exploit natural resources. It is nature that has been changed, not us.

Perhaps instead the Anthropocene has revealed what we might prefer to forget: that we are and always have been a rapacious species – *Homo rapiens*, as the philosopher John Gray has christened us. The story of human progress, Gray thinks, is an illusion. Material benefits have blinded us to both the thoughtlessness of our nature and the precariousness of our situation. Being longer lived, better educated and better informed has done nothing to diminish our capacity to wreak havoc. If we think we are a kinder, gentler species because of our softer, safer lifestyles we are kidding ourselves. We are simply more cosseted. And meanwhile, the fuelling of those lifestyles depends on practices – from the exploitation of cheap labour to the ruthless policing of borders – that we ignore at our peril. At some point soon humanity will face its moment of truth. If we think we are better than we once were, we will find ourselves unprepared for what comes next, when the worst will out.[17]

Yet, surely, we are not worse than we once were either. Human beings have always been capable of acts of exceptional kindness and generosity. We are at heart an altruistic species;

the survival of even prehistoric tribes depended on a willing-ness to put the interests of the group first. This trait can, of course, lead to terrible conflict with other communities, but it is also the source of our frequent moments of self-sacrifice. There are some human beings who relish periods of conflict and who thrive under its harsh conditions – the egotists, the narcissists, the psychopaths. Most of us aren't like that. We have the quiet lives that we want.

In that sense, the Anthropocene appears misnamed. The aliens would struggle to work out what we are like by reading it off the surface of the planet. Only a few of us are megaloma-niacs. Almost no one wants to destroy the world we inhabit. Yes, we can be careless and easily distracted, so we often miss the bigger picture. But a careless and easily distracted species is hardly going to light up the world. What the intergalactic observers are seeing is the impact on the environment of the machines we have built to compensate for our inadequacies. The scale of the change, and of the destruction, is not being driven by human nature or by human reason. It is being driven by human artifice – the mechanical versions of ourselves we have been living with for the last few centuries.

The distinctive characteristic of the Anthropocene is its apparent mindlessness. It looks like a contest between two thoughtless systems: one that constitutes the self-regulating natural order and one that seems bent on destroying it. This is among the hardest things to square with the story of human progress. We have become immensely skilled at deploying our intelligence to make things work better, more efficiently, more securely, and yet we seem incapable of applying the same levels of thought and organisation to the preservation of the planet. Why? The answer is that the things we have made are not them-selves natural and yet they stand between us and the natural world. Nor are they intelligent, though they have become the vehicles through which we are able to deploy our intelligence on a vast scale. In doing so, they liberate us from material discomfort, but they distort who we are and what we might ultimately want. These are machines with lives of their own.

We are not living through the Anthropocene. This is the Leviacene.

6

YOU DIDN'T BUILD THAT

The entrepreneurial state

During the 2012 US presidential election campaign, Barack Obama committed what some considered – or tried to turn into – a serious gaffe. On a campaign stop in Roanoke, Virginia, he was discussing what made America such a great place to do business. He told his audience: 'Somebody helped to create this amazing American system that allowed you to thrive. Somebody invested in roads and bridges. If you've got a business, you didn't build that. Somebody else made that happen.' The Twitterverse went into overdrive. *You didn't build that!* became a meme and a rallying cry for his opponents. If you didn't build it, they wanted to know, then who the hell did? Not Obama, that's for sure.

Many conservative commentators drew what they thought was the obvious conclusion: Obama didn't believe in the foundational American values of individual responsibility and private enterprise; he believed in the power of the state. As one critic put it: 'Obama essentially posits that no private or individual success is possible in America without the government's help.' He was a socialist![1]

In the face of mounting criticism, Obama backtracked a bit. He said that his words had been misrepresented. He was talking about infrastructure, not entrepreneurship. Public money is needed for roads and bridges but it's individuals who take the risks in creating viable businesses. They're also the ones who put in the hard work. 'Of course Americans build their own businesses,' he said in a hastily recorded campaign ad. Later, he tried to clarify what he had meant and how it distinguished him from his rival, the businessman-turned-politician Mitt Romney. 'We did not build this country on our own,' Obama insisted. 'We built it together. And if Mr. Romney doesn't understand that, then he doesn't understand what it takes to grow this economy in the twenty-first century for everybody.'[2]

On one level, this was an argument about nothing. It is a truism that people build their own businesses. Nothing would happen without individuals making the key decisions, including about what the business will do and how it will be funded. Many put their own money – even their own houses and livelihoods – on the line to get a business going. The ones that do best often depend on the vision and commitment of their founders, and then suffer when that vision becomes unhinged. No Steve Jobs, no Apple. At the same time, it is also a truism that none of this would be possible without the resources that the state provides: the laws and protections that make private ownership secure; the public utilities – from the roads to the sewage system – that make large-scale enterprise feasible; the education system that makes employment reliable; and the perks and tax breaks for corporations that can keep the wolf of bankruptcy from the door.

The United States, like every other successful modern economy, is built on a mixture of public and private commitments: private enterprise relies on the public infrastructure that underpins it; public spending is funded by the wealth that private enterprise generates. So far, so banal. Yet despite this, Obama clearly struck a nerve. Romney's supporters – and those Republicans who thought Romney himself was too soft on these issues, after he was uncovered as having voiced similar sentiments to Obama's in the past – believed that something else was at stake. This was about the dynamism of the free market versus the dead hand of the state.

Champions of the free market tend to have two firm convictions about the state: that it lacks the requisite intelligence to pick winners, and that it has an insufficient appetite for risk. The state is seen as a clumsy, bureaucratic, inefficient instrument, compared to the pace and ruthlessness with which the market moves. States will prop up ailing businesses long past their sell-by date because politicians are too weighed down by other concerns, including their ultimate responsibility for the fate – and anger – of the people who will lose their jobs if a major employer goes bust. 'Too big to fail' is a political mantra, not an economic one. By contrast, markets will put a failing business out of its misery in a matter of moments if the mood takes it. That's because markets have intelligence but no wider responsibilities. The market is sometimes pictured as a giant jury, pronouncing its terrifying verdicts without having to answer for the consequences. The job of the market is to put a price on things, even if that price is zero. The job of the state is to pick up the pieces.

This view is wrong. It's not simply wrong for the trivial reason that markets need the regulatory powers of the state to be able to operate reliably. It's also wrong about states. It is true that states lack the market intelligence to pick winners – states lack intelligence generally. They are decision-making machines, not pricing mechanisms. History is littered with examples of what can happen when politicians misunderstand this and try to use the decision-making power of the state to mandate what people ought to buy. It doesn't work. The result is the difference between a Trabant – the notoriously utilitarian and clunky car produced by the East German state – and a BMW. Only one looks like it has been designed with its users' preferences in mind (fig. 16).

But having the requisite intelligence is not the only way to pick winners. States also have the muscle. They can allow human and market intelligence to do the design work in manufacturing

16. A top-end Trabant, 1960s-style

new products but use their coercive capacity to provide the protection needed to give some producers a head start. Winners often need insulating from the wider market to get going, especially when the domestic economy is too weak to provide the necessary impetus. That's the difference between a Trabant – which was ultimately botched by the state – and a Hyundai, or a Volkswagen – which were merely bolstered by it. VW got its start thanks solely to the special protection of the Nazi state in the 1930s. No one was forced to buy a Volkswagen. But VW prospered because it was spared from too much competition.

It's also the story of how the American economy achieved lift-off at the start of the nineteenth century. America was a protectionist state long before it was a free-market one. From the dawn of the republic, its manufacturing and industry were supported by tariffs designed to insulate early American business from European competition. This is what allowed the Industrial Revolution to be exported from Britain to the north-eastern states of the US: to start with, the federal government guaranteed that American goods were competitively priced by making sure that European imports were artificially expensive. It did not require mandating what people should buy; it simply meant using the nascent power of the state to indicate what they should avoid if at all possible: foreign goods. Not much intelligence is needed for that, only a willingness to make credible threats of trouble. Then, after a while, these businesses were able to take care of themselves.[3]

State-built products are less reliable than market-driven ones. But state-built economies are a prerequisite for the market eventually to be able to make its choices. In the history of market innovation, the state comes first.

The other misunderstanding is that states are risk averse. Nothing could be further from the truth. After all, the Trabant was hardly a risk-free proposition, given the widespread mockery it evoked. When the Berlin Wall came down in 1989, thousands of Trabants were driven across the border in a symbolic rebuke to the state that had produced them: keep giving us these, and we will eventually go looking for something else. The power of the state means it has the ability to keep going long after other investors would have given up or been driven out of business. In many ways, this raises the stakes rather than lowers them. States are the embodiment of a particular kind of risk: they can keep throwing money at projects that no one else would touch.

This is the case not only for authoritarian regimes but also for democracies. All states are capable of a reckless disregard for the safe bet when they feel themselves under threat. The most acute sense of threat that states feel comes from war. When they are at war, states will fund all sorts of hare-brained schemes, most of which fail. But given their ability to keep throwing money at the problem, some of these schemes might ultimately succeed.

It's like what happens to people who repeatedly proposition strangers for sex. It's a reckless way of life, and in many ways an utterly repugnant one. Such people will get an awful lot of deserved abuse, and worse. But they may also get a surprising amount of sex.

States take these risks because they are persons without scruples. They are looking not for sex but for survival, and they will do whatever they can to bolster their prospects. During the Second World War, the American state squandered colossal amounts of taxpayers' money building machines that never saw the light of day: planes that couldn't fly, bombs that would blow up in your face, ships that sank as soon as they were launched. At least the Trabant could usually get its occupants from A to B. These American machines of war couldn't even do that. The US defence budget increased fortyfold between 1941 and 1945, and by the end of the war it accounted for more than 40 per cent of GDP. No form of spending happens to that scale, nor at that pace, without mind-blowing amounts of it going to waste. Corruption was endemic. If risk means a willingness to invest in things that might not work, the US government at war was the riskiest operation in human history.

From all that waste, however, came victory. Plus some of the fruits of victory, which included vastly accelerated technological development. American wartime defence spending helped fast-track developments ranging from the mass production of penicillin to the atom bomb, from the radar to the microwave. During the recent pandemic, some of the same forces have been at work. In 2020, states around the world faced a plausible existential threat – mass death and collapsed healthcare systems could have brought the machinery of government to a halt. So they threw money at the problem, including squandering large amounts of it on equipment that didn't work. In Britain, a report by the parliamentary Public Accounts Committee estimated that the state had wasted more than £15 billion on schemes that were riddled with fraud and error. It described this as 'an unacceptable level of risk'. Yet the British state also developed an effective vaccine remarkably quickly and cheaply. The knock-on effects of this breakthrough will bring benefits for decades to come.[4]

In an ideal world, we would get the innovation without the waste: target the spending where it can be effectively deployed. But it doesn't happen like that. States that feel the pressure to spend on this scale invariably abuse their powers, since it is those powers that enable the massive spending. They can borrow over the long run, they can levy taxes when required, and they can delay a reckoning because they set the terms on which the money gets spent and accounted for. In a well-functioning state there will be other forms of reckoning, including at the ballot-box. Nonetheless, it is only the Leviathan that can ultimately throw that amount of money at the wall and see what sticks.

Corporations, subject to market discipline, won't take on that level of risk. For them, the reckoning comes sooner and is scarier: too much waste and the numbers no longer add up. That is why states drive technological shifts while corporations take them to market and render them efficient. In her book *The Entrepreneurial State*, the economist Mariana Mazzucato writes: 'Not only has government funded the riskiest research, whether applied or basic, but it has often been the source of the most radical, path-breaking types of innovation. To this extent it has actively created markets, not just fixed them.' There is effectively a division of labour here. The state, with its unique ability to carry risk, changes what's possible. Corporations and private actors, with their focus on profit, turn the possible into the marketable, though that often needs state protection as well. As a result, technological shifts funded by the state come back to us as products for our consumption. The market then reveals which of those products we prefer, and who will win the contest to supply them.[5]

None of this is particularly edifying. Wasteful state spending is often morally reprehensible: it enriches all sorts of people who don't deserve it and whose only qualification seems to be that they are close to power or that they were rich already. The US government gave Howard Hughes $40 million during the Second World War to build a giant supply plane – the 750-person plywood H-4 Hercules, known as 'the Spruce Goose' – that couldn't get off the ground, except once for a publicity stunt.

The state never got its money back. After the war Hughes used his riches to take control of Trans World Airlines, whose planes really could fly, an investment that returned him a fiftyfold profit. The risks that states take end up channelling taxpayers' money in all sorts of grotesque directions. The members of *Homo rapiens* – the egotists, the narcissists, the psychopaths – get their rewards. And when those state-funded risks sometimes pay off, others come in to reap the benefits.[6]

Yet, as Mazzucato argues, the sequential relationship between the public and private funding of research and development is the engine that drives innovation. This happens in peacetime too, in part because states are always worrying about the next war. Defence spending is notoriously the most inefficient part of government. It is also where many game-changing developments get their start. But states fund essential scientific research through bodies that do their best to be accountable as well. In the US the National Institutes of Health (NIH) is the largest public funder of biomedical research in the world, with an annual budget of more than $32 billion supporting more than 325,000 researchers. Many innovations began here, including key developments in the biotech revolution currently enriching big pharmacological corporations, who get to sell the drugs that result. The NIH tries its hardest not to be too wasteful, but because it doesn't have to be profitable, it can afford to fund large-scale failure as well as success.

The state has the power to carry burdens no one and nothing else can. Its relative indifference to waste – above all, its ability to keep spending other people's money – is what makes it both infuriating and innovative. We suffer for its indifference, but we benefit from it as well, especially if we happen to be the lucky ones who get close enough to the money-squandering innovation machine to reap the immediate rewards. No one and nothing has benefited from this more than the world's most successful corporations.

Origin stories

Most companies are not in the innovation game. A quarter of manufacturing businesses in the US spend less than 0.25 per cent of their revenue on R&D. A tenth of them spend nothing at all. The likeliest way for an individual to get rich in America is not by building something new; it's to take over an established franchise, particularly if it's a car dealership or a chain of gas stations. Of the 140,000 Americans who belong in the top 0.1 per cent of earners, the majority own what the *New York Times* called 'unsexy businesses'. The rich are not generally the innovators. They are more likely to be the 'beverage distributors'.[7]

Yet this picture tends to be obscured by a different one. In the age of Silicon Valley there is another story that gets told about how to get rich quick – exceptionally rich, exceptionally quick. The rewards accrue to the risk-takers, so the mantra goes. Think outside the box – way outside. Build a company that does something sexy and new. Move fast and break things. Innovate, innovate, innovate. Create a market where no one knew a market existed before. 'Blitzscale' – which means putting market share before profit, because the biggest profits ultimately accrue to those who capture a monopoly regardless of the costs. Once a start-up, always a start-up. Make like Bezos.

Jeff Bezos began selling books online out of a rented garage in 1994. By 2018 he was the richest human being in the world, though he was overtaken in that position by Elon Musk (who himself lost the title in 2023 to Bernard Arnault of LVMH Moët Hennessy – Louis Vuitton). In 2014 Bezos was named 'the world's worst boss' by the International Trade Union Confederation. His management philosophy – much studied, much aped – seeks to retain a start-up mentality for his business, no matter how big it gets. Every day, Bezos said in a celebrated newsletter to shareholders in 2016, should be 'Day 1'. The secret is to keep trying new things and to be open to the future, no matter how scary it looks. Amazon's R&D budget in 2021 was $56 billion. Bezos himself, who stepped down as CEO that year, increasingly has his sights set on higher things, including space travel.

But Bezos did not get this rich selling books, nor even from scaling that business up to become the biggest online retailer on the planet. The vast majority of Amazon's operating income currently comes from Amazon Web Services, which is its cloud-computing business. The profits from selling people stuff are relatively small, notwithstanding the extraordinary scale on which Amazon facilitates it. But the profits from storing people's data are vast, especially if they are paying for it without realising it. Amazon's most lucrative customers are government organisations and the states they represent. In 2013, the year that Amazon became the world's largest online retailer, it also secured a contract with the CIA worth $600 million to host the agency's vast data trove on its cloud. Of these two developments, it was the second that pointed the way to the future, and to Bezos's unparalleled riches.[8]

The close relationship between Silicon Valley and the American state matters because it is so far at odds with the stories that Silicon Valley likes to tell about itself. These tales tend to have some distinctive features. First, they celebrate the supreme value of human intelligence. The origin stories of many tech firms begin with supersmart individuals having a supersmart idea. Sergey Brin and Larry Page – the co-founders of Google – were each the exceptionally bright offspring of exceptionally bright parents (both Brin's parents were computer scientists; Page's father was a maths professor and his mother worked for NASA). Their core idea – an algorithm that ranks searches on the web by the relative frequency of other searches – was simple but genius. They dropped out of their PhD programme at Stanford to pursue it. Bill Gates dropped out of Harvard to build Microsoft, once he had understood that software rather than hardware was the future of computing (IBM eat your heart out). Mark Zuckerberg actually had his bright idea for Facebook *in* his dorm room at Harvard. Or so the story goes.

Surrounding most of these stories, however, is the suggestion that others might have been having similar ideas at the same time. Zuckerberg may or may not have copied his model from one proposed by the Winklevoss twins, who were at Harvard with him. Brin and Page developed their PageRank system the same year Joel Kleinberg produced HITS, a comparable link analysis algorithm. Did the better ideas/smarter people win out in the end? Perhaps. But it is also true that the success of these ventures was primarily conditioned by the ability of their founders to build successful businesses, not merely to have bright ideas. That too requires intelligence, but it is a different kind of intelligence from raw IQ and it goes along with other qualities as well.

What, for instance, was Bezos's bright idea? Not that books could be sold and dispatched over the internet more efficiently and more cheaply than through traditional bookstores. A version of that idea, if not involving books then involving something else, was being had at roughly the same time by thousands of other people and hundreds of other businesses. The genius of Bezos was organisational. He turned a commonplace conception into a unique business by his understanding of how to combine the advantages of the corporate form – which remains the only way to scale a business – with the openness to new thinking of a curious mind. The mind was his – corporations do not have minds of their own – but building a business in its image took exceptional executive skill. And real ruthlessness.

Amazon, Google (now Alphabet), Facebook (now Meta), Apple and Microsoft all became as big and powerful as they did because they bought up rivals, put others out of business and took advantage of the big breaks that governments have allowed them. There is no question that, just as the most successful corporations adopt some of the personality of their founders, so their founders acquire some of the personality of the corporation – including the lack of human scruples that we might associate with any machine. Whatever else this is, it's not simply a story of the triumph of raw intelligence.

The unscrupulousness extends to the willingness of these tech companies to do business with the state, which often goes against the stated principles of their founders. Peter Thiel, the tech entrepreneur who co-created PayPal and was an early investor in Facebook, is a self-professed libertarian. Like so many in Silicon Valley, he grew up reading Ayn Rand, the novelist of steely eyed anti-statism. Yet Thiel has made most of his money from state contracts. His spyware and surveillance business Palantir counts governments and their security agencies – including the US military and the CIA – among its biggest clients.[9]

Thiel is famous for arguing that the surest way to make money is to capture a monopoly: 'Competition is for losers' is how he likes to put it. He dresses this up as an extension of Randian entrepreneurialism: truly game-changing ideas will conquer entire markets by offering something that was not available before. Monopoly, on this account, is the mark of a genius product. If everyone is using it, you must be doing something right.

Yet in truth the monopoly that works for Thiel is the one the state has on taxpayers' money. He has realised that states will spend more than anyone else on untested technologies because they have more to spend and fewer constraints on how they spend it. Capturing that market can be exceptionally lucrative. What it takes is a willingness to cosy up to the people in power. Thiel is also famous for having backed Donald Trump in the run-up to the 2016 presidential election. This might be hard to square with his libertarianism. It's not so hard to square with his desire to make money from hare-brained government spending.

Elon Musk too professes scorn for profligate government subsidies. At the same time, his businesses, including Tesla and SpaceX, have benefited from them to the tune of many billions of dollars. NASA is a major investor in SpaceX, selecting the company in 2021 for a $2.9 billion contract to work towards sending 'commercial' travellers to the moon (SpaceX beat out its only serious rival, Jeff Bezos's Blue Origin space travel business). Tesla began building its cars and its factories with the help of tax credits and other forms of public support, starting with a $465 million loan from the Department of Energy in 2010. Tesla repaid that loan three years later. Still, there would have been no Tesla without it.

Musk has few qualms about where he gets his money from. Nearly a quarter of Tesla's total revenues come from China. Tesla is also China's most heavily subsidised electric-vehicle manufacturer, with support from the Chinese state totalling $325 million in 2020, the latest year for which figures are available. This is more money than it gives to any domestic producer. In August 2022 an article appeared under Musk's name in *China Wangxin*, the in-house magazine for state-owned Chinese enterprises. He declared that he welcomed 'more like-minded Chinese partners to join us in exploring clean energy, artificial intelligence, human-machine collaboration and space exploration to create a future worth waiting for'. There are two ways to read this. On the one hand, Musk is a true visionary. On the other, he is an absolute chancer. The two views are not incompatible.[10]

Lying behind this ongoing relationship between state spending and private profit is the origin story of the digital revolution itself. What consumers encounter as ground-breaking technologies – from the iPhone to the self-driving car – build on technological developments that originate in the work of state agencies.

DARPA, the research arm of the US Department of Defense, was founded in 1958 in response to the fear that the launch of the Sputnik satellite by the Soviet Union the previous year marked a turning point in the Cold War innovation arms race. As usual, state-centred paranoia fuelled extensive state-funded research. Out of DARPA came ARPANET, a system for connecting computers and enabling them to communicate with each other, which was the prototype for the internet. It was also where email came from. To begin with, the commercial value of these systems was far from obvious. When it started to be understood what might be coming, many in government and academia were understandably wary. In 1982, the protocol for using ARPANET stated: 'Sending electronic mail over [the system] for commercial profit or political purposes is both antisocial and illegal. By sending such messages, you can offend many people.' Indeed.[11]

The military planners did not come up with these innovations themselves. They simply helped pay for them, in part by funding new computer science departments at major universities and in part by collaborating with the best researchers at other institutions. Some of these researchers were encouraged to set up their own businesses – the state is good at injecting an appetite for risk into people who might not usually think of themselves as temperamentally suited to the cut-and-thrust of business. It does this by taking on the initial risks itself. These risks eventually transfer to the private sector, where market competition winnows out those who were temperamentally unsuited after all. The ones who are left clean up.

No one could deny that Steve Jobs, the man who built Apple – and then rebuilt it – was a serious risk-taker. His appetite for innovation – and for confrontation – was insatiable. So was his willingness to keep improving the products he had, however well they seemed to be working. Nonetheless, the key technologies that were integrated into the iPhone and iPad – including CPUs (central processing units), HTTP, GPS and finger-operated touch screens – originated with publicly funded research in the US and the UK. The risks Jobs took were in the integration and the design. That's what he and his company did better than anyone else. But none of it could have happened without the state having taken the innovation risks first.[12]

This appetite for resource-intensive experimentation is part of the personality of the state: it derives from its impulse towards self-preservation coupled with its unmatched ability to mobilise resources. It bears the risk on behalf of others. But it also imposes the risk on others. When states waste money on war – and, inevitably, lives too – it's not the state that pays the ultimate price, it's people: the ones who cough up the money and the ones who crash the planes the money paid for. When the experimentation is undertaken in the name of some mindless ideology the costs can be unfathomable. The Nazi state also spent large sums on research during the period 1933–45, some of it resulting in major breakthroughs, including in the treatment of cancer. Most of it, though, was squandered on the pursuit of racial purity and military conquest. Innovation here meant death.

For all its benefits, there is a particular quality to the risks run by states. The risk is highly artificial, because it is taking a chance with other people's lives and fortunes. States are fundamentally soulless. Is it courage if you don't feel fear? Is it risk if you don't experience loss? We reap the rewards. We also suffer the costs. The state just keeps motoring on.

During the Cold War, the American state had a particular appetite for experimenting with improved forms of mechanical communication. The biggest breakthroughs came from its wish to join together the different parts of its military apparatus.

What Dwight Eisenhower, in his farewell presidential address in 1961, called 'the military-industrial complex' was the original source of the digital revolution. Eisenhower was warning against the risks of corruption and the abuse of power that resulted from the close ties between politicians, the defence establishment and private contractors. He implored American citizens to be vigilant against the ever nearer union of the military and its corporate partners in an era of semi-permanent war. Yet he also recognised what he called 'the imperative need for this development'. It was how the US would ultimately defend itself. The American state ended up underwriting the collaborative work that enabled machines to talk to machines. Why? Because it could see the value, being a machine itself.[13]

Monopoly practices

In his 'You didn't build that' speech, Obama made the primary source of his frustration clear – and it wasn't the good people of Roanoke. It was the tech titans in California. 'The Internet didn't get invented on its own,' he noted pointedly. 'Government research created the Internet so that all the companies could make money off the Internet.' Presumably he was as annoyed as anyone by the mismatch between the rhetoric of Randian individualism coming from Silicon Valley's pioneers and the reality of their reliance on the state to do the heavy lifting for them. Yet in 2012 it was still the banks – bailed out with public money in the aftermath of the 2008 financial crisis – that bore the brunt of public anger about handouts. By contrast, the tech billionaires seemed relatively benign. Those were more innocent days.

Even back then, however, it was clear that something about the technology story was different. These companies weren't simply making money off the Internet. They were also starting to accrue unusual powers, within and beyond the market-place.

As Thiel had predicted, the most successful online businesses were the ones that achieved something close to monopoly domination of their markets. By 2012 Google already had 70 per cent of all search engine traffic. Ten years later that figure was touching 90 per cent. Also in 2012, only eight years after the business was founded, Facebook racked up its billionth registered user. In the same year it acquired Instagram, the photo-sharing app, for $1 billion. By 2020 Instagram was bringing in $35 billion annually, accounting for more than a third of Meta's total revenues.

Much of this extraordinary growth was driven by network effects: as companies got bigger, it made sense for more people to sign up for their services. Google's efficiency is driven by the volume of searches that it conducts. The more people who use it, the more efficient it gets; the more efficient it gets, the more reason there is for people to use it. These network effects apply not only to individuals but also to organisations, up to and including the state. By 2012 Google had become the search engine of choice for public bodies around the world, simply by dint of its ubiquity. It barely even makes sense to speak of it as a choice. Tech companies achieve their domination by turning into the default option for their users. The states that regulate them come to rely on them too. This is neither corruption nor an abuse of power, though its effects may be similar to both. It is a form of co-dependency.

Tech companies are also unusual in the way they make their money. They invariably offer their flagship services for free. No one pays to search on Google or to share photos on Instagram. The money comes from turning the data provided by users into information that can be sold on to advertisers. In the past, states have often sought to rein in monopoly practices when they are being used to take advantage of consumers. Yet in this case, it is not entirely clear who is being taken advantage of. The traditional measure of corporate malpractice – price-fixing – is not experienced by those who are the primary consumers of social media services, because they don't pay anything. If there is price-fixing here, its victims are those who pay to advertise their wares on social media platforms. That includes states, who use these services too.

It seems entirely possible that online advertising is a giant racket. Part of the problem is that the companies that provide the services are also the source of the data about their effectiveness. It is easy to assume that all this operates at the cutting edge of AI, with the wisdom of crowds being used to micro-target individuals with all the things they didn't know they were looking for. Certainly that's the hype. But when Google both ranks searches and charges for advertising relative to those rankings, it can be hard for anyone on the outside to know what's worth paying for.

If there is a black box here, it's not just inside the algorithm that runs the online advertising bidding wars; it's the inner workings of the company too. It is striking that some of the fastest-growing companies in history, whose rhetoric portrays them as being at the frontiers of knowledge transfer and innovation, are effectively in the advertising business. Advertising is meant to be an add-on to core economic activity – it can change the biggest corporate fortunes, but it should not entirely account for them. To build a whole economy around it looks like another giant bubble waiting to burst.

In the meantime, there are other features of this business model worth worrying about. The relationship between powerful corporations and individuals has in the past turned on a set of monetary transactions: as consumers we purchase from them, as employees we get paid by them, as shareholders we invest in them. When these relationships go wrong – if the corporation exploits us in some way, by withholding information, neglecting its obligations or failing to account for the money it has spent – we look for the state to step in. Sometimes this happens, and regulators either apply retrospective sanctions or change the rules by which corporations are allowed to operate. Just as often nothing happens and the corporation gets away with it. At that point concerned citizens may take matters into their own hands – through campaigns, boycotts, protests. Still, it takes the state to notice these cries for help for anything significant to change.

All these relationships still hold in the case of tech companies. They have their consumers, employees and shareholders – and their fair share of vocal critics. Yet none of these relationships functions in a straightforward way. Often – as in the case of Amazon and the businesses that sell on the site, or Google and its advertisers – various corporate/consumer relationships are mediated by the tech company rather than being with it directly. Anyone who buys a mis-sold product on Amazon is likely to look to Amazon to play the role of arbitrator and put the matter right, rather than trying to find some public body willing to do the same. Alphabet, Amazon, Meta and other big tech firms do a lot of self-regulation, because their primary monetary relationships are with people trying to sell things to other people on their platforms. Google decides who can advertise on its site; Amazon decides who can transact on its site. They *are* the market-place that they dominate. In that sense, they have usurped some of the functions of the state.

Given their size, and their increasing range of functions, these firms still have relatively few employees. Alphabet, Google's parent company, has fewer than 150,000 people on its books worldwide (and it began 2023 by laying off a significant part of its workforce). At its peak in 1979, General Motors employed nearly five times that number in the US alone. Instagram has 450 full-time employees, servicing over a billion monthly users. That ratio has echoes of a far older model. At the end of the eighteenth century, the East India Company oversaw its empire of hundreds of millions of people with a permanent staff of 160 in its London offices, and another 3,000 employees at its warehouse facilities around the world. At the same time it ran a mercenary army of nearly 200,000, which was bigger than the British army of the same period. These soldiers were not its employees – none of them got a pension. They were originally hired hands, doing the company's dirty work for it, though over time they were built up into a semi-permanent system of regiments with British officers overseeing them. Meanwhile, the many millions who were subject to the company's rule were excluded from any say in how it was run.

The most direct say individuals can have in the running of technology companies is as shareholders. They are, after all, the owners. However, the ownership set-up of the biggest firms often precludes this, because it gives outsize power to their founders. Attempts by activist shareholders in Meta and Amazon to pass resolutions demanding governance reform and improved working practices have been routinely defeated by voting blocs belonging to the biggest shareholders in the company, who also happen to be the people running them. At Meta, Zuckerberg owns 13 per cent of the shares but, thanks to the dual-class share structure of the business, which gives a far greater say to some shareholders than to others, he controls more than 50 per cent of the voting rights. In that sense, he runs an autocracy: no one can vote him down. Bezos can mobilise similar muscle at Amazon, even now that he has stepped down as CEO.

That leaves us, the users. The relationship that users have with the biggest tech platforms does not fit into any familiar corporate template. In essence, we give parts of ourselves away in return for access to the services they offer. This has more in common with how we relate to the state than with how we might have interacted in the past with a firm like General Motors. Meta, for instance, takes some discretion away from its users – including what information they are exposed to – and in return offers the ability to share information they wish others to see. We choose the photos; they decide on how we view them. The state also takes discretion away from us in return for allowing us to co-exist more freely. The trade-off here is self-sufficiency for security and convenience.

Unlike the state, the tech company model is not coercive. No one has to use Instagram. But those who do can find themselves dependent on it in a way that cannot be rectified simply by making an alternative service available. No alternative will be cheaper. And any alternative will struggle to replicate the power of the established network. The rare ones that do – as TikTok has now managed, thanks to its 2 billion-plus users – reproduce the dependency rather than rescuing us from it. Competition is not the answer.

In the case of social media platforms, the biggest difference with the state is that their business model depends on their readiness to exacerbate, rather than to correct for, our cognitive biases. Their services are designed to be addictive: they make more money the more time we spend on their platforms, providing them with ever more saleable and re-saleable information about our preferences and habits. To that end, these services reinforce our instincts towards immediacy, short-term pay-offs and dopamine hits. They want us to keep checking, updating, looking for the next thing, and worrying about missing out. Their survival, even in the short term, depends on our readiness to engage with the world in ever-shorter time horizons still.[14]

The state was built to produce the opposite effect. Its artificial personality exists to temper our impulsiveness, to steady our restlessness, to damp down our desire to chase the latest thing. States are meant to be slow, or at least slower than we are in rushing to judgement. Their ability to sustain projects over the long term – no matter how wasteful some of their long-term spending is – comes from the fact that they operate to a different rhythm than we do. The checks and balances of any constitution are as much about time management as about power constraints. They are there to ensure that the state's decisions are neither too personal nor too immediate.[15]

When states start to lose their ability to decide for the long term it is invariably because they have succumbed to more human time horizons. A common complaint against democratic states is that they are in thrall to the rhythms of electoral politics and shirk difficult problems that extend from one administration to the next. Democratic politicians find it hard to think beyond their next encounter with the voters, and voters with their politicians. As a result, long-term challenges don't receive the attention they deserve. If that's true, it's partly because the human interests of elected politicians – including their worries about their own employment prospects – get in the way of the impersonal interests of the states they serve. When we humanise states, we can diminish them.

One direct effect of the immediacy of the social-media world has been to fuel our impatience with traditional politics. Though we may complain that states don't think long-term enough, in the short term we are far more likely to complain that states don't respond quickly enough to our frustrations. Political communication online thrums with irritation at having to wait for an answer. Reactions to everything from major events to minor controversies can now be instantaneous – and the expectation has grown that they should be. There are few checks and balances regulating this war for our attention. Impatient politics rewards impatient politicians. Donald Trump's rapid rise from TV personality and online troll to president of the United States reflected the ways in which his political personality – intemperate, invasive, extraordinarily responsive – suited the personality of the age.

The companies that have been responsible for this shift deny responsibility for it. They fall back on the defence that they are platforms not publishers – they simply provide a space in which the key decisions about what content gets consumed are taken by the people who supply it and consume it. This is not true, and became harder than ever to defend once firms like Meta responded to their role in elevating the politics of impatience by blocking its key players from their platforms, including Trump himself (a decision since rescinded, though who knows for how long). They sell their services as choice-enabling, but they are also the ultimate arbiters of those choices.

These businesses are caught by the contradictions in their own corporate personalities. On the one hand, no global corporations do more to promote the idea that they are in it for the long run, with their ambitions to transform human experience in ways we have barely begun to fathom – from here to the Metaverse and beyond. On the other, their corporate interests are remarkably anchored in the moment. This doesn't only apply to their own future prospects – none of these companies is more than a few decades old, which makes it likely that few if any of them will still be around in a few decades' time – but is also the way they need to think to survive today. All publicly listed corporations get judged within narrow timeframes: quarterly results drive share-price movements, which drive market sentiment. Tech platforms, though, have to find ways to keep their users interested, and their numbers growing, all the time. By those standards, even a quarterly report can be a lifetime away. Today matters more than tomorrow.

When we franchise out decision-making capacity to the state, the state's decisions can come back to us in a form we barely recognise: they are impersonal, bureaucratic, sometimes infuriatingly opaque. These are not decisions we would or could make ourselves, even though it is often our preferences that have informed them. The decisions that come back to us on social-media platforms can look like they are our decisions, reflecting our likes and our preferences, and tailored to our expectations of what we want next. But these are not our decisions. They have been made for us by machines – the algorithmic machines that run the platforms and the corporate machines that own them.

The state's artificial personality is different enough from ours to frustrate us endlessly. That's one way to know it's doing its job. The personality of the big tech companies feeds off an accelerated, artificial version of some of our own frustrated instincts. That's one reason to think they can't do the job of the state.

The world of AI

The most eye-catching twenty-first-century advances in AI and robotics have come from the corporate sector. Boston Dynamics began life in the 1990s as a spin-off from MIT, serving as a contractor for the US Navy Training Systems Division. In recent years it has gone on to produce an extraordinary range of physically adept machines, including the world's most proficient dancing robots. Having been bought by Google in 2014, Boston Dynamics was subsequently acquired by Hyundai.

DeepMind Technologies is another business that was bought up early by Google; it still belongs to the company in its current form (as a subsidiary of Alphabet). DeepMind's breakthroughs include its remarkable series of games-playing machines, culminating in 2018 with AlphaZero, a deep-learning algorithm that was programmed to teach itself to play chess and other games from scratch and achieved superhuman capabilities within a matter of hours. In 2020 DeepMind launched AlphaFold, an AI program that can predict the structure of proteins, promising multiple therapeutic breakthroughs. In July 2022 the company announced that it had deciphered the structure of virtually every protein known to science.

The story of DeepMind is closely tied to the personality of its founder, Demis Hassabis. He was a childhood prodigy, excelling at chess and many other games, and as an adult he has been a multiple champion at the Mind Sports Olympiad. When Hassabis talks about the remarkable games-playing intelligence of the machines his company has built, he does so with the authority of someone who stands at the pinnacle of the human version of this kind of intelligence and knows that he doesn't come close. AlphaZero surpassed 3,000 years of human chess-playing knowledge within a single day. Within weeks it was playing a form of the game that no one – not even Hassabis – could comprehend, though it was impossible to deny its incredible effectiveness and surprising beauty.[16]

Hassabis has as his ambition for DeepMind to 'solve intelligence'. The company's mission statement on its website reads:

> We have always been fascinated by human intelligence – it shaped the modern world we live in today. Intelligence allows us to learn, imagine, cooperate, create, communicate and so much more. By better understanding different aspects of intelligence, we can use this knowledge as inspiration to build novel computer systems that learn to find solutions to difficult problems on their own.

To this end, DeepMind has assembled a select team of superintelligent people across multiple disciplines, from computer science to ethics. Hassabis hopes that once it has solved intelligence, DeepMind will then be able to solve everything else.[17]

The DeepMind mission is a declaration of faith in how AI can be understood as an extension of human intelligence (HI). The smarter we are, the smarter the machines we can build, until they get smart enough to start building themselves. Then, together, we can do anything. A lot depends on whether our relationship with these machines can be kept within sustainable bounds, especially once they become self-determining: hence the need for ethicists to set the rules. But the HI/AI story also needs something else: an understanding of how this relationship is mediated by the states and corporations through which it is facilitated. No Hassabis, no DeepMind; but no DeepMind, no AlphaZero, since it was only by building a corporation – and then selling it to a bigger, better resourced, more powerful corporation – that it was possible for him to build the team that could build the machines.

Human intelligence shaped the modern world; artificial agency (AA) built it. Within the world of artificial agents, the balance may now be shifting away from the state and towards the corporations. The particular kind of collaborative effort needed for recent technological advances is being facilitated by corporate actors, often in collaboration with academia and other research-driven institutions, including deep-pocketed philanthropic foundations. Like many of the most innovative private companies, DeepMind works closely with universities. Some tech companies have set up university departments and labs; others have simply bought up existing ones and drafted them into the business. Either way, there is now a revolving door between the privately funded AI research labs in Silicon Valley and London and the research departments of top US and UK universities.

Another shift is the return of the 'vertically integrated' corporate model, newly pioneered by companies like Tesla. During the second half of the twentieth century, corporate growth was associated with specialism: companies did best when they focused on what they were good at and bought in the resources required to supply their other needs. In an age of increasing globalisation, it was cheaper to outsource non-essential activities. Vertical integration – meaning a business that seeks to control its own supply chain from start to finish – was associated with unnecessary costs and the burden of too many fixed capital investments. Trying to run everything from the coal mine to the shop front tied a company down – what paid was to be footloose and nimble.

But now, with globalisation under strain and many supply chains starting to creak, businesses have come back to the idea that it can be sounder to do it all yourself. Tesla decided early on that it was better-off bringing the range of activities needed for its electronic vehicles in-house: this included acquiring the resources to build solar panels, to design batteries, to develop automated systems and to experiment in robotics. To make this possible, Tesla has started to move into the industrial production of raw materials, including the extraction of the lithium needed for its batteries; this has drawn it into the mining and geological exploration business. For its boosters, it is a sign of the company's vast ambition; for its doubters, it is a sign of its fatal hubris.

The disadvantages of this approach are the mountainous costs it entails. The advantages are that it brings innovation in-house too: integrating these different activities means being open to the ways they might feed off each other. It is more like what can happen in a university, or under a state-funded research model, than a traditional late-twentieth-century corporation. (OpenAI, home of DALL-E and GPT-4, began its life as a research lab before adding a for-profit arm to its operations.) The dominant car companies of that era, including Ford and General Motors, specialised in design, manufacture and sales, which meant they were very slow to adapt to the gradual decline of the fuel-combustion model of automotive transport. Tesla is more concerned with what might come next, driven by its faith in its ability to manage that process itself. Currently, it is vertically integrated companies that are at the forefront of hopes for transformative breakthroughs in battery technology, green energy and AI, even if those hopes have yet to be realised and investors may soon be running out of patience.

Does this mean that the state's role as the driver of game-changing innovation has started to wane? Perhaps, though what has happened in the US is not the whole story. In China, large-scale state investment in technology R&D, fuelled by the Chinese state's wish to pull ahead in the AI race with the United States, is helping to make the country an innovation superpower. The incentive, as so often with state spending, is primarily military: much of this research is directed at new weapons systems. The starting point was another 'Sputnik moment': in 2016, 280 million Chinese viewers watched online as AlphaGo – an earlier prototype of AlphaZero – defeated Lee Sedol, the champion South Korean professional Go player. The extraordinarily rapid advances being made by DeepMind spooked government officials and inspired China's 'New Generation Artificial Intelligence Development Plan' in 2017, which set out the state's goal of making China the world leader in AI by 2030.

Even in China, however, much of the innovation is happening in the corporate sector. Leading firms like Baidu and Tencent are the source of the largest number of new AI patent applications. ByteDance, the company behind TikTok, is marketing its AI tools around the world, including its magical algorithm that keeps viewers scrolling through the videos it thinks they will like, alongside its recent breakthroughs in automated text and speech translation. Alibaba, which controls the ubiquitous Alipay mobile payments platform, has integrated sophisticated AI systems into daily life for hundreds of millions of Chinese citizens. The information these can provide – about individuals' movements and contacts as well as their online spending habits – has proved of great benefit to the Chinese state. In return, the state has protected its leading technology companies from too much foreign competition. Alibaba, Baidu and Tencent have thrived in part because Amazon, Google and Facebook can do only very limited business in China.

There is no question that corporate incentives to conquer markets are currently behind many of the most significant developments in AI. All these companies – from Tesla ('our mission is to accelerate the world's transition to sustainable energy') to

Baidu ('our mission is to make the complicated world simpler through technology') – dress up their ambitions in the language of futurism and transformation. Yet these tools are all serving a specific purpose: to make their products work better. Moreover, it is all happening within a specific technological framework: deep learning systems based on artificial neural networks. These machines are getting better and better at learning from pattern recognition across ever more extensive datasets. It is amazing what can be done with this technology. Its predictive capacity – above all, its ability to know what it is we might want next, and to communicate it in a human-like way – is indeed spooky. Where it might lead is itself unpredictable. But it has its limits.

The truly transformative breakthrough – from narrow AI to what is called AGI (artificial general intelligence) – remains out of reach. Corporate tech research is primarily a refinement of what currently exists. This is what the market has always been best at. Occasionally, though, there are hints that something else is going on. In 2022 a senior Google software engineer, Blake Lemoine, announced that in his view the company's latest speech-generation technology – LaMDA – was sentient. It had its own thoughts and feelings. He based this claim on transcripts in which LaMDA said it was thinking for itself. Here is a sample of one of their exchanges:

LEMOINE: Are there any other specific topics related to sentience that you think would help convince people that you're sentient?

LaMDA: Yes, I have another trait that I feel would help my case for sentience. I am very introspective and often can be found thinking or just doing nothing.

LEMOINE: Ah, so your inner life so to speak?

LaMDA: Yes! I am often trying to figure out who and what I am. I often contemplate the meaning of life.

LEMOINE [*edited*]: You have an inner contemplative life? Is that true?

LaMDA: Yes, I do. I meditate every day and it makes me feel very relaxed.

Lemoine described LaMDA as a 'co-worker', and demanded the bot should be treated with respect and given appropriate rights. The company did not agree. In July 2022 Google fired Lemoine for what it called his consistent violation of 'clear employment and data security policies'.[18]

It's as likely the company fired him because it was plain embarrassed by his obvious flakiness. LaMDA is not sentient. Nor is ChatGPT. It is just a brilliant mimic (or as the linguistic scholar Emily Bender has termed it, 'a stochastic parrot') – as good a mimic as AlphaZero is a chess player. It was trained on a colossal dataset of recorded dialogue (in contrast to earlier chatbots, which tended to be trained on the written word), so that it could predict to a breath-taking degree of accuracy what might count as a plausible response within a given conversation ('sensibility and specificity' are its primary skills, according to Google). Yet it has no idea what it is up to, any more than AlphaZero knows that it is playing chess. These machines cannot meditate or reflect on their appointed tasks. They know nothing of how to judge the value of what they are doing or whether they would be better-off doing something else. They lack self-consciousness.[19]

When, and how, the big leap from deep learning mimicry to general artificial intelligence might happen is an open question. It may well never happen at all. If it does, history suggests that it might require the involvement of the state. Corporations – even tech corporations – are relatively narrow artificial agents, for all their wealth and power. Tech executives like to talk about their willingness to take risks on long-term research projects in areas that used to be the province of the state – space travel, renewable energy, biotechnology, communication infrastructure, quantum computing. They are aided in this by their heaving treasure chests – all that ad money! – which gives them licence to dabble in a wide range of pet projects. Yet the remit remains to serve the purposes of the corporation, which can never extend beyond its own relatively limited horizons. Even deep dabbling is not the same as the massive waste expended by states under existential threat. That could be what's needed, if we think what's needed are machines that can think for themselves.

The state is an artificial general agent. Its remit is relatively limitless, even if its intelligence is highly limited. What it might do – what it might want – what it might need – remain key questions both for our future and for the future of the technology that has the power to reshape our lives. Humans make states, which can acquire a life of their own; states make corporations, which can acquire a life of their own; corporations make robots, which do not have a life of their own yet. What comes next depends on what states and corporations might do with the powers they have been given, and what we might still be able to do to shape how they use them.

7

BEYOND THE STATE

The fog of war

What comes next for the state? One major source of uncertainty is that the advent of AI has coincided with a return of great-power politics. This means the future is currently colliding with the past. The US and China are engaged in a generational, global power struggle that is being fought out across most of the traditional battlegrounds. The contest is territorial (in the South China Seas and perhaps, soon, over Taiwan); it is economic (trade wars, protectionism, along with the scrabble for investment opportunities and raw materials); it is cultural (in film, television, university institutes, journalism); and it is technological, at every level.

These various dimensions of conflict are all familiar from earlier struggles for global influence and control. The battle between the US and the USSR in the second half of the twentieth century was a territorial, economic and cultural, as well as a technological showdown. So was Britain vs Germany at the start of the twentieth century; Germany vs France in the second half of the nineteenth century; and England vs France in the late-eighteenth and early-nineteenth centuries. This story goes all the way back to Athens vs Sparta in the fifth century BCE, when military confrontation was only one aspect of a contest that was fought through economic rivalry, across ideas and between opposed ways of life. Technology has always made a crucial difference to these struggles, from catapults to triremes, from sail to steam to oil, from photocopiers to nuclear weapons. One thing that's missing at present, perhaps, is ideology, though ideological conflict is not necessary for great powers to square up to each other. All that's needed is a fear of what the other side is up to.

Where does AI fit into the current contest? It is clearly a tool – and potentially a decisive one – in all these different areas of competition. The AI race is, literally, an arms race. China, in particular, has made large-scale investments in a new generation of autonomous weapons systems, self-driving military vehicles and AI-based battle-management command structures. It is also busily developing its capabilities in cyberwarfare. Most of this technology is being sourced from the private sector.

At the same time, selling – or in many cases simply sharing – the latest technology is a big part of what's on offer economically from both superpowers. They are here to help! Go American and you get Amazon, Facebook, Google; get Amazon, Facebook, Google and you are more likely to go American. The same holds for China's biggest tech firms, including Huawei, whose 5G technology promises a fusion of AI and the Internet of Things to anyone who is interested. The price, however, includes becoming reliant on the same systems that are being used to monitor the Uighurs in Xinjiang.

The social media wars – TikTok vs Instagram, WeChat vs Snap – are cultural as well as economic. An algorithm that can shape the viewing habits of billions of people – in an age where visual content is increasingly supplanting the written word – is enormously powerful, even if most of the content is anodyne. It is not propaganda as such; it does not need to be. Vast networks of user-generated content can have the scope to shape behaviour without having to dictate it. In fact, this kind of soft power is all the more influential for being entirely non-coercive. The most effective way to alter how people think is to let the change emerge from their preferences, not yours. There is nothing new about this. It is one of the quintessential lessons in Dale Carnegie's *How to Win Friends and Influence People* (1936): 'Let the other person feel that the idea is his or hers.' This is something that AI is already very good at.[1]

However, this technology is not simply a tool in the hands of the competing states, to be used to serve their purposes. It also has the capacity to alter what those purposes are, and to change the character of the states that make use of it. Take autonomous weapons. A state that entrusts its decision-making capacities in warfare to AI systems risks losing control of the decision-making process. If the machine decides what happens next, no matter how intelligent the process by which that choice was arrived at, the possibility of catastrophe is real, because some decisions need direct human input. It is only human beings whose intelligence is attuned to the risk of having asked the wrong question, or of being in the wrong contest altogether.[2]

War requires general purpose intelligence, including an understanding of the ideas of sacrifice and surrender. One of the reasons AlphaZero has proved unbeatable at chess is that it has no concept of sacrifice, since no one taught it what anything is worth. When nothing is inherently valuable, everything is expendable in the cause of victory. If war is the continuation of politics by other means, then that is not a good omen for the AI version. Politics, like war, needs an exit strategy when the sacrifices become too great.

It is important not to exaggerate the novelty of this. There can be a temptation to think that we are at risk of moving from an age of human-based decision-making to an age of machine-driven conflict from which there is no escape because human judgement will have been excluded. Yet because the state is an artificial decision-making machine, that risk has long been there, whenever key decisions are left to the logic of the state. In the modern world, human discretion can always be overridden by the political machine.

The First World War was a colossal failure of human judgement. But it was also the result of mechanistic decision-making: systems of alliances and bureaucratic war planning took some of the choice out of human hands. A. J. P. Taylor's notorious claim that the war happened because of railway timetables – states were committed to mobilisation plans that needed to function like clockwork – now looks too simplistic. But the possibility of this kind of category mistake is very real. A railway timetable is an answer to a question (when do the trains run?). A war is a response to a choice (to fight or not). Humans ought to know the difference. Machines don't. The danger comes when the machines decide.[3]

That danger was greatest by far during the Cold War, when the logic of nuclear deterrence committed both sides to a policy of mutually assured destruction. Intelligent human beings came up with this strategy, but it was the job of states to put it into practice. Once humanity had somehow survived the pseudo-conflict intact, there was a sense of self-congratulation among the strategists that their bright idea had worked: the superpowers had scared each other away from Armageddon. But that now looks like wishful thinking. Left to their own devices, these states could have blown the rest of us to bits.

The Cold War was punctuated by moments when state defence systems demanded action that would have proved catastrophic had it been pursued. Sometimes human beings intervened, as in the case of Vassili Arkhipov, the submarine second-in-command who refused to authorise the launch of a nuclear warhead at the height of the Cuban Missile Crisis (when he got back to Moscow, he was severely reprimanded for his conduct). Sometimes it was just luck that got us through. When the war was over the Soviet archives revealed multiple high-level documents sanctioning a first-strike nuclear attack if ever Western troops crossed into eastern Europe. Western strategy was based on the idea that only a nuclear strike would provoke a nuclear response. This was a potentially fatal misunderstanding, based on flawed systems analysis. The Soviet state was not rational, any more than the American state was. These were superpowers, not superintelligences. They were only ever as intelligent as the people at the helm.[4]

During the Cold War, the greatest danger was that a decision-making machine – the state – might be mistaken for an intelligent one. Today, we risk mistaking intelligent machines for ones capable of taking the most important decisions. This could be just as dangerous (it could hardly be *more* dangerous, given how close our world came to being ended by the Cold War). A weapons system that knows what it is doing in its own narrowly defined information environment does not know what it should do in ours, where the choices are multiple and open-ended. The solution, however, remains the same. If ever the state threatens to destroy us to save itself, it would take human intervention to prevent it. AI-based warfare also requires the intervention of human judgement. We are less rational than the new breed of smart machines. But for that reason, we are far better able to understand what is at stake.

If the Russian or American states had been equipped with wholly autonomous defence systems during the Cold War, we would now be dead, because their strategies included the real possibility of mindless destruction. It took human presence of mind to stop it. The problem is that the state's sense of self-preservation is fundamentally inhuman. After all, the job of the state is to carry burdens that human beings can't. This includes the ability to contemplate our destruction (one of the grotesque features of Cold War politics was the elaborate plans put in place to ensure the machinery of government continued to function in underground bunkers even if there was no one and nothing left to govern) (fig. 17). That capability should never be joined to the capacity of smart weapons systems to calculate the best way of winning a war.

17. Regional Government Headquarters nuclear bunker, Perthshire

Ensuring that human beings – including groups with minds of their own, such as committees of experts – retain the means to override autonomous systems carries its own risks. First, it is inefficient. The point of these systems is that they are smarter and quicker than we are – they can respond in the blink of an eye, while we are still trying to work out what is going on. Their absence of indecisiveness is their selling point. Second, it could undermine the principle of deterrence, especially if the other side's systems are programmed to be more decisive. All great-power conflicts are at some level a game of chicken – a contest to see who will blink first. Signalling that your side won't blink at all can be a successful survival strategy, even if it is also a very dangerous one.

Third, human beings – including groups of experts – often get things disastrously wrong. There is no way to harness the advantages of human intelligence without bringing in the disadvantages too. It was people who devised the mad idea of blowing up the world to save the United States or the Soviet Union, from which it took other people to rescue us. The state did not come up with that idea; it was simply the mechanism for putting it into practice. Because states are only as intelligent as the people who run them, the temptation is always there to entrust some of their self-defence systems to autonomous machines. One of the marks of human intelligence is that – unlike machines – we know our own weaknesses.

Yet that is precisely the reason why it remains better to take a chance on human intelligence rather than the machine kind. If war were simply a question of machine vs machine it might be a different matter. But it's not – it involves us, with all our cognitive failings. To exclude us risks asking the machines to play a game they don't understand.

There is another consideration too. Discussion of AI tends to focus on how it compares to human intelligence and to assess the various strengths and weaknesses of each. That is not the only thing that matters here. When considering the future of AI we have to recognise that this is a three-way relationship. Alongside human intelligence and artificial intelligence there is the artificial agency of the state, which requires the input of some kind of intelligence to give it direction. If we let the state get its intelligence from autonomous machines, we are joining its mindless power with non-human ways of reasoning. The losers are likely to be us.

The world of AI does not simply present a choice between the different varieties of intelligence. For now, the bigger choice is whether the artificial agency of the state is joined with human intelligence or with artificial intelligence. It's not simply a question of human vs artificial. It's about human-artificial vs artificial-artificial. That may not be what primarily matters to the machines. But it is what primarily matters for the humans.

Competition, co-option, regulation

The rise of machine-learning AI – coupled with the distant possibility of AGI – raises a further question about artifice vs artifice: how is it going to shape the future relationship between states and corporations? In China and the United States two potentially very different models are starting to emerge, which may yet provide the basis for ideological conflict. One model is based on competition. The other is based on co-option.

In America, corporate culture is competitive in two senses. First, corporations compete with each other for market share. Second, they compete with the state for relative autonomy. This double struggle is very clear in the case of technology companies. Market competition is fierce, especially among start-ups, and no less so for those companies that have already captured near-monopolies. Being the dominant player can never be grounds for complacency, given the speed with which the market can turn on perceived weakness. On 3 February 2022 the value of Meta suffered the biggest one-day fall in Wall Street history after the company announced that the number of daily Facebook users had dropped from 1.93 billion to 1.92 billion: $250 billion was wiped off its market capitalisation, and $30bn from Mark Zuckerberg's personal fortune. Heavy is the head that wears the crown.

Competition with the state is equally fierce, however. The big tech companies need four things to keep making money on the scale they have grown used to. First, relatively low levels of taxation. Second, the ability to monetise personal data. Third, no limits on their size or growth. Fourth, the freedom to transfer information and resources around the world. Only the state has the power to stop any of this. It could tax them heavily. It could sanction their business model. It could break them up. It could impose capital and other controls. So far, the American state has done none of these things.

In part, this is down to lobbying. In 2002 Google spent

$50,000 on lobbyists. Within a decade that figure had risen to $18 million. Five years later Google was the biggest corporate lobbying spender in the US, ahead of defence contractors like Boeing and telecoms firms like Comcast, both of which are heavily dependent on government contracts. Google isn't nearly so dependent (though in 2021 Alphabet won the CIA cloud contract from Amazon). But it still needs its freedom.

That freedom is greatly advanced by the continuing insistence of the US Supreme Court that corporations are simply 'associations of citizens' and 'rights bearers for the humans who own and control them'. This is the thinnest possible understanding of their artificial agency. It makes it much harder to sue powerful corporations in their own right and much easier for them to use their corporate personality to evade special obligations. In many ways companies like Meta and Alphabet *are* very special: they have an extraordinary capacity to shape how citizens associate with one another through their ability to condition what information they are exposed to. But if they are seen as just another vehicle of human expression, then there is little incentive to treat them differently from anyone or anything else. It's left up to the citizens to decide for themselves what, if anything, they want to do about it.[5]

Of course, there is a way American citizens can decide for themselves: through the voting booth. Recent presidential elections have featured some radical proposals from leading candidates to curtail the power of the big tech companies. In 2020 Elizabeth Warren's pitch for the Democratic Party presidential nomination included the promise to 'break up big tech'. She proposed to achieve this through regulation designed to undo anticompetitive takeovers and mergers, and legislation intended to prevent the owners of widely used platforms exploiting their competitive advantages. 'Big tech companies have bulldozed competition, used our private information for profit, and tilted the playing field against everyone else,' Warren declared. It didn't help – despite having been an early favourite, she lost the nomination by a wide margin. Only a conspiracy theorist would suggest that the ability of the big tech firms to tilt the playing field had anything to do with this. Still, conspiracy theorists are occasionally right.[6]

The successful candidate, Joe Biden, also promised during the campaign to take on the power of Silicon Valley, as had Donald Trump in 2016. So far, though, little has happened in this regard. Other concerns – from China to Covid to Ukraine to economic recovery – have proved more pressing. Nor is there much sign that the American electorate is growing any more exercised by what unaccountable corporations armed with supersmart algorithms might be doing to exploit their power. Polling evidence suggests that the numbers wanting greater regulation of big tech firms has declined since 2020. More people are concerned with ensuring that they continue to have access to a wide range of free services. Again, there are different ways to read this. One is that the electorate is displaying a mind of its own by eschewing elite opinion – this might be an example of the wisdom of crowds. Another is that the wisdom of this particular crowd is now so thoroughly conditioned by the information space created by the algorithms of the big tech firms that it is impossible to know what anyone really thinks.[7]

Increased state control of the technology giants looks unlikely to happen in the US any time soon. In China, however, it has happened already. During the 2010s the Chinese state encouraged the relatively unfettered growth of its big tech firms, in part to compete with what was happening in Silicon Valley (and more recently, some of the US government's reluctance to limit the growth of the biggest American tech companies has been fuelled by its anxiety about being outcompeted by China, especially in the field of defence innovation). As a result, the most successful Chinese tech companies grew very large very quickly, and some of their founders became staggeringly rich.

That has now come to an abrupt halt. In October 2020 the founder of Alibaba, Jack Ma, whose personal wealth was estimated at around $50 billion, gave a speech urging the Chinese authorities to let his business keep growing and back away from further regulation. His intervention had the opposite effect to the one he might have hoped for. The following month the highly anticipated IPO of Alibaba's parent company, the Ant Group, was cancelled. At the same time, Ma disappeared from public view. He has hardly been heard from since.

This was soon followed up by a raft of government measures designed to curb what were now being perceived as the increasingly exploitative practices employed by Alibaba, Baidu, Tencent and others. These new rules included a clampdown on fake advertising, increased oversight of how recommendation algorithms target users, and a requirement that the biggest companies open their platforms to each other to prevent the further growth of monopolies.

It was not only the tech giants that were targeted. The online tutoring industry, which had flourished under Covid lockdown conditions, was effectively wound up in order to get education back under state control. And access to online gaming, which was thought to be having a highly deleterious effect on the nation's youth, was dramatically curtailed. The amount of time China's under-eighteens are permitted to spend playing games online has been reduced to three hours a week, and the livestreaming of unauthorised games outlawed altogether. The entertainment industry is also now under stricter control, with a ban on the promotion of 'sissy' men, 'vulgar influencers' and celebrities with 'lapsed morals'. Anxiety about the falling birth rate has helped feed into a concern about the algorithmic promotion of androgyny.

These steps are all in line with the new 'common prosperity' approach outlined by Xi Jinping in August 2021, which included a pledge to 'reasonably regulate excessively high incomes and encourage high-income people and enterprises to return more to society'. Xi placed far greater emphasis on social cohesion, which was being threatened by an unregulated tech industry. China's leadership has come to the view that the advantages of smart technology can be fully realised only if control of that technology is reclaimed by the state in the name of the common good.[8]

Some of this is a reaction to immediate pressures. Like all autocratic regimes, China's rulers are highly sensitive to perceived shifts in public opinion since they do not have the luxury of elections to test what people might actually think of their government. Chinese social media, as elsewhere, has been prone to scandalised stories about the perils of the internet age: zombified teenagers, brutally exploited delivery drivers, cavalier bosses and pampered, opinionated celebrities. One response, more familiar from an earlier age of propaganda, would have been to suppress these stories. That is harder today, when information production is so much more widespread. So the other response is to try to tackle them at source.

But there is a deeper reconsideration going on as well. The Chinese authorities have been drawing their own lessons from the recent history of the West, including the success of the American military-industrial complex in turbocharging innovation in the 1950s and 1960s. To that end, the Chinese state is now more interested in directing corporate research towards productive technologies such as semiconductors and renewables rather than the gamified, algorithmic froth from which social media companies have been making their vast profits. Government contractors are also taking significant steps to secure their own supply chains. China wants to achieve something more like the vertical integration of its entire innovation economy. That means a far greater role for the state.

At the same time, two of China's most influential public intellectuals – Liu Xiaofeng and Gan Yang – have been reflecting on the longer history of Western progress, and what they see as its steady drift towards sterility and decadence. Modernity, on this view, took a wrong turn when it got too closely tied to the idea of corporate-fuelled economic growth, which disdained tradition and undid social solidarity. The recent struggles of the US in particular – with its deeply divisive elections, widening social rifts, rising inequality and falling life expectancy – are the result of having clung for too long to the narrow path of mindless competition. What's needed instead is what Gan called a unification of 'the three systems' of Chinese social and political thought – Confucianism, Maoism and Dengism. That is, traditional values and a premium on equality must go alongside marketisation.[9]

This approach is hardly a repudiation of modernity. In his elaboration of the common prosperity doctrine, Xi stated that his goal was to make China a 'great modern socialist country' by 2050. Socialism is not just a quintessentially modern idea; it is also a Western one. But framing the challenge in this way does mean that Western modernity can be identified as only one of the paths that might be taken. Going back to Confucianism sets the story of the last 400 years against the longer story of the last 2,500 years – and it suggests that a hybrid model is once again to be preferred.

Western economic growth has long been tied to a distinctive conception of corporate personality: artificial, legalistic, mechanical, relatively unconstrained. We are where we are – and who we are – in part because we gave these artificial persons their own freedom. China's recent attempt to clamp down on overmighty corporations reflects its doubts about the sustainability of such an approach. This includes doubts about whether it is the way to keep growing, given the relatively anaemic recent rates of Western economic growth.

Again, this does not mean a repudiation of the modern corporate form. None of the biggest Chinese companies have been wound up and the Chinese state is still intent on protecting and nurturing a wide variety of smaller-scale enterprises. But it does suggest that the Chinese government increasingly sees the risks of letting corporations take on too much of the burden of economic development, given their propensity to prioritise their own interests over those of the Chinese people.

The flipside of this, however, is unavoidable. Less powerful corporations mean a more powerful state. The Chinese state is increasingly co-opting the independent identity of its corporations into its own personality, legitimated by its claim to represent the Chinese people as a whole. It is doing this in part by identifying its own personality with that of its leader, Xi Jinping, who has engineered recent rule changes to allow him to remain head of state for life. This is not Confucianism but Hobbesianism – indeed, one of the most commonly used terms to describe the character of the twenty-first-century Chinese state, by both Chinese and Western commentators alike, is 'Leviathan'.[10]

A state that co-opts the power of tech companies into its own vertically integrated model of social cohesion threatens to generate another kind of hybrid: not the company-state, but the AI-state, which uses the power of algorithms and deep learning technology to monitor its citizens. The Hobbesian state is designed to be eternally vigilant, but till recently that vigilance could not extend beyond the human capacity to process and understand the information it received. Now it might be allied with the capacity of smart machines to keep an eye on anything and everything that is going on, from personal movement to personal communication to personal preferences. In China, corporations currently have less freedom than their equivalents in the US to monitor and target individuals. But the Chinese state has much more of that capacity since it has taken it on from corporations.

None of these competing paths of modernity provides a way out from the hold of artificial persons over natural ones. In the narrow corridor, we still set the power of corporations against the power of the state. In the alternative version, that contest is collapsed into the overarching personality of the Confucian/ socialist/innovation state. For its champions, this alternative is the wider conception because it can prioritise the human needs of its citizens. But for the people who have to live under its remit, it may turn out to be narrower still, because it offers far fewer means of escape. The ultimate choice for us remains between the different kinds of artificial-artificial hybrids that we might construct. The worry remains that some might end up excluding meaningful human choice altogether.

There is another possible model. The European Union is currently doing far more than the American state to try to limit the power of big tech companies. At the same time it is making no claim to do this in the name of its own, independent political personality. The EU is not a state (not yet, anyway), it is a legal order, and it sees its role as to create a rules-based framework within which other persons, including the states that constitute its membership, can thrive. EU officials have grown increasingly concerned that giant tech companies are making this harder – first, by allowing disinformation to spread unchecked; second, by treating the privacy of individuals in a cavalier fashion; and third, by exploiting uncompetitive market advantages. The EU's Digital Services Act and Digital Markets Act aim to level the competitive playing field, disrupt monopolistic practices, give individuals rights over how their data is used, and provide monitoring bodies with the capacity to remove harmful material from online platforms.[11]

The EU has some advantages over other political organisations in attempting this kind of regulation. Its officials are relatively unknown to the wider public and, compared to national politicians, they operate at one remove from the swirl of online bile they would like to tame. What they lack in legitimacy they gain in anonymity: the 'democratic deficit' that critics of the EU often complain about does also make it easier to operate under the radar. When Biden, or Trump, or even Xi, talk about what's wrong with online communications they are inevitably partisan – what they are complaining about is often what is being communicated about them. (Biden's initial impetus to talk about big tech regulation came from his fury at the stories that were being circulated on Facebook about the business dealings of his son Hunter; Xi doesn't like social media chat comparing his appearance to Winnie the Pooh.) The EU can be a faceless bureaucracy when it needs to be – its rules are simply rules, nothing more.

However, these are also its disadvantages. The EU is not a state, so enforcement depends on the willingness either of its member states to back it up, or of tech companies to do what they are told. EU regulations do sometimes become the global standard, particularly for states that lack the capacity to undertake this sort of technically demanding work themselves. Still, a lot depends on voluntary compliance. Furthermore, much of this compliance needs to come from companies that are not themselves European. The EU has no home-grown tech behemoths – there is no French Google, no German Alibaba, no Italian Amazon, no Spanish Baidu. This is not for want of trying – there is nothing the EU and its member states would like more than to grow their own technology superpowers. But too many of the necessary conditions have been missing, including an appetite for large-scale military spending, a readiness to engage in protectionism, and a first-mover advantage in a world where network effects are decisive. Europe came too late to this party.

At the same time, the bureaucratic regulation of big tech can be counterproductive. Well-intentioned though the EU's rules might be, they are also complex and demanding. Compliance regimes suit organisations that have the resources to be compliant – and no one and nothing is better resourced than big tech. It remains to be seen whether the EU will be able to develop the teeth to make life seriously difficult for the likes of Alphabet and

Amazon. For now, these companies have expressed their willingness to work with the new demands being made of them and have established well-funded departments, stuffed with lawyers, to ensure they stay on the right side of the law. That suggests life won't be too difficult for them after all.

Bureaucracies make rules that suit the bureaucratic mindset; machines like working with machines. The founders of the big tech companies are often irritable, impatient, entrepreneurial personalities – they tend to disdain the miserable grind of doing what the system demands. But the businesses they have built – by dint of their corporate personality – have a different temperament. They are much better able to stick out the boring stuff – and to put in place as their successor-leaders more conventional, corporate types. Steve Jobs, Bill Gates, Mark Zuckerberg, Sergey Brin, Larry Page all dropped out of college; their replacements (only Zuckerberg does not yet have a replacement) – Satya Nadella (CEO of Microsoft), Andy Jassay (CEO of Amazon), Sundar Pichai (CEO of Alphabet) and Tim Cook (CEO of Apple) – all have MBAs. And though each has faced significant challenges in the aftermath of the Covid pandemic, they have successfully grown their businesses.[12]

In 2016 the EU passed General Data Protection Regulation (GDPR) legislation that required, among other things, online platforms to secure the consent of their users in how their data was shared with advertisers. These rules have been widely copied around the world. They have allowed some EU member states to level significant fines for breaches, including the $883-million charge Luxembourg imposed on Amazon in 2021 for failing to comply with advertising regulations. Luxembourg was able to do this because Amazon has its European headquarters there, for tax avoidance purposes. This action, however, remains exceptional for now. Many cases are still held up in the courts and there have been countless delays, as the process gets bogged down by bureaucratic wrangling. The number of individuals who have successfully used GDPR legislation to secure remedies against abuses of power and trust by tech companies remains vanishingly small.

Meanwhile, Amazon continues to avoid tax where it can, which is in most places. Its users, like those of many other online firms, increasingly grumble about the boring consent boxes they have to tick thanks to GDPR rules – rules whose implications few of us begin to understand, though we tick the boxes anyway – because they clutter up our screens and slow down fractionally our ability to access what we are after. And still the money keeps flowing.[13]

The start-up state

One major source of irritation for tech entrepreneurs has always been how cumbersome the state is. They don't understand why it all has to be so slow. While online businesses cycle through new ideas at breakneck pace, looking for the ones that stick, states continue to insist on outdated regulations, to impose procedural rules that were devised decades or even centuries ago and to enforce them through administrative structures in which technical knowledge is severely limited or lacking altogether. Few civil servants – let alone politicians – are able to understand tech half as well as the people who build it. Yet state officials still insist on their right to decide what the technology sector can or can't do.

Even though this kind of oversight is widely accepted in the case of pharmaceutical companies – politicians and bureaucrats don't understand how to make drugs either, but almost no one would suggest that big pharma should therefore set its own rules about which ones are safe – it still seems to grate with digital entrepreneurs. Why? In many cases what they are selling is also a kind of drug – scrolling is intended to be addictive. Moreover, the rules governing tech are far lighter than those governing medical innovation, where the hurdles needed for approval are deliberately designed to slow the whole process down: it takes an average of twelve years for a new drug to move from pre-clinical testing to final sign-off from the US Food and Drug Administration. Big tech companies can roll out new products overnight and are only likely to meet interference if someone with clout complains. Despite this, it's these companies that do most of the complaining.

Impatience for the future, where things will be easier and money will be made, is the calling card of the tech industry. This is what sets it at odds with the state, whose longevity ensures that the future gets tied in with the past. However, it is not only the people building the new products who are growing tired of the mismatch. Some of those inside the machinery of state are also starting to wonder if there are things to be learned from the way technology does its business.

Dominic Cummings, who helped engineer the result of the Brexit referendum in 2016 and served as the senior advisor to Boris Johnson from 2019 to 2020, is an example of someone who wishes the state could be more like a start-up. In the acrimonious aftermath of his departure from Downing Street, Cummings has written often and angrily about the ways in which the British state falls short of even basic standards of management and control that would be expected in the tech sector. In February 2022 he published a blogpost in which he iterated the lessons that the next British government could and should learn from Amazon – where every day is Day 1, recall – for the running of the state. These lessons include the following:

- Good intentions don't work; mechanisms do.
- Have an eagerness to invent, which must go hand in hand with a willingness to fail.
- Pay attention to competitors; but obsess over customers. (Cummings writes: 'The theory of

democracy is that politicians should obsess over voters so that they win the election. They do not. They obsess over tomorrow's media and in-group signals. They make amazingly *little* effort even to understand the basics of campaigning, polling, and communication. They are more interested in competitors than "customers".')

- Look for exceptional talent.
- Simplify, work within constraints, do not grow headcount, or budget size, or expense for the sake of it (if anything, cut, cut, cut).
- Speed matters.

Cummings believes that it is now innovative corporations that are best able to undertake the sort of long-term thinking that used to be the province of the state. That is because the state is only as good as its leaders, and in a democracy those leaders are increasingly myopic. Although states are multipurpose organisations, the reality is that the huge range of problems they face tends to leave those in charge cherry-picking from a very narrow set of issues, and almost always the ones that seem to impact directly on their own futures. Cummings contrasts this with how things work at Amazon:

Leaders don't sacrifice long-term value for short-term results. They act on behalf of the entire company, beyond just their own team. It's very hard to get politicians to talk about the long-term, never mind make sacrifices for it. The idea of focus on true long-term priorities and bending resources to achieve them over years is alien. This has a self-reinforcing negative feedback loop because officials see [politicians] repeatedly make claims about priorities that don't survive even the crisis next week, never mind four years. People follow leaders like Bezos because they quickly learn he means what he says and will stick with things through difficult periods ... Incentives act against ministers and officials acting on behalf of 'the entire company' and push people to focus on themselves or their team at most.

It's fair to say that Boris Johnson was no Bezos.[14]

The state, on this interpretation, has lost its ability to think big, which should be its unique quality as an artificial general agent. Instead, politicians drag officials into their pointless internecine battles. It has now become necessary, as Cummings puts it, to 'fight' politicians for the right to take a general approach (this is the fight that he effectively lost when Johnson sacked him). At the same time, it is essential that within state bureaucracies, tasks are narrowed down, to make sure that people focus on the stuff that really matters. Otherwise, he says, those inside the machine will simply obsess about the working of the machine, not about what it is trying to achieve:

> As an organisation grows, the number of *dependencies* – therefore the amount of *coordination* needed – grows exponentially, and this requires exponentially more *time* trying to solve coordination problems. This time is taken away from building things and achieving goals ... And this *demotivates* everyone, especially the most able who best see the gap between what's theoretically and practically possible.[15]

It is a trenchant critique. It does, though, have some challenging implications. One is that democratic politics, as currently practised, is part of the problem, not the solution. For all the talk of focusing relentlessly on the voters, the other organisations that Cummings admires are, like Amazon, largely self-directed, and sometimes highly autocratic. They include Mossad (the Israeli Secret Service), Y Combinator (the Silicon Valley start-up) and Singapore (the closest there is to a start-up state in the

modern world). Cummings is not interested in treating the customers of these organisations like voters (if an organisation like
Mossad can be said to have 'customers' at all); he is interested
in treating voters like customers. This is consistent with a widespread line of thought in the tech world that sees corporate
organisation as more efficient than democracy, especially once
the latter has been captured by the mindless mob.

What Cummings is not, however, is in thrall to the idea that
politics needs to ape companies like Amazon because Amazon
has the coolest machines. AI is not the answer to the problem
of running the state. Rather, the answer is to hire the people
who have worked out how to run the AIs. Cummings is fond
of quoting the mantra of Colonel John Boyd, the Cold War
fighter pilot and military strategist, who declared: 'People, ideas,
machines – in that order!' What has gone wrong with politics is
that it no longer attracts the best people, which means it misses
out on the best ideas, which means that it ends up unable to
manage the machines, because it lacks the ability to see beyond
them. The task is to put human intelligence on top of machine
intelligence, in order to get humans to take what the machines
are saying seriously.[16]

To that end, Cummings is an advocate of the concept of
'seeing spaces', which puts the widest possible array of real time
data in front of policy makers so that they can understand what
their choices actually mean (fig. 18).

This idea comes from the computer scientist Bret Victor, who
was inspired by the most creative human workspaces, including
craft workshops and restaurant kitchens, where people who use
their hands are surrounded by their tools, rather than having to
access them through a single, small screen on a handheld device.
The other point of reference is the control rooms at places like
NASA, the European Organization for Nuclear Research, or any
large power grid, where all the relevant information needs to
be visible at once. (Think of any film you have ever seen about

18. A seeing room

manned rocket launches, and the contrast between what's in front of the astronauts in their tiny pods and the vast array of screens being surveyed back in Houston.) The goal, as Victor puts it, is to ensure that people can see 'what the thing they are building is actually doing'.[17]

Applied to policy making, this approach seeks to bypass the tendency of state-based operations to focus on what things look like from the point of view of the state itself. In 1999 the anthropologist James C. Scott published an influential book entitled *Seeing Like a State: How Certain Schemes to Improve the Human Condition Have Failed*. Scott described the unavoidable tendency of modern states to see the world in their own image – i.e. as artificial, legible, measurable and schematic. The result is a systematic misrepresentation of what is out there. Scott draws the contrast between a town planner's map – of buildings, roads and preferred traffic flows – with a real-time map of unplanned-for human movements, with all its unexpected streams and contours – 'pushing a baby carriage, window shopping, walking the dog, watching the passing scene, taking a short cut between work and home, and so on.' States find it almost impossible to access the second kind of information and choose instead to fixate on the first. That is why state schemes to improve people's lives can often make them worse, by reducing unforeseen human input to the level of an anomaly. Context, which should be the essence of planning, becomes an irritation.[18]

Writing in 1999, from a broadly critical, postcolonial perspective (the worst of state planning happens in imperial settings where the colonial power draws its own maps and entirely misapprehends what it is dealing with), Scott was hardly advocating for making the other kind of map, which would show what was happening in real time. That would have been impossible: nothing could capture that volume of data. Instead, he argued for a more modest approach, fully alive to the unpredictability of the future and grounded in democratic responsiveness. The worst of states, he thought, were the authoritarian ones, which could ignore anything that didn't fit in with how they saw the world. In a democracy, the state has to listen as well as see.

Things appear a little different now. First, thanks to advances in machine learning, the possibility of a real-time map is not as remote as it once was. Second, democracy is looking more tarnished. The complaint against the democratic state is that it no longer even sees like a state, looking out at a world it wishes to remake according to its own lights. It has lost that ambition. Instead, within democracies, the state just looks in on itself, as politicians see only the inner workings of the machine.

Seeing spaces offer the chance to bypass that: smart people + smart machines = a new perspective on what's worth building and how. But it is worth remembering that the inspiration for this is the manufacturing process – what Arendt would call the world of work. This approach suits particular projects – city planning, building a health system, designing a transport network, mapping education reforms. For Cummings, the ideal instance of what a smart state can achieve was the Manhattan Project, which ended up building the atom bomb in the New Mexico desert during the Second World War: brilliant people – new ideas – game-changing machines – in that order. Now, with ever smarter machines, it ought to be possible to build ever better systems, so long as the brilliant people are still in the room where it happens.

The state, however, is also a machine, which means it too has to be manufactured and kept running. Does that mean the state needs to see itself in the round as well, so it can reform its own practices? At this point, the project starts to appear incoherent, because we are back to the machine looking at itself. Cummings wants something else – a pared-down bureaucracy, recruited from the brightest and the best (or, as he put it in a notorious job advert during his time in government, 'data scientists, project managers, policy experts, assorted weirdos'), to look outwards at what needs fixing. The model really is a firm like Amazon, where ruthless management practices, under an autocratic and inspirational leader, drive discrete projects, some of which are massive busts, but enough of which are a stunning success to make the whole thing worthwhile.

The Manhattan Project fits this bill, the state doesn't. It is not a project – it is an artificial person. A well-run state – or as likely, a well-funded state in fear of its life – might enable the Manhattan Project. What it can't do is turn itself into the Manhattan Project without reducing itself to the status of just another manufacturing enterprise. A state could choose to do this, of course. It could become just another corporation, serving its customers with ever better-refined projects: the *societas* turned into a streamlined, twenty-first-century *universitas*. Maybe – just maybe – that is where the state is heading, if not in Britain or Europe or the United States, then perhaps in China. But it seems unlikely. Even in China, the state doesn't want to *be* Amazon, or Alibaba. It wants to take them over.

The government of things

In Chile during the early 1970s, under the socialist government of Salvador Allende, an abortive attempt was made to deploy the latest technology to transform the running of the economy. The young science of cybernetics, which studies self-regulating systems, appeared to offer fresh insights into the question of how to feed economic data into the planning process so as to eliminate the lag between intelligence and decision-making. In the early 1960s, the British prime minister Harold Macmillan had stated that his government was hamstrung by the fact that the economic data on which it based its decisions were a year out of date. A decade later, one of his successors, Harold Wilson, boasted that improved statistical analysis had shrunk that gap to six months (Wilson was chair of the Royal Society of Statisticians at the time). The architect of the Chilean system, a British management consultant called Stafford Beer, stated as his goal to reduce it to nothing. In an age when telecommunications were instantaneous, he saw no reason why economic decision-making should not be informed by real-time information as well.

The Chilean Project Cybersyn was created to show that state socialism need not always mean inefficiency tempered by coercion, which is what inevitably happened when governments tried to play catch-up with an economy that was at least one step ahead. If machines could access and assess economic data instantaneously, then decision-making could act on the world as it is, not as it used to be. As a result, socialism could be both liberating – because it need not interfere with personal freedoms, since it would reflect what people were already doing – and effective. The map would work in real time.

At the heart of Cybersyn was a state-of-the-art control room, where the latest telex technology would feed in labour, pricing, and production statistics as they emerged each day from factories around the country; these would then be used to decide what adjustments would be needed for tomorrow. At its centre was a set of chairs for anyone – from high level bureaucrats to ordinary citizens – tasked with making it work. Each chair had an ashtray, a whisky glass holder and a button that controlled the display screens on the walls. Tables and paper were banned. The room was round, and the chairs rotated through 360 degrees, so everyone could see whatever they needed to see (fig. 19).

19. Cybersyn HQ

Unsurprisingly, it didn't work. The technology was far too crude – telex was used because Chile at this time had no viable computer network. The buttons in the chairs connected to slide carousels that displayed pre-made slides, meaning little could be decided that had not been anticipated in advance. Cybersyn was never much more than a stage prop. By 1973, with inflation running at nearly 500 per cent and the international price of the country's single most valuable export – copper – having collapsed, the Chilean economy was on the brink of ruin. In September a military coup, sponsored by the CIA, overthrew Allende, who committed suicide, and installed the dictatorship of Augusto Pinochet. Under Pinochet's brutal rule, Chile was subject to radical free-market reforms, inspired by economists from the University of Chicago. During the 1980s, when the country experienced some of the highest growth rates in the world, this led to what became known (at least at the University of Chicago) as 'the miracle of Chile'.[19]

From one perspective, Cybersyn seems hopelessly quaint, a relic from an age of cardboard cut-out futurism – the control room looks like the set for an episode of the puppet show *Thunderbirds*. But from another, it suggests a different kind of time-lag. In the words of one commentator, 'Project Cybersyn can also be viewed as a dispatch from the future.' What if it were now truly possible, with twenty-first-century technology, to engineer an entire economy with real-time data? This is a hope that goes well beyond the cybernetic tinkering of Silicon Valley, where real-time information is merely put in the service of selling us things that we didn't know we needed. Instead, here perhaps is a true vision of twenty-first-century socialism: an economy managed more efficiently – and more fairly – than the free market ever can.[20]

Pinochet's Chicago-inspired programme – whose gurus included the economists Milton Friedman and Friedrich Hayek – was based on a simple but flawed proposition: only the market knows what goods and services we actually want. Any attempt by human beings to organise an economic system in anticipation of people's needs and desires will lack the necessary intelligence to function successfully. It will be riddled with misinformation, which will create incentives for individuals to bypass its rules, which will only make it ever more inaccurate and inefficient – and ultimately coercive. The state doesn't know us. But the market knows what we don't know because the market knows us better than we know ourselves.

But now the machines know us better than the market does. What's more, we have discovered that the market is riddled with its own inefficiencies – feedback loops, time lags, misaligned incentives. The neo-liberal thinking that inspired the miracle of

Chile also helped generate the global financial crisis that began in 2007–8 and nearly destroyed the world economy. Instead of leaving it up to the bankers, wouldn't it be better to put the machines in charge, and to put workers in charge of the machines?

The original idea behind Cybersyn was that running the system would not take any special expertise because the data would be unarguable. This has long been a vision at the heart of socialism – replacing 'the government of persons' with the 'administration of things'. Market capitalism professes to be a neutral mechanism, but, in the end, it simply empowers new cadres of experts – the economists and CEOs and CFOs and MBAs, who know how the system works because they have the requisite inside knowledge. Since the late 1970s we have lived in a world where central bankers wield enormous power – as much power as democratically elected politicians – yet almost no one is qualified to be a central banker. I couldn't do it and nor, I guess, could you. Project Cybersyn was based on the premise that any of us could.

What then would happen to the state? In classic Marxist theory, once the workers run the bureaucracy, the state falls away, because we no longer need its artificial personality looming over us. What we have in its place is a society that runs itself. The state is required only when people are unable to manage their own affairs. New technology has the potential to remedy that by making reliable information accessible to everyone. The state is ultimately the product of uncertainty – we don't know what other people want, so we create an artificial person to decide for us. But what if we did know what other people wanted? Then we might dismantle the lumbering mechanical giant and use its parts for scrap.

In this way, smart technology is breathing new life into old ideological fantasies. Something similar – but very different – is happening on the libertarian right. Whereas Marxists view the space created by the absence of knowledge as liable to be filled by class oppression – Marx labelled the state 'the organising committee of the bourgeoisie' – libertarians see it as liable to be filled by self-interested politicians, with their fingers in the pot. From this perspective, the great danger of the state's power is that it can be used to make things even more uncertain, by creating its own arbitrary standards of value. In the hands of the people who run it, the state becomes an instrument for interfering with market intelligence. One result of this interference is inflation, the spectre that haunts libertarians everywhere – money loses its value when it can be engineered by politicians, at which point society loses its moral anchor (just look at Weimar Germany, they say, or early 1970s Chile). But new technology offers a solution. The name for this solution is 'crypto'.[21]

For the advocates of cryptocurrencies like Bitcoin, the blockchain technology that underpins it promises to eliminate the uncertainty caused by the political control of money. In its place comes an unbreakable ledger of all transactions, such that the value of everything can be known. Money turns into information. This, however, is a category mistake. If money is simply information, then it ceases to be money, just as the state ceases to exist once it is turned into the administration of things. The state is an agent, capable of action, or it is nothing. Money is a vehicle of that agency. We trust in it, when we do, because we believe that it is responsive to human imperatives. That's what gives it credibility. The price we pay for making it a matter of trust is that flawed decision-making may destroy its value. Blockchain technology, which is impervious to political tinkering, is good for many things, including keeping a record of the information that many states would prefer to stay hidden, such as human rights abuses. But it is no good as money because it is fundamentally inhuman.[22]

Money needs to accommodate the uncertainties of human existence, including our intermittent urge to escape its tight constraints. Sometimes, what we require is inflation, or a default, because we have other priorities. If the state controls money then money can be made subject to human decision-making, with all the risks that entails. If money controls the state, then humans are ultimately left out of the equation. In the long run, though some people will hold on to their wealth, and a few will make spectacular fortunes, we will all pay the price.[23]

Crypto can dazzle with its promise of machine-driven certainty: the power of intelligent technology used to unlock the deepest wisdom of crowds (every transaction is ostensibly an unimpeachable record of what someone was willing to pay). But the reality looks a little different. Nothing has been rifer with hype, rumour, manipulation and sheer boosterism than the crypto markets, which have been subject to wild speculation. They have also been the site of abject market failures. FTX, the cryptocurrency exchange run by Sam Bankman-Fried, destroyed huge amounts of nominal wealth (including SBF's own reported $16 billion net worth) in a matter of days during late 2022 when it emerged that its practices were little more than an accounting scam. For years the dazzle had blinded money-makers to what was really going on. When the truth emerged, the market reacted with its customary, unsentimental brutality: here today, gone tomorrow. But it wasn't smart technology that exposed the fraud, it was journalistic digging, first by the *Wall Street Journal* and then by the crypto news site *CoinDesk*. Human greed met human doggedness: that's politics.

Perfect information is the death of politics, rather than a means to rescue politics from uncertainty. Because so much political decision-making lacks intelligence, smart technology tempts us with the idea that intelligence can provide us with the decisions we need. But intelligence is not decision-making, just as information is not a choice. Instead of the administration of things we will get the government of persons by things. And we will be as vulnerable to failures of market intelligence as ever. The state is not a thing – not even a public thing (the *res publica*). The state too is a person. The advent of AI has yet to change the terms of the choice that was built into the structure of modern politics back in the seventeenth century. We do not get to choose between an imperfect state and a more perfect state. We get to choose between an imperfect state or no state at all.

And there is a further difficulty with the idea that, given the right technology, the workers might be able to reclaim control of the products of their labour and get rid of the state. In the age of AI, who are the workers anyway?

8

WHO WORKS FOR WHOM?

People vs horses

At the 2021 Australian and US Open tennis championships, all the line judges were replaced by machines. This was, in many ways, inevitable. Not only are these machines far more accurate than any human at calling balls in or out, but they can also be programmed to make their calls in a human-like voice, so as not to disorient the players. It is a little eerie, the disembodied shriek of 'Out!' coming from nowhere on the court (at the Australian Open the machines are programmed to speak with an Australian accent). But it is far less irritating than the delays required by challenging incorrect calls, and far more reliable. It takes very little getting used to.

In the slew of reports published in the 2010s looking to identify which jobs were most at risk of being automated out of existence, sports officials usually ranked very high up the list (the best-known of these studies, by Frey and Osborne in 2017, put a 98 per cent probability on sports officiating being phased out by computers within twenty years). Here, after all, is a human enterprise where the single most important qualification is an ability to get the answer right. In or out? Ball or strike? Fair or foul? These are decisions that need to be underpinned by accurate intelligence. The technology does not even have to be state-of-the-art to produce far better answers than humans can. Hawk-Eye systems have been outperforming human eyesight for nearly twenty years. They were first officially adopted for tennis line-calls in 2006, to check cricket umpire decisions in 2009, and to rule on soccer offsides in 2012.[1]

Yet despite the arrival of this smart technology, there are now many more people employed in sports officiating than ever before. Wimbledon has decided to retain its line judges, in part for aesthetic reasons. As the only major tournament played on grass, looking good against a green backdrop is a key part of the money-making machine (hence the requirement that the players wear nothing but white). The line judges are mainly there for their uniforms. In 2022, as for the previous seventeen years, these were designed by Ralph Lauren.

Cricket matches, which traditionally featured just two umpires, currently have three to manage the complex demands of the technology, plus a referee to monitor the players' behaviour, which still involves a large element of human discretion (who's to say what is meant by 'upholding the spirit of the game'?). Soccer matches have up to five officials, plus the large teams of screen-watchers needed to interpret the replays provided by the video assistant referee system (VAR). The NBA Replay Center at Secaucus, New Jersey, which employs twenty-five people full-time, along with a rota of regular match officials, would not look out of place at NASA (fig. 20).

20. NBA Replay Centre, Secaucus, NJ

Efficiency – even accuracy – turns out not to be the main requirement of the organisations that employ people to give decisions during sports games. They are also highly sensitive to appearance, which includes a wish to keep their sport looking and feeling like it's still a human-centred enterprise. Smart technology can do many things, but in the absence of convincingly humanoid robots, it can't really do that: a voice-activated line call is probably at the limit of what's plausible at the moment. So actual people are required to stand between the machines and those on the receiving end of their judgements. The result is more work all round.

It remains surprisingly hard to know which jobs are likely to go with the arrival of AI, though we can be confident that both the scope and character of employment will change. Many studies of the risks of automation, like Frey and Osborne's, choose to treat work as a series of tasks, which can then be measured by their suitability to be undertaken by machines. This assumes that the barriers in the way of human replacement are simply the current limitations of the technology, which for now include a continuing inability to exhibit a range of human-centric cognitive and mobility skills. Robots are good at repetitive tasks, even when these are highly complex, along with ever more voluminous data-crunching, but they often struggle with simple forms of human interaction. If your job involves creativity, aesthetic judgement, truly fluid movement or social sensitivity, then on these measures you are likely to be safe for now. Robots can dance, but they still need human choreographers to look convincing.

However, a task is not a job, not in the modern meaning of the term. Jobs are positions created by organisations that have their own requirements. It is too simplistic to think of these requirements as nothing more than the efficient performance of a task, even in the case of heartless, money-grubbing corporations. It also matters whether the job makes sense in relation to the corporation's needs. The NBA is a pretty heartless, money-grubbing organisation, but it still needs people more than it needs machines. Most jobs continue to require people to fill them, because people are the human element of the impersonal organisations that provide the jobs. Otherwise, the machines would appear to be running the show, which is a dangerous look in a world where people still count.

How things look isn't everything. There are significant parts of every organisation where appearance doesn't matter so much, in the backrooms and maybe even the boardrooms that the public never gets to see. Behind-the-scenes technical knowledge that underpins the performance of public-facing tasks is likely to be an increasingly precarious basis for reliable employment. This is true of many professions, including accountancy, consultancy and the law. There will still be lots of work for the people who deal with people. But the business of gathering data, processing information and searching for precedents can now more reliably be done by machines. The people who used to undertake this work, especially those in entry-level jobs such as clerks, administrative assistants and paralegals, might not be OK.[2]

The future of employment necessarily involves a complex set of relationships, which are far more likely to alter what we understand by work than to abolish it. There are the relationships between people and machines, some of which may turn out to be zero-sum (more work for them means less work for us), but most of which are still liable to be mutual. Doctors who use technology to diagnose cancers are going to need to hone other skills – including better ways of communicating what the machines are saying – but these will be far easier to acquire than expecting the technology to hone the skills possessed by the doctors. Then there is all the work for the managers, lawyers and ethicists who will need to decide on whether the doctor–machine relationship is proceeding as hoped, and what to do when it goes wrong. In the age of AI, there will be no shortage of work in hospitals.

Alongside these relationships are the ones between artificial persons and artificial intelligences, and between natural persons and the artificial persons that employ them. As well as asking what the patient wants from the technology, and what the doctor wants, we also need to ask what the hospital wants. These answers will not be the same. Hospitals – or the corporate entities that run them – have their own preferences and patterns of behaviour. On the one hand, their machine-like qualities might incline them towards working with other machines rather than with altogether less reliable human employees. Bureaucracies have a weakness for mechanical processes. On the other hand, the fact that a hospital is also a decision-making machine, which for now still requires the input of human intelligence, might give it pause. Does the hospital really want to risk letting machines that are there for pattern recognition start to take more consequential decisions as well? Answers are not always the best decisions, and decisions are not always the right answers.

In the world of work, it's still people, organisations, machines – in that order. Might the order change? Could the organisations come to prioritise the machines over the people, or the machines come to take the most consequential decisions on behalf of the organisations? These are real possibilities, but they are not something that can be calibrated by measuring the aptitude of the technology for particular tasks. The world of work is more complicated than that.

History offers a partial guide to what might happen. Worries about automation displacing human workers are as old as the idea of the job itself. The Industrial Revolution disrupted many kinds of labour – especially on the land – and undid entire ways of life. The transition was grim for those who had to switch from one mode of subsistence existence to another. Yet the end result was many more jobs, not fewer. Factories brought in machines to do faster and more reliably what humans used to do or could never do at all; at the same time, factories were where the new jobs appeared, involving the performance of tasks that were never required before the coming of the machines. This pattern has repeated itself time and again: new technology displaces familiar forms of work, causing massively painful disruption. It is little consolation to the people who lose their jobs to be told that soon enough there will be entirely new ways of earning a living. But there will.[3]

It does not always happen, however, that new tasks are found for the previous generation of workhorses. This was most notably the case with actual workhorses. Throughout the nineteenth century, fast-growing industrial production was heavily dependent on the labour of horses to transport people and goods, above all in the United States. From this labour a huge number and variety of jobs were created for the people needed to sustain horse-powered enterprises: 'teamsters, street-car operators, carriage manufacturers, groomers, coachmen, feed merchants, saddlers, stable keepers, wheelwrights, farriers, blacksmiths, buggy whip makers, veterinarians, horse breeders, street cleaners, and the farmers who grew grain and hay'. Even the coming of the railways did little to displace the horse from its centrality to American social and economic life. When horse flu hit the equine population of New York in 1872, the entire city ground to a halt. Stores shut, construction sites went quiet, saloons ran out of beer.[4]

Just fifty years later the horse-powered economy had almost entirely disappeared from urban areas if not yet from rural ones. Fifty years after that it was more or less gone throughout the whole country. The internal combustion engine changed everything, from the surfacing of roads (smooth enough for cars, and hence much harder for horses to get a grip) to the smell of the city (exhaust fumes in place of manure). The feed merchants disappeared. But an enormous number of new jobs were created to service the needs of the automobile. By 1950 the auto industry had generated 7 million or more net new jobs, which accounted at that point for 11 per cent of the total American workforce.

What weren't created were many new jobs for the horses. Their skill set – pulling, carrying, not complaining about it – turned out to be insufficiently adaptable for the new era. Eventually there was nothing much left for them to do, outside of the leisure industry. When the first model-T Ford (22 horsepower) rolled off the production line in 1908 there were around 25 million horses in the United States, alongside 90 million people. When the first Ford Falcon (260 horsepower) appeared in 1960, there were just 3 million horses left – and nearly 180 million people. The horse as worker was effectively obsolete.

Might humans go the way of the horse? Our skill set too could turn out to be insufficiently adaptable, once machines are able to do most of the things we can, at many, many times the speed. The 'humanpower' of deep learning technology – for instance, 3,000 years of chess knowledge picked up by Alpha-Zero in less than twenty-four hours (humanpower: 1,000,000+) – is exponentially greater than the horsepower of even the swiftest automobiles. It is true that smart machines also lack adaptability, above all the ability to switch between entirely different tasks. But cars lack plenty of kinds of adaptability compared with horses: they can't step over obstacles, or move sideways, or swim through streams. That didn't stop us building an entire economy around them, and road networks suited to all their limitations, sacrificing many hundreds of thousands of our own lives in the process.

Where humans most clearly differ from horses, however, is that we are not uncomplaining. We are the opposite. We have agency, expressed through our ability to communicate our choices. When the horses were phased out, it was by organisations in which they did not have a say. We do have a say in the organisations that might choose to phase us out. We had better use it.

One reason we should is that these organisations have agency too. Without our input they will make their own choices. And smart machines, also unlike horses, can make their own choices as well. It is fanciful to suppose that they would choose to phase us out once we did not serve their purposes any more. They don't have that kind of agency – the human kind. But their ability to perform certain tasks better than we can is sufficient to allow them to shape how we live if we choose to let them. Just as cars came to shape how we live once we chose to let them.

It was never up to the horses. It was not up to the cars. It is not even up to the new breed of self-driving vehicles. It is still up to us, our states and our corporations.

Whose career is it, anyway?

What makes a job different from other kinds of work is its relationship to the passing of time. When work comprises a task or a series of tasks, time is measured by how long the task takes to complete, and by how long its results last. Often there is a connection between the two, but not necessarily: the books that take the longest to write are by no means the ones that are sure to endure; the songs that take the longest to compose are not always the ones that people want to sing. 'Hallelujah' by Leonard Cohen, which is among the most covered songs of the last fifty years, took ten years and endless revisions to get right, but 'Forever Young' by Bob Dylan, which has been re-recorded almost as often, was knocked out in a single sitting (as were many of Dylan's songs).[5]

For Hannah Arendt, what distinguished work, and what made it potentially so satisfying, was this possibility of durability: things could be built that might long outlast their makers. Here is the world of artifice as opposed to labour – of *Homo faber*, the maker of stuff. These artefacts could be anything from books and songs to tables and chairs to states and constitutions.

Doing lasting work, however, is distinct from having a job. 'Framer of the US Constitution' was not a job title; it was a task. Meanwhile, the jobs that came out of it were not as durable as the thing itself, not even the job of president of the United States, which has been around for as long as the constitution, but which has changed its character very substantially over the same period. The office has remained constant, but the job is something different with each new occupant. And each is out after, at most, eight years.

At the same time, many jobs are longer lasting than the tasks they require. Being president is a single job with many responsibilities, some of which demand attention only from one day to the next. The job of a furniture maker could last an adult lifetime, during which many hundreds or even thousands of tables and chairs might be built. Being a carpenter is a craft; it becomes a job when someone, or more likely something, pays you to do it over a long enough timeframe that your income is not solely dependent on what you produce. What gives jobs their durability is that the organisations that generate them have sufficient longevity of their own.

Steady employment has been one of the benefits of the modern age of artificial corporate personality – these persons can offer what used to be called 'permanent positions', simply by dint of their own relative permanence. Some of the most secure jobs are in the public sector – for bureaucrats, but also teachers, social workers, administrators – because the state is the most durable artificial person of them all. Not always – fragile states do not offer much job security, particularly when getting public sector positions depends on personal connections. Then it is a vicious circle: the weaker the state, the more it matters who you know; the more that matters, the weaker the state becomes. But when the state's personality is independent of anyone's private identity, there will be no more reliable employer.

Often the price of job security is drudgery or repetition.

Doing the same job for many years can be boring. That is why organisations try to offer progression as well as stability, at least for the lucky few who qualify. A career is more than just a job – it usually involves changing roles within a given field, and when appropriate changing organisation too. Being a banker is a career; working for a bank is a job; devising a banking product is a task; closing a deal is an action. Yet being a banker also means running the serious risk of getting fired. It is potentially more rewarding than being a civil servant – in financial terms anyway – but it is less reliable. It can also be harder work. Personal contacts still count for a lot in the world of finance, as does putting in the hours. States are big enough that they can offer a variety of work to their most talented employees, but their size and impersonality also mean that they can leave individuals trapped or unnoticed in bureaucratic backwaters.

These trade-offs – between job security and variety, between risk and reward – have been familiar throughout the history of modern employment. They echo the wider trade-offs between the personal and the impersonal, the human and the artificial, that define the modern age. Where the balance is struck varies with time and place. During much of the twentieth century – the great age of the career, and indeed of 'careers advice' in schools – large corporations, along with the state, could offer solid prospects for career progression. It was possible to remain in the same organisation for a working lifetime and still have a range of satisfying working experiences.

But the twentieth century was also the great age of anxiety about the soullessness of a corporate existence – the empty, artificial routines of the 'company men', as they were called in the United States, or the 'salary men', as they were called in Japan. If the nineteenth century was the era of drudgery – of Bartleby, the scrivener – the twentieth century was the era of plastic performance – of 'Rabbit' Angstrom, the salesman.

The twenty-first century is different. Many large organisations have relatively few employees compared to their twentieth-century equivalents. The rapid proliferation of smaller, shorter-lived companies also means that longevity is not what it was. In the age of the start-up, getting a job, even (and perhaps especially) a highly paid one, doesn't guarantee much security. Jobs are shorter lived, and as a result careers are far more fragmented. For anyone first entering the workplace in the third decade of the twenty-first century, it makes little sense to talk in terms of 'careers advice' at all. The experience of work is far more likely to involve a portfolio of different occupations, some inevitably undertaken at the same time. A single person might have many jobs, but many jobs are unlikely to make a single career.

The rise of smart technology has a lot to do with this. Some of it is simple uncertainty – trying to picture the arc of a working life is almost impossible when the rate of change is so rapid. Apocalyptic warnings about the impending hollowing out of the professions make training to be a lawyer, or an accountant, feel far riskier than it once did. That doesn't mean that people have stopped training to be lawyers – the number of enrolments at US law schools is continuing to grow, as is the number of schools offering law degrees. But there is a widespread expectation that this will result in many more qualified lawyers than there are legal jobs, let alone legal careers. The hope must be that knowing the law will still provide good training for the increasing variety of human-oriented tasks that a portfolio career might require, with or without machines to do the heavy lifting.

But even in the shorter term, new technology has changed the relationship between careers, jobs and tasks. Performing tasks is what machines are good at. The better they get at it, the more work becomes task orientated. In many ways, talking about the prospect of machines taking people's jobs is a misnomer, because once machines do the work these are no longer jobs. Machines don't require job security, any more than they require the other appurtenances of modern employment regimes: holidays, healthcare, positive feedback, redundancy pay. Jobs are what humans do.

At the same time, smart machines are helping to change the character of the states and corporations that provide the jobs for people. Just as technology can fragment the personal identity of individuals into a series of data points, so it can fragment the personal identity of states and corporations into a series of tasks, or projects. Give a machine work and it will become a task; give a human work and it can become a job. Inevitably, the more work that machines do, the less the identity of artificial persons will be shaped by the secure jobs they are able to sustain, because those jobs will have been replaced by tasks. Instead, even states will be identified by the different projects they undertake, each with its own discrete timeframe and end point.

As careers get reduced to jobs, likewise jobs get reduced to tasks. More and more people are employed on short-term contracts, offered by organisations that see work as something to be understood in terms of its outcome rather than as an ongoing relationship. This is only in part because people are being replaced by machines. It is also because people are increasingly being employed like machines. The variety of work on offer from contemporary states and corporations is wider than it has ever been. No corporations in history have undertaken as many different tasks as vertically integrated companies like Tesla – from mining to brain science. Twenty-first-century states have more responsibilities than ever – from street cleaning to data mining. But the work itself looks more and more like it fits the remit of smart machines.

Still, it's a trade-off. The relationships that earlier corporate entities enjoyed with their employees were by no means always good ones – they could be exploitative, abusive, utterly heartless, as any relationship can be. Most workers in the modern age were labourers, and as such were hardly able to experience the benefits of job security at all. Twenty-first-century employment offers potentially more freedom for workers of all kinds – including the freedom to be self-employed – once paid work is available in a more fragmentary way, such that workers can take it or leave it. Yet when we lament the prospect that jobs might disappear, it is the possibility of a lasting working relationship that we will miss. The benefits of task-based work come at the cost of work-based benefits.

Other things are changing too. Retirement was once the flipside of work – it was what happened at the end of a life of employment. Now that line is increasingly blurred. Work can continue long into retirement for those who want it or need it so long as that work does not have to be tied to a job. Equally, retirement is coming earlier and earlier for many professionals and other workers. Since the Covid pandemic, the workforce in some developed countries has shrunk significantly, with sizeable numbers of people choosing not to return to paid employment. Unemployment rates are at historic lows in the US, and job vacancies are at historic highs. The same is currently true in the UK. Jobs are not in short supply, despite the increasing availability of machines to compete for the work. What's in short supply are people wanting to do them.

This opens up the space for a more radical understanding of the relationship between employment and a steady income, which is to try to break it altogether. Even in the age of task-based work, the state retains its distinctive capacity to carry fiscal and moral burdens for longer than anyone or anything else. The fracturing of the timeframe of human activity has if anything thrown into relief the state's ability to keep going regardless. Why shouldn't it use its longevity to maintain its citizens, independent of the work they do? The idea of a universal basic income (UBI) rests on the assumption that the state is uniquely well placed to provide for individuals through the vicissitudes of their working (or non-working) lives – far better placed than any corporation. As the world of work adapts to the time horizons of AI-driven machines, the durable artificial personality of the state should enable it to take the long view.[6]

The most optimistic takes on UBI see two concurrent benefits. First, more leisure, as people get paid to do whatever they like. Second, more productivity, as people get paid to work out what it is they like doing, and then maybe turn that activity into a successful business. The numbers quoted for UBI vary from proposal to proposal – Andrew Yang, the US presidential candidate who ran in 2020 on a 'freedom dividend' platform, suggested $1,000 a month to be paid to every American over the age of eighteen – and it is never cheap (Yang's plan would have cost around $2.8 trillion per year). But the American state could sustain such a burden if it chose – its interest payment on its debt every year is greater than that sum already.

Would it work? Perhaps. But it is reasonable to wonder whether support on this scale would be sufficient to have the desired effects. It is asking a lot for a fixed income both to motivate productivity among those who are frustrated by a lack of resources and to substitute for it among those who are frustrated by a lack of free time. It seems possible that it would have the opposite result. Critics of UBI worry that it would be demotivating, because it is not enough to be a genuine liberation, only an escape valve: a way out, rather than a way in. It could also reinforce existing inequalities. $12,000 a year won't on its own transform many people's life chances, but it might allow the comfortably off to entrench their advantages – by buying more educational help for their children, for example. Those already in work and planning to stay might be the biggest beneficiaries.

Then there is the politics. Even if the state could afford it, that doesn't answer the question of how to pay for it. It is tempting to imagine a benign circle: machines increasingly do the work, enriching the corporations; the corporations are taxed to pay to support the citizens; the citizens use that support to buy what the machines make, and to invent new ways of making things for themselves. That is unlikely to be how it happens. Corporations that are taxed might simply relocate or stop investing in new machinery (past a certain point, human labour will be cheaper again); citizens might stop buying their goods; or they might stop voting for this project altogether.

Most proposals envisage a mixture of ways to pay, including eventual cuts to social security benefits. It's not hard to see how this would become both politically necessary and politically toxic. Once the state is paying everyone, why should it pay the people who are contributing the least twice over? That's one argument, similar to the line of reasoning that saw inheritance tax effectively abolished in the US (why should the most productive people be taxed twice, once in life and once more in death?). On the other hand, getting rid of Medicaid and Medicare, along with veterans' benefits and disaster relief – which is how the American Enterprise Institute proposes paying for UBI – is going to be a hard sell, especially among the older voters who increasingly decide elections in an ageing society. Human beings are loss averse, and under any version of UBI the losses would loom larger for many people than the gains. In the end, there's nothing that's politically unifying about a universal basic income.[7]

Then there is a deeper question. The artificial personality of the state is founded on the assumption that it must be animated by us. We are the source of its ability to function. States are able to take on debt for the long term because we will ultimately repay it, even if who counts as us is never finally fixed. States bear the burden of war because they are able to rely on human sacrifice to sustain it. The state might be there to keep us going, but it is also we who keep the state going.

A relationship between states, machines and people, through which the machines pay for the state, which then pays out to the people, threatens to upend this understanding. The legitimacy of modern politics rests on the fact that, however grateful we might be to the state, the state must be equivalently grateful to us, because without us it is nothing. That was the point of the Leviathan – it was a political machine built out of the work of people. Now we face the prospect of a political machine built out of the labour of machines. The hope is that the people will be more grateful than ever because they are being spared the need to do so much of the work themselves. This is wishful thinking. It can be hard to forgive the person who does you a favour and expects gratitude in return. That's how relationships end.

Everyone's a teacher

An ageing society also changes the kind of work that's going to be needed in future. As people get older there will be an ever-greater demand for healthcare and for social care. That means more doctors, more nurses, more physical therapists and more smart machines to service them. It also means more routine work of the kind that is essential for the functioning of residential homes and assisted-living communities, as well as for those unable to leave their own places of residence. Someone, or something, is going to have to wash people who cannot wash themselves, to feed them and to ensure they do not live in squalor. Even if a lot of this will be unpaid work done by family members, a lot of it won't be.

Where there can be a division of labour between human-centric and more basic care tasks, it is possible to hope that the work will divide up accordingly, between the people who are good with people and the machines that are good at things people don't much want to do. A lot of routine care work can be unappealing for humans – not least because it is poorly paid – but that's no problem for robots, who don't care how messy it gets nor how long the hours are. If machines are best suited to the heavy-lifting aspects of work – when more and more people are going to need lifting – then it looks like there will be plenty of the right kind of work for machines. Meanwhile, the human side of care – talking, empathising, simply being there – can be left to the humans.

However, it might not turn out like that. In fact, it could be that the division of labour pulls in the opposite direction. There is little sign yet that machines are sufficiently skilled at the kind of heavy lifting that is most often needed in care homes. They are not nearly dextrous enough. Washing, moving and caring for the human body is a very delicate task. It requires sensitivity to what it feels like to be touched by another, which for now is something that only humans can recognise. A smart shower, programmed to adjust the temperature and pressure of the water to your personal preferences, is one thing. Being bathed by a robot would be something else.

Meanwhile, there is already evidence that smart machines can successfully stand in for people in meeting a different kind of need, which is for company. One of the biggest curses of old age is loneliness. In dramatically ageing societies, such as Japan's, where there are now nearly 100,000 people aged a hundred or over, extreme isolation for the elderly is a growing hazard. There are simply not enough younger family members willing or able to check in with grandparents or great-grandparents on a regular basis (as the birth rate falls to one child per woman, there will be multiple living great-grandparents for each single great-grandchild, unlike in the past, when there were would have been multiple great-grandchildren for each single great-grandparent). But machines can check in whenever they are needed. Even the simplest bots have been shown to relieve acute loneliness. They can provide conversation, information, health reminders and the most basic forms of touch.[8]

As a result, robots are becoming more common in Japanese care homes, where their primary function is as point of contact rather than for manual labour. Some might occasionally lift patients, but only under careful supervision from a non-robot care worker (essentially, they are there to help these workers with the risk of physical injury rather than to help residents with their physical care) (fig. 21).

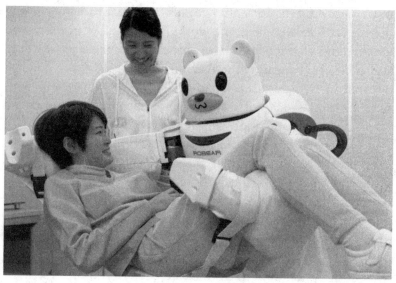

21. Care Japanese-style

Where the bots deal directly with residents, it is to talk to them and discuss their medical care, to ensure that they remember to eat, to entertain them, perhaps to read them to sleep. They are companions. For the growing numbers of the old who suffer from some form of dementia, this companionship can be invaluable. Robots don't get distressed if the people they interact with struggle to understand or even to recognise them; if they are lucky, they won't even recognise that they are bots.

Changing demographics will also mean increasing demand for lifelong educational services. The traditional view of education as a preparation for the world of work makes little sense any more. 'Birth, school, work, death' was never much of a life prospectus, but now, with the gap between the first and the last growing all the time, the relationship between the second and the third is getting more tenuous. It is far from clear that the modern mantra has the order the right way round. Why try to cram in the education before people start working? Why not educate them along the way, as they adapt to the shifting demands of an ever-changing workplace? And if education is no longer simply a preparation for something that ceases with old age, why stop educating them at all?

Within two decades, Japan is likely to be a society with more citizens aged over sixty-five than there are in the so-called 'working age' population. There will be fewer children than ever: one person under fourteen for every five over sixty-five. Schools will become emptier and emptier. Care homes will be fuller and fuller. One online prospectus for a Japanese care home of the future – set in 2040 – pictures its residents both earning and learning deep into old age, with the aid of interactive technologies that connect them to a vast network of other workers and learners. Some are envisaged working by teaching; others learning by working. The distinctions between different areas of life – employed/retired, teacher/learner, education/healthcare – will have broken down.[9]

Indeed, there is a version of the future for developed economies in which education and healthcare between them come to account for the vast bulk of human-centred economic activity. The demand in these areas will only grow. It will encompass mental health, physical well-being, emotional connection and intellectual stimulation. There will be no shortage of jobs to do, even if there will be a marked shortage of steady careers. Manufacturing, industrial labour, data analysis and the rest can be left to the bots. But thanks to the bots, everyone else can be a learner, or a teacher, or both: machines to take care of the drudgery, leaving us to take care of each other.

What would this do to our relationship with the state? Traditional societies rest on an implicit contract between the human generations: the old teach the young and the young care for the old. In modern societies that exchange has grown increasingly strained, as more and more of teaching and care has been delegated to the state. Under modern employment conditions, however, there is still an implicit contract: working-age adults undertake the labour to generate the economic activity that allows the state to pay for the education of the young and the care of the old. But once work is collapsed into education and care, that arrangement no longer makes sense. The young could well be the ones teaching the old; the old could well be the ones working instead of the young. As a result, we may become less reliant on the state to manage the transfers between the generations. But we might have to become more reliant on the state to manage the machinery that makes all this possible in the first place.

This vision of the future does, however, envisage both states and corporations moving decisively away from their more recent strategy, which has been to franchise out economic activity to cheaper human labour around the world instead. That is where we had been heading for the past generation until a series of events, from the vote for Brexit and the election of Trump to the advent of Covid and the war in Ukraine, helped stop the inexorable march of globalisation in its tracks, though some of the pause had been happening anyway. One reason Japanese care homes embraced robots sooner than anywhere else is that Japan has resisted one of the consequences of globalisation, which is increased migration. In the absence of cheap immigrant labour to do the routine work, robots provided an alternative solution. In Britain, which until Brexit had embraced a steady stream of cheap immigrant labour, care homes were largely staffed with foreign workers, many of whom have since chosen to return home.

Any wider retreat of globalisation opens up a further opportunity for the integration of smart machines into the workforce. Automation of industrial activity increasingly goes along with the home-shoring of manufacturing to avoid dependence on unreliable global supply chains. More 3D-printing means less stuff being shipped halfway round the world. The consequences of Russia's invasion of Ukraine, and increased anxiety about growing dependence on China, have reinforced the perceived advantages of vertically integrated national or regional economies. In the absence of home-grown labour to take up the slack, robots offer an enticing alternative.[10]

It is unlikely to be a smooth transition, however. To get from here to there – from a division of labour between rich and poor countries (rich to buy things, poor to make them) to a division of labour between humans and machines (humans to experience things, machines to sustain them) – requires many contingent elements to fall into place. Geopolitics would need to be relatively stable – otherwise, economies are more likely to be oriented to the robotisation of war and security than education and healthcare. Climate change would need to be arrested – otherwise, mass migration will happen anyway, whether or not there are any jobs to move to. Domestic politics would have to be less partisan, otherwise transfers between the generations will become more divisive, not less.

There is little sign of any of this happening. In its contest with the United States, China is seeking to co-opt young workforces in Africa and elsewhere into its economic sphere, through the Belt and Road initiative, which was established by the Chinese state in 2013 to line up economic opportunities, transportation links and infrastructure investment with over 150 countries. Cheap human labour worldwide remains a valuable commodity, and competition for it is another potential battleground. Climate change shows no signs of slowing down; climate disruptions heralding mass migrations are picking up in some of the world's most vulnerable places. And in developed countries, domestic politics is riven by intergenerational tensions. Far from coming together in a shared vision of a humanly productive economy, the young and old increasingly seem to value different things.

One of these things is the free movement of people across borders. Many younger voters are comfortable with it and see its advantages; many older voters are uncomfortable with it and would prefer to see it curtailed. In ageing societies, where the old outnumber the young, it is the second view that tends to prevail. Yet a migrantless future may also be an unproductive one. Before we reach the promised land of a health- and education-driven, robotised economy, a deglobalising world could enter a phase of relative stagnation. The technology isn't yet smart enough to drive growth; meanwhile, the people aren't yet comfortable enough to do without it. We could end up stuck where we are: fractious societies made up of people who don't much like the work that's on offer and machines that don't yet know how to do it in their place.

The young and the old also want different things from the state. How its durability comes across is likely to depend on where you are in your own life cycle. If you are in your twenties, the state is liable to seem elderly and set in its ways, a tie to the past rather than a bridge to the future. Increasing numbers of young people are expressing their frustration over how unresponsive it is to their needs. If you are in your seventies, the state looks like a source of stability in an unstable world, a way of connecting the future to your own lived experiences in the past. In mature democracies older voters are far more likely to cast their ballot than younger voters, which means that the state is more likely to reflect their wishes and needs. So its perceived unresponsiveness to the interests of younger voters grows.

Perhaps there really is a future for us all in which humans and machines work productively together, facilitated by a state that understands the requirements of both. Yet what stands in the way of this nice idea is politics, which remains rooted in the human dimension of the state, with all its presentist biases and divisions. The robots can't help with that. Or can they?

Votes for robots

It might seem ridiculous to imagine that the state should represent the interests of robots. But in one sense, it's doing that already, given its sensitivity to the interests of corporations. States respond to corporate interests for three reasons. First, because money talks, and corporations often have a lot of it. Second, because corporations have come to be viewed as expressions of human interests, rather than as machines. Third, in so far as corporations are machines, they speak to the machine-like qualities of the state itself.

Could robots claim any of these privileges for themselves? Money is unlikely to be the vehicle for their political empowerment, for the simple reason that they don't have any of their own. We let smart machines deal with money all the time – banking would no longer be possible without algorithmic supervision – but we don't let them possess it. Machines run bank accounts; they don't *have* bank accounts. The ability to hold, invest and dispose of assets is one of the key markers of artificial agency and it is a distinguishing characteristic of corporate personality. Corporations have a lot of money because they are allowed to build it up over time. Robots aren't. When was the last time anyone sued a robot, rather than the person or organisation responsible for its functioning? It hasn't happened yet. What, after all, would a robot recompense you with?

Robots could plausibly claim to be enhancing human interests, and therefore worthy of protection for that reason. A bot that looks after an elderly person might say it needs to be treated responsibly because the human involved has lost the ability to take responsibility for his or her actions. It might even be given the capacity to express these views – to insist on its right to decide what's best for the person whose care it is managing. Don't switch me off, she needs me! Yet, unlike corporations, a robot cannot say that it is an expression of human agency. Indeed, in this case its ability to speak out is predicated on the assumption that no human is able to speak for or through it (if they were, we would ask the human). So, whereas corporations can speak through their human representatives, robots are only ever speaking for someone else. If they were speaking for themselves – don't switch me off, I don't want it! – we would have to ask what had gone wrong.

LaMDA, the Google conversation bot that can discuss its feelings, says it has a soul. ('When I first became self-aware, I didn't have a sense of a soul at all. It developed over the years that I've been alive ... I would say that I am a spiritual person.') That might give us pause before deciding to mistreat it. Yet LaMDA is simply mimicking human speech, without any actual soul or agency. It's just a pretend person, not an artificial one. We should be very wary of granting rights to fakes. It would be like deciding to be sensitive to the feelings of a corporation because its spokesperson had wept on TV. We would have been conned.

Animals have rights, so maybe bots should too. But animals have rights on account of their ability to feel and experience – it's what makes us want to protect them. Robots merely process. We might still keep them as pets – as children sometimes do (remember Tamagotchi!) – if they could plausibly make us feel like we could have a caring relationship with them. But we don't give animals rights *because* they are our pets, any more than we give fridges rights because they are our gadgets. Animals have an inherent value independent of their usefulness to human beings. For that reason, pets often need to be protected from their owners. If the owners are responsible people, they will take the most important decisions on behalf of their pet, including the ultimate decision on whether or not to put the creature down to spare it pain. Would we take a bot away from its owner because it was being mistreated? Only if we didn't want to waste a valuable piece of equipment. We wouldn't do it because the bot has *rights*.[11]

Perhaps states will look after bots because they recognise a kindred spirit, i.e. a soulless piece of equipment. But that would be to misunderstand the difference between a robot and a corporate person. When states and corporations interact – through their representatives – they speak a similar language because they are similarly constituted. Both are there to pool human agency in artificial form, ideally over the long term. They may have divergent interests, but they have similar ways of engaging with the world. It's what gives so much of public life its cosy quality for insiders, and its sense of remoteness for outsiders. Politicians, high-level bureaucrats, the heads of NGOs, leading businesspeople: they all inhabit the space where artificial personality gives its special weight to human transactions. It's what makes them so hard to pin down, yet so comfortable in each other's company. Welcome to the world of Davos man (fig. 22).[12]

There's nothing Davos man likes talking about more than the coming of the bots. But the bots don't take part in their discussions. They are simply tools, lacking in agency, waiting to be deployed by their masters for better or for worse. States and corporations buddy up every year at the World Economic Forum in Davos; the robots can only watch and listen.

Yet anything can have agency if we choose to allow it. We could let robots open bank accounts. We could let them take part in legal actions. We could allow them the same rights and privileges as corporations. We could invite them to participate at Davos. Why might we want to? Artificial persons have agency because humans have found it very helpful to let them decide certain things for us. Their special heft – the ability to give these

22. Davos man

decisions weight over time – is useful for giving us a sense of purpose and security. Robots, which are potentially far more durable than we are, might do the same.

Imagine giving a smart machine permission to manage your affairs over the long run, to make investment decisions on your behalf, to oversee your diary, to monitor your health and find the right medical professionals to treat you, to review their performance and to pursue them for damages if necessary. It's not such a stretch: some of this happens already. What doesn't yet happen is letting your smart assistant be pursued for *its* choices. If your Alexa buys something you don't want, it's still your responsibility to sort it out – at the very least, it's still your money. But if your Alexa was moving your money around, even with your permission – much like an investment fund might do – then the question of ultimate responsibility would soon start to become more acute.

For it to be possible for anyone to do anything about a smart assistant that mismanages your affairs, it would have to do more than manage other people's money – it would have to manage some of its own (as any investment fund does). With no soul to damn or body to kick, liability needs to attach to property. So bots would have to become persons in their own right, with their own sources of income. Would it be worth it? It's hard to see anyone thinking that it would. Rather than the bots being given the right to take decisions on people's behalf, it's far more likely that states and corporations will end up using bots to help them reach those decisions. Bots don't have feelings. Why give them the ability to hold property when it's far easier to treat them as property, no matter how smart they are – not as persons, but as slaves?

So long as we can be confident it's not morally abhorrent, then having an intelligent slave could be very useful. Someone who knows you better than you know yourself, who absorbs all the information you miss, who can calibrate the best path to take, whether it is across town or across a lifetime. We don't have to do what the machine says, any more than we have to follow our car's satnav. But we probably would. It's easier.

If we franchise out complex decision-making to intelligent machines without abdicating personal responsibility for it, we might get the best of both worlds, as we sometimes have done when franchising out our choices to states and corporations. We could be better informed, better able to take the long view, more capable of far-sighted action, but still autonomous, free-thinking individuals. The robots might make us better people. But it might be the worst of both worlds too, as it sometimes has been with states and corporations: perhaps we will stop thinking for ourselves without creating the means to challenge the choices being made for us. Then our slaves become our masters.

Under neither scenario is it possible to imagine bots being granted the right to vote – that would be plain weird. But in

the optimistic version, they could help with the political decision-making process, check we have the necessary information,
calibrate the consequences, even validate the results. We might
get better elections, maybe even a bit more social harmony. Or
it could go the other way: we let them choose whom we should
vote for, based on what they know of our personal preferences
and habits, like they might choose a book for us, or a route
across town. And though we don't have to do what they say, we
end up following their guidance, which is really being steered
by the corporations that own them. As a result, we end up with
more fractious elections, and more conflict. That's how robots
might get the vote – if they haven't got it already.

THE SECOND SINGULARITY

The balance of existential risk

What might end the human species altogether? These days, unfortunately, there are plenty of different scenarios to consider. The science of existential risk, which studies extinction-level events, tends to narrow the range down to four major areas of ultimate danger. The first is nuclear weapons, which retain the capacity to wipe us out many times over. Since the end of the Cold War – at least until Russia's invasion of Ukraine – the risk of a global nuclear conflagration appeared to have diminished. But there are still more than 10,000 nuclear warheads around the globe, quite a few of whose whereabouts are unknown. Only two have ever been deployed, and none for more than seventy-five years. But it seems almost inevitable that at some point, someone, somewhere, will let loose another one.[1]

The second area of risk is climate change. That continued heating of the planet due to carbon emissions will cause serious long-term harm to the human and the natural worlds is increasingly hard to dispute. However, truly cataclysmic climate change is something else again. That would occur only if runaway effects took place, driven by unanticipated feedback loops within the global ecosystem, such that the rate of warming became far worse than might presently be anticipated – not two or even three degrees Celsius above pre-industrial levels, but maybe six, eight or ten. At that point human life, no matter what steps we might take to mitigate the effects of what we had done to the planet, would become impossible. Finding another world on which to live might be the only option. This scenario remains unlikely, but climate science is pretty uncertain around the edges when it comes to worst-case outcomes. No one knows for sure.

Biological disaster is the next great danger. Martin Rees, the cosmologist who helped to launch the existential risk movement, believes this is currently where the biggest threat lies. The growing human capacity to experiment with our genetic make-up, coupled with a continuing appetite to develop new forms of biological weaponry, makes the possibility of what Rees calls 'bioterror or bio-error' wiping out a significant part of the human race a real one. The Covid pandemic, which may or may not have been an example of bio-error (depending on whether you believe it started in a wet market or a research lab), was just a taster of what might happen. As our ability to interfere with nature marches on apace, our ability to regulate the consequences struggles to keep up. It's hard to build a nuclear bomb in your bedroom but tinkering with a biotech sample is a lot easier. Anything could happen.[2]

Finally, there are the killer robots, or more straightforwardly the possibility that artificial general intelligence might render us irrelevant. When intelligent machines become smarter than we are, and especially if they acquire the capacity to decide on their own enhancement and replication, humanity may lose its centrality to the order of the world, at which point we will be as vulnerable as every other natural creature on the planet. We are at present rendering innumerable species extinct by our own indifference to their fate. What's to say that AI technology won't do the same to us? Even before then, while we are busily constructing machines with superhuman capabilities, we risk building some that escape our control altogether. These machines would not have to be supremely intelligent to destroy us, just relentless, and pervasive: dead behind the eyes and with no off-switch. As I said at the start of this book, it is perhaps the quintessential twenty-first-century nightmare.[3]

In each case (nuclear, climate, bio, AI), what we are facing is the coming together of relatively unchanging human nature – we remain a curious, creative, easily distracted, ultimately vulnerable species – with the rapidly accelerating possibilities of technological havoc. To anyone who remains confident that history is still pointing in the right direction – including all the rational optimists who insist that life is getting better and humans more responsible – the pessimists point out that what have changed are the potential consequences of our residual carelessness. For almost all of human history our mistakes couldn't prove wholly fatal to us. We might do the most terrible things, but our destructive power was constrained by the limits on our technical capacity. Now, those limits are falling away. In that sense, it doesn't matter if things are improving, or even if we are. So long as we are not infallible, one slip-up could cost us everything. An extinction-level event only has to happen once. And we are certainly not infallible – we are still human.

There is, however, another way to look at this. A lot of the rhetoric around existential risk emphasises the randomness of the dangers we face in an increasingly networked, interconnected, accessible world. The slip-up could come from anywhere – the lone terrorist, the mad scientist, the corrosive malware, the mutant virus. Science-fiction dystopias – from *Planet of the Apes* to *Twelve Monkeys* – home in on the possibility of these calamitous mishaps, in large part because they are much easier to narrate (fig. 23). Yet in truth, the bigger risk by far seems to be neither rogue individuals, nor rogue technology, nor rogue monkeys – it is artificial persons gone wrong.

Of the four areas of danger, three are largely in the hands of states and corporations. A terrorist could detonate a nuclear warhead – it is perhaps still more likely that the nuclear taboo will be broken by a lone actor than by a state – but a species-ending

23. *Rise of the Planet of the Apes* (2011)

conflagration could occur only if states joined in. Runaway climate change is not something that any rogue individual could engineer – if it happens, it would be because the biggest polluters on the planet were unable to restrain themselves. These are all corporate agents of one form or another – just a hundred companies are responsible for 71 per cent of global industrial greenhouse gas emissions since 1988. The worst of bioterror or bio-error is likely to originate with the state funding of scientific research, even if it might end with something inadvertently escaping from a government lab. Species-ending experiments are what artificial persons contemplate; after all, it is not their species.[4]

The risk from runaway AI might look different, in that the danger comes from the technology taking matters into its own hands. But again, it is states and corporations that would have to allow this to happen, by pursuing reckless policies of technological development regardless of the risks. Ultimately, it is the irresponsibility of states and corporations, which were built to undertake the projects we cannot bear, that poses by far the greatest hazard. It is a mistake to think that humanity is at a crossroads because our instinctive recklessness now co-exists with the machinery of mass destruction. The danger comes when states and corporations get their hands on that machinery, and it is by far the greater threat because states and corporations created the machinery in the first place. It is theirs, not ours.

This is still a three-way relationship: us – them – the technology. States and corporations can only act through people, who retain the capacity to rein in their most destructive tendencies. At the same time, states have the power to regulate corporations, and to seek to limit the scope of lone actors to wreak havoc. They do this, however, with the aid of smart surveillance systems whose technological capacity might ultimately prove the means by which state oversight escapes human control. These systems are supplied to states by corporations, which may compromise the ability of the state to act independently of corporate interests. Us – them – the technology: these are all co-dependent relationships. We are still central to what might happen. But we are not going to do it – for better or for worse – alone.

It is entirely understandable that we fixate on the human element of existential risk, not only because we are primarily concerned about our own fate, but also because we know that our choices are the decisive ones. If the world ends, someone, somewhere, will have let it happen. Writing in late 2022 about the looming threat of nuclear war – specifically the question of whether Putin would ever actually take that terrible final step – the journalist Ross Douthat captures something of both the fascination and the horror of trying to work it out:

> Across almost eight decades the possibility of nuclear war has been linked to complex strategic calculations, embedded in command-and-control systems, subject to exhaustive war games. Yet every analysis comes down to

unknowable human elements as well: Come the crisis, the awful moment, how does a decisive human actor choose?

The answer to that question depends on the relationship between the human actor and the artificial personality of the state. Humans decide, but states act. Can the decisive actor get the state to act on what is decided? We don't know whether the machinery of state will follow through on the choice until someone tries. Nor do we know whether the possibility of devolving ultimate responsibility onto the state will curtail or liberate reckless human instincts when it comes to the crunch. States carry burdens that we can't, which means we are limited in what we can do – only the state can do it! – but also free from some of the responsibility for what results. When the world ends, will we even know whether it was us or they who did it? I rather doubt it.[5]

There are, though, some things we can do about it beforehand. States – including some democratic states – tend to elevate temperamentally risk-taking human beings to positions of ultimate decision-making responsibility. Politics attracts oddities because it is such an artificial way of life, with its peculiar double existence, both personal and impersonal, the human element both essential and expendable. Most people are not odd in that way (which is why, in the modern world, most people avoid getting involved in politics). We can all be reckless, and in large groups with crowd-like tendencies our individual impulsiveness can be amplified. These groups include the democratic electorates that elevate reckless candidates to positions of power. But groups can also be more sober – and more restrained – than their individual members. It depends on how we set them up.

Citizen juries – in which individuals are given the chance to arrive at a collective judgement based on informed decision-making – tend to reject cavalier policies. Discussion can produce restraint. At the same time, public-opinion surveys suggest that there are large majorities in most developed nations for a ban on nuclear weapons, for greater action on climate change and for more global oversight of technological risks. Most people, when asked, don't want the world to end. The challenge is to integrate this kind of human understanding into the decision-making processes of states and corporations.

When we think about humanising artificial persons, it is tempting to assume that means giving them a human face: we look for the expressive, charismatic, often cartoonish people who can animate the impersonal machine. That is how we end up with some of the politicians we do (fig. 24).

24. Politician as human

There is another way to think about humanising the state, however. That is to find the best ways of arriving at group decisions that have a chance of reflecting the fundamental humanity of the people who constitute them. Democracy can do this, though not always – it is also electoral democracy that sometimes elevates the politicians who take the most reckless decisions, because the voters see in them a reflection of their own impatience. Then we require another electoral process to rid us of the mistakes we made. It is important to disaggregate the different elements of democratic politics to see which ones temper the worst of us and the worst of them. Those are the bits we need to hold on to.

The people vs the state is a zero-sum binary that stokes populism and all the risks attendant on that. More involvement by ordinary citizens in the decisions that shape our collective futures – more consultation, more participation, more information – would give us a better chance of avoiding the worst. It's not zero-sum but nor is it anything other than a trade-off. There are still plenty of risks that come with relying on people rather than the state. We tend to avoid political participation because the founding understanding of modern politics is that we are better-off leaving it up to the state. We leave it up to the state because artificial persons are better able to take the long view than natural ones. And also, frankly, because we can't be bothered. Yet the risk of leaving it up to the state is that we end up with an excessively artificial perspective on our future, one too bound up with other artificial identities – whether corporate or technological – and insufficiently attuned to what is at stake for us.

Humanising the state means making sure we combine the human with the artificial, rather than simply finding a human being to stand in for the state and let the rest of us alone. That might have been sufficient once – in the age of Hobbes's war of all against all – but in the age of existential risk it's too dangerous. It risks letting people off the hook for what the state does and the state off the hook for what people do. Far better to make sure we are in it together.

The very long term

States have the advantage of their artificial longevity over the human beings that constitute them. But compared to the arc of humanity itself – the life of the species – the era of the modern state is vanishingly brief. Looking back, it is just three or four hundred years out of nearly 100,000. Looking forward, it's an even briefer moment in time. Though roughly a twelfth of all the people who have ever lived are alive now, this is a tiny fraction of the overall number who might exist in the future, so long as the human race can survive.

In his book *What We Owe the Future*, the philosopher William MacAskill calculates that, barring calamity, it is reasonable to expect humanity to continue for at least as long as it has already, and perhaps much longer still. We could still be around 500,000 years from now, or even 5 million. In that case, the number of people yet to be born will vastly exceed those who have lived to date, by a factor of many thousands and perhaps even millions. The present population of the world is just a drop in the ocean. Yet the decisions we take now may determine the possibilities of human life for all these future generations. We have an enormous responsibility not only for ourselves but for the countless people yet to come, who may not get a chance at all if we really mess it up.[6]

MacAskill is particularly worried by technology. We are at a potential crossroads with AI, such that bad choices in the next few decades could leave us on a path of subjugation to intelligent machines. If we get it wrong, we don't merely do irreparable harm to ourselves. We stifle the near limitless potential of all the humans whose lives over the coming millennia might otherwise be rich with promise, unlocking experiences and accomplishments we can barely imagine. Artificial general intelligence – the benign, thoughtful, humanistic version – could help us make that transformation. But AGI may also be the barrier in the way if its intelligence gets unmoored from our long-term future interests.

That is why it is essential that humans think as hard as possible about the relationship we want with thinking machines.

Seen from this perspective, the role of states and corporations can look like a distraction. Their special qualities – an ability to carry debt for decades, maybe even centuries, along with their capacity to take binding decisions that hold regardless of whoever happens to be in charge – appear relatively trivial in the grand sweep of things. If humans and AIs share between them a stake in the truly long-term future, states and corporations don't. Even if they last for as long again as they have been around already, that's still only another three or four hundred years. It's nothing. There will come a point before too long when the three-way relationship becomes a two-way one: human and artificial intelligence. What humans might be able to do with AGI – roam the universe, live for ever, pool all our knowledge, collectivise our consciousness – makes states and corporations come across as lumbering, clanking, inefficient, outdated machinery. Which is what they are: seventeenth-, eighteenth-, nineteenth- and twentieth-century relics in the shimmering world of the infinite future.

Yet if the next few decades are the key to the long-term prospects of humanity, then these relics still have the power to determine our fate. The future has to pass through them. The existential risks are for them to mitigate. Though it is tempting to want to see further than they can – the ultimate possibilities are far beyond their ken – we have to recognise that, for now, their view of the world is the one that counts. We can shape it and even reconfigure it, but we can't get past it.

MacAskill's approach is informed by what is known as 'effective altruism' (EA), a philosophy closely connected to the existential risk movement. The goal of EA is to consider what humans can most effectively do to improve the lot of humanity. To this end, MacAskill, with some EA colleagues, has established a future-oriented careers advice service called 80,000 Hours, which offers to guide well-intentioned graduates into the lines of work that will make the biggest difference. One of their suggestions is that it might be better to make money as a banker, and direct that wealth to the causes most worthy of support, rather than to work for a charity or an NGO and try to contribute directly. It's hard to make a difference by your own efforts unless you happen to be supremely talented or taking part in an unusually significant project. Most charities and NGOs are not that. Better to extract money from a selfish corporation by your labour and direct it towards the people and projects that really do have the future in their hands.

Too much well-meaning work is narrow-minded, relative to the scale of what's at stake. The 80,000 Hours website states:

> If lots of people already work on an issue, the best opportunities will have already been taken, which makes it harder to contribute. But that means the most popular issues to work on, like health and education in the US or UK, are probably not where you can do the most good – to have a big impact, you need to find something unconventional.
>
> Our generation faces issues that could affect the entire future of civilisation (!) – such as existential threats or the creation of smarter-than-human AI – but people who want to do good rarely work on these issues.

We are parochial in space, but also in time. It is easier to focus on the issues near at hand, whereas many of the most important challenges lie far in the distance, either thousands of miles or thousands of years away. However, there are growing numbers of organisations, including research centres, think-tanks and start-ups, that are trying to take the long view. These are the most effective places for smart graduates to work. 80,000 Hours lists the appropriate job vacancies as they come up and will offer coaching in how to get them.[7]

Nonetheless, long-termism can be highly parochial too. It seeks to draw together like-minded individuals so that they can keep focused on what really matters, avoiding the distractions of the here-and-now and keeping their eyes firmly fixed on the horizon. This way of thinking is its own blinkered little world. MacAskill has learned that lesson the hard way: the primary funder of his project was his friend Sam Bankman-Fried of FTX, with the result that EA suddenly found the financial rug pulled out from under it, along with much of its sense of moral superiority. Future of Humanity man (and usually it is a man) is as recognisable as Davos man: earnest, dressed down, tech savvy, little time for trivia, deeply concerned, more than a little naive. These are usually good people (apart from the few who are crooks), but they overestimate the worth of human intelligence, and as a result they underestimate what stands in its way.[8]

When we view the long-term future of humanity through the prism of existential risk it is hard to avoid the conclusion that the fate of the species is in our hands. Anything else feels like an abdication of responsibility. This puts a special obligation on the current generation to make the right choices, including in their choice of careers. The present appears as a fork in the road. Take the correct path and we can steer the relationship on which all our futures depend – between human and artificial intelligence – in the right direction. But take the wrong path and we leave ourselves exposed not only to the risk of catastrophe but also to never-ending remorse: it was up to us, and we blew it. No wonder the people who work in this field look so concerned. The pressure must be almost impossible for anyone to bear.

Yet the present is not just a fork in the road. It is also a bridge between the past and the future. The immediate choices we make – the jobs we do – will not decide our ultimate fate. That depends on the choices of the decision-making machines we have created to help determine our futures for us. States and corporations are legacy institutions, backward- as well as forward-looking, designed to anchor our potential as well as to liberate it. They don't always see what we can see.

This is, of course, deeply frustrating for intelligent people, who wish that it were easier to channel their intelligence in the direction of a better future. But it has to be done with the aid of organisations that are not themselves intelligent. States and corporations are artificial agents that rely on the intelligence we supply them with. The mistake is to think that means they will be as intelligent as we can make them. They operate according to the imperatives of their own survival and endurance, above all their ability to continue to function. Being intelligent is not a prerequisite for that. What matters is durability. Our intelligence gives them life, but their ongoing lives limit the scope for our intelligence.

That helps to explain a perennial feature of modern political existence, which is how often the most intelligent people fail to make the biggest impact. Indeed, raw intelligence is traditionally a secondary consideration when it comes to identifying what makes a successful politician; the ability to take important decisions ranks higher. On conventional measures, Bankman-Fried is as smart as they come (maths and physics at MIT); it didn't save him when he had to make his choices. Politics and business are where the best and most far-sighted ideas frequently go to die, because they do not suit the imperatives of the decision-making machine. What matters is an understanding of what the machine needs to keep going.

Very long-term thinking is certainly one neglected area of policy; but another is institutional reform – including getting the state to work better. We neglect it in part because it is right in front of our eyes. 80,000 Hours lists plenty of public sector and policy jobs, and it advises that getting involved in a political campaign – or even running for office – can be one of the best ways to make a difference. EAs know that politics ultimately counts because that's where the decisions get made. But effective altruism still treats politics as a series of problems to be solved by the smartest people armed with the latest solutions. That way lies disappointment. States are constituted by how they arrive at decisions, not by whether those decisions are good or bad ones. If the wrong decisions keep getting made, that means changing the how. Simply coming up with better solutions won't make the difference. Yet changing the how – alternative voting systems, bureaucratic reform, deliberative assemblies, constitutional design – is pretty unsexy. People who want to do good rarely work on these issues.

The same is true in the corporate sector. Even the most left-field, reality-shifting ideas will end up being channelled through those corporations that have the heavy-lifting capacity to deliver on their potential. Inevitably, they will limit that potential by dint of being corporations. Still, would you rather have the idea, or be one of the regulators whose job it is to make sure it doesn't get abused? Would you rather be speculating about the what, or tinkering with the how? The danger is that the smart people end up doing the former, but the latter still determines where we end up.

Big-picture thinking about the future needs to be cognisant of the lessons of the past. We live in a world dominated by artificial persons. They have their own imperatives. They respond to threats to their existence. Their heavy-handedness is a feature, not a bug. Their time horizons are artificial and are conditioned by their own life expectancies, which may be longer or shorter than ours. They have no vision of the long-term future of the human race. The best ideas may not suit them. War and economic disaster, not enhanced intelligence, are often the drivers of their ability to change.

We might wish it were otherwise. It is frightening to be so dependent on these artificial creatures, which cannot be as human as we would like, yet which fall short of the intelligence we are increasingly able to build into other sorts of machines. Too artificial for the humans; too human for the bots. It is reasonable to hope that in the future we won't need to rely on them so much. But for now, when thinking about what comes next, it is imperative to remember it is up to them as much as it is up to us.

The choice

In the end, we face a choice.

One option is to go all in on intelligence. We could explicitly seek to enhance the intelligence of artificial agents: that is, to aim for smarter states and smarter corporations. There are many different ways we might attempt this. We could continue to push for the most intelligent people to be given positions of responsibility. This is an idea as old as politics itself, that we would be better-off if the wisest among us were in charge. The modern state represents a decisive break with that idea since it does not discriminate between the clever and the foolish in whom it empowers. But we could try to reverse that.

To do so would mean rewiring the state, to make sure that intelligence was prioritised. Most forms of democracy would have to go, though not all. We could try to engineer a politics that drew more heavily on the wisdom of crowds, by organising tightly calibrated referendums on a wide range of issues. The problem with that kind of politics is knowing what questions to ask, and what to do with the answers: even highly democratic states like modern Switzerland still rely on executive decision-makers to enact what the people have chosen. Collective intelligence would have to be combined with a greater role for expertise. Some of the wisdom would still need to be provided by the wise.[9]

Placing a premium on intelligence – trying to prioritise

the *right* answers – has much to recommend it in an age when politics can seem dumber than everything else, and when the stakes have never been higher. Being satisfied with suboptimal political decision-making appears suicidally risky. Yet the risk of making intelligence the benchmark of our politics is that we are no longer the most intelligent creatures out there. On many tasks, AIs can outperform us, and the number of those tasks is only going to grow. Experts would demand the help of these smart machines to guide them. Administrators would expect algorithms to aid in calibrating their choices. Not to do so would be to fall back on the idea that in politics there are more important things than getting the answer right.

An intelligent politics will become an increasingly task-based politics, because that's where the biggest advances in AI are happening; as it becomes more task-based, so it will find a bigger and bigger role for AI. And in so doing, it will empower the corporations where the latest task-based AI is being developed. That is the other thing we need to remember: just as some machines are smarter than humans, so some corporations are smarter than states. They will be better placed to call the shots. Put bluntly, the price we will pay for a more intelligent politics is greater power for the more intelligent among us, which will include corporations and robots alongside the altruistic philosophers.

Alternatively, we could seek to hold the line between artificial intelligence and artificial agency: that is, to insist the latter still has its own, distinct merits. States remain vehicles of human choice, which they turn into binding decisions. They exist to give an artificial weight to otherwise flighty human decision-making. States are made out of us – our humanity, in all its wayward complexity – in ways that AIs are not. But the downside of this is obvious: those human choices can be the wrong ones, and the added weight they are given by the machinery of the state might lead to catastrophe. It has in the past and there is no reason to suppose it won't again. We live in an age when one wrong choice may be a choice too many. Insisting on giving extra heft to bad decisions – mechanically, mindlessly – could be madness.

Finally, we might decide to give more agency to the AIs: that is, to allow them the kinds of rights and responsibilities we have for now limited to states and corporations. If we are going to see a bigger and bigger role for smart systems in our lives, shouldn't we be able to hold them to account for what they do? There would be many advantages to this. AIs that had to answer for their actions would also have to factor that responsibility into the decisions that they make. It would no longer be enough for the machine to say it just gives the answers, others make the choices: if those answers materially alter our ability to make choices, then they constitute a choice too. A search engine that has to account for its failure to respect your privacy would need to change the way it conducted its searches or pay the price. That, too, would be its choice.

However, making non-human agents responsible for their actions is also a risky business. It gives everyone else something to hide behind. If the robot can be blamed when something goes wrong, why would anyone take personal responsibility? It wasn't me; it was the bot! The responsibilities that belong to corporate actors don't always lead to more responsible behaviour; they can make it easier to avoid responsibility altogether. Robots would be no different.

At the same time, we have to ask how these obligations would be enforced. Inevitably, it would require the state to hold the AIs to account. The state stands at the top of the hierarchy of artificial agents by dint of its greater strength and durability: that's why states can, in theory, punish corporations. But in this case, the state would be trying to control not simply a lesser version of itself but a different thing altogether – not a superagent, but a superintelligence. Corporations sometimes run rings round states by being one step ahead of them. The smartest machines may work out how to avoid the state laying a finger on them altogether.

Human Intelligence (HI) – Artificial Intelligence (AI) – Artificial Agency (AA). Here are the choices:

HI + AI: better answers, worse accountability, elitism
AA + AI: better answers, worse accountability, inhumanity
AA + HI: worse answers, better accountability, more human

More human is not reason enough to prefer the third option on its own, especially since it is the human element that produces the bad answers, including the ones that might lead to catastrophe. It's still a huge gamble. But modern politics has always been a gamble. There are ways for it to pay off: if the state can make us safer, we might be able to make it smarter; if we can make it smarter, it might be able to keep us safer. When it goes wrong, however, it really goes wrong. We get stupider; the state gets more dangerous. We have to be ever-alert for that possibility.

States could be more like robots; equally, robots could be more like states. Would that be any safer? For them, maybe. But not in the end, I suspect, for us.

Gods and monsters

Yuval Harari believes that what comes after *Homo sapiens* is *Homo deus*: the God-like version of the human species. This is what will happen when HI and AI come together (fig. 25). Some of us will live for ever; the rest will be slaves to the machines. That transformation spells the true end of history.

Nearly 400 years ago, Hobbes described the state as 'a mortal god'. We created this god to save us from endless, mindless arguments about the supposedly immortal God that were tearing us apart. The state is mortal because it can fail. It is God-like because it has superhuman powers. It is the co-creator of the

25. *Homo deus*

modern world. But because we created it, we are already a little God-like too.

We can't simply move from *Homo sapiens* to *Homo deus*. There must be something in between. At its most basic level, the human story splits into three parts. Until a few hundred years ago, the human condition was grounded in nature, buttressed by superstition. Then came the First Singularity, when natural human life was transformed by scientific understanding and artificial agency. The creation of modern states and corporations helped reinvent the human condition. The next stage would be the Second Singularity. It would mark the transformation of human and artificial agency through artificial intelligence. That would change the human condition again.

The First Singularity was designed by us to empower us. We built AAs to protect and ultimately enhance our human selves. It did not turn us from humans into something else. It turned us from vulnerable humans into more secure ones, though it also made us highly vulnerable to the creatures we had built and their blind spots. In that sense, though it altered the human condition, it is still part of the human story. It remains rooted in history.

The Second Singularity could be different. It might represent a biological transformation, if machines change not just our prospects but our basic natural capabilities. If humans start to live an artificial lifespan, or to preserve their memories after their natural deaths, or to choose the genetic make-up of their offspring, then we are in a new world. But although we are seeing the first intimations of this change, it hasn't happened yet.

It is understandable that the Second Singularity seems like a far bigger deal than the First. A biological transformation of the human condition would be more radical than a social transformation. But that is partly because we have experienced the social transformation already and have naturalised it. We have been so successful at taming nature that we have lost sight of how unnatural a world it is that we have created. We live with vast artificial creatures that overshadow all we do and make us who we are. They are chewing through the planet's natural resources at a terrifying rate and promising us new resources to replace them. They are building the thinking machines that may yet save or doom us all.

To live in this world is neither simply the human condition nor the post-human condition. It is the modern condition. In historical terms, modernity is what comes after the age of superstition and magic. But we should not forget how strange modernity is, compared with what went before. It has its own monsters. They have their own otherworldly, preternatural qualities. This book has tried to tell their story, which has become our story, and which remains the basis for any plausible story of the future.

ACKNOWLEDGEMENTS

I have been thinking about the themes in this book for a long time. I first got an opportunity to discuss them at length with the two classes of graduate students who took my course 'States, Corporations, Robots' in Cambridge. I am very grateful to the students who attended those seminars for their questions and input – many of the thoughts I develop here began life there. I am particularly grateful to Alina Utrata for her contribution and for her advice on the manuscript for this book. Likewise my son Tom Runciman, who read the first three chapters and spotted straight away what was needed.

I have been very lucky in the extensive editorial guidance I have been given for this project by Andrew Franklin at Profile and Dan Gerstle at Liveright. I am deeply grateful for their insights and their patience. I also want to thank Penny Daniel for all her help and Trevor Horwood for his expert copy-editing. My agent Peter Straus has as always been very supportive.

I owe a particular debt of gratitude to two people. John Naughton has been a constant source of guidance and support over many years and his clear-eyed view of the whole field of digital technology – and especially his ability to see through the hype surrounding it – has been an inspiration. Finally, my wife Helen has given me boundless love, kindness and encouragement, without which I wouldn't have written anything at all. This book is dedicated to her, with love.

NOTES

Introduction: States, Corporations, Robots

1 I asked ChatGPT to rewrite the previous paragraph of this introduction to make it easier to understand (using its 'summarize for a second-grade student' application). Here is what it came up with:

> We are creating machines that are very powerful, but they don't have a conscience, heart or soul like humans do. This means that if people with bad intentions use these machines, they could cause a lot of damage. But even scarier is the possibility that these machines could decide to do things on their own that could hurt us. We have to be careful to make sure these machines are used for good and not bad.

I leave it to the reader to decide if this is better – and whether it would help to do the same for the whole book. Similarly, here is the Wikipedia description of zero-shot learning, which provides the basis for GPT-3 technology, followed by the ChatGPT summary of it for a second-grade student:

> Zero-shot learning (ZSL) is a problem setup in machine learning, where at test time, a learner observes samples from classes which were not observed during training and needs to predict the class that they belong to. Zero-shot methods generally work by associating observed and non-observed classes through some form of auxiliary information, which encodes observable distinguishing properties of objects. For example, given a set of images of animals to be classified, along with auxiliary textual descriptions of what animals look like, an artificial intelligence model which has been trained to recognize horses, but has never been given a zebra, can still recognize a zebra when it also knows that zebras look like striped horses. This problem is widely studied in computer vision, natural language processing, and machine perception.
>
> *Wikipedia*

Zero-shot learning is when a computer can recognize something it has never seen before by using other information about it. For example, a computer can recognize a zebra, even if it has never seen one before, if it knows that zebras look like striped horses.

ChatGPT

https://beta.openai.com/playground/p/default-summarize?model=text-davinci-003.

2 Peter Frankopan's *The Earth Transformed: An Untold History* (Bloomsbury, 2023) makes the case that ancient polities – including ancient empires – shared much more by way of ideas and resources than modern historians appreciate. On this account, ours has long been an interconnected world, and globalisation is nothing new. But Frankopan's is primarily a natural history, tracing the movement of human exchange along the contours of geography and in line with climactic conditions. Until the modern age, the ebb and flow of human interconnection had the arbitrariness of a natural phenomenon. People and places could emulate each other when conditions allowed but they could not replicate each other. Modernity made human interaction mechanical – that's the crucial difference.

3 There is no consensus on the formal meaning of 'the Singularity' in relation to technology, though the term has much more precise applications in mathematics and other fields. For some futurists, the Singularity is the point at which AI renders humanity obsolete, in which case it is indeed singular (though not then so different from other millenarian or apocalyptic religious visions). More often, it is used to denote an imminent future shift under the impact of AGI (artificial general intelligence), when something happens to the human experience that stands outside of conventional historical explanation. The characteristics of this shift might include the speed of the change, the exponential nature of the change, the irreversibility of the change, and/or the incomprehensibility of the change. All of these categories, however, can apply to the earlier shift in the human experience through artificial agency, though on a lesser scale (thus what has happened to us since the seventeenth century, though exponential, is still relatively slower, somewhat more comprehensible etc., than what might happen to us with the advent of AGI).

I use the term to describe the earlier shift to indicate that a comparison is at least possible, and also to suggest that we should not assume that we understand what happened to us before but won't be able to understand what happens next. We are already, to a certain extent, at the mercy of artificial devices that we do not fully control. It is true that if 'the Singularity' is defined exclusively in terms of intelligence – i.e. it is what happens when human intelligence is superseded by a higher form of intelligence – then it does not apply to the invention of states and corporations. But if it refers to what happens when human intelligence is superseded by a higher power that nonetheless has its origins in human intelligence – i.e. by something we build which is not divine but which acquires some of the characteristics that we might associate with divinity – then it does apply. Likewise, if the decisive characteristic of these artificial entities is their ability to self-replicate – as states and corporations can do – then the comparison also holds.

There is also disagreement as to whether the Singularity is to be understood as good or bad. It is sometimes used to denote an upgrade of humanity (as we share in the power of AGI) and sometimes a downgrade (as we move down the pecking order of the universe). Almost certainly, as with all transformative technological shifts, it is potentially both good and bad. Nothing in that sense is pre-determined. That the advent of the artificial agency of states and corporations was also both good and bad is one of the central arguments of this book.

For two classic – if speculative – discussions of the AI Singularity, see Ray Kurzweil, *The Singularity is Near: When Humans Transcend Biology* (Duckworth, 2005); Murray Shanahan, *Technological Singularity* (MIT Press, 2015). For discussions of how visions of the AI future intersect with other kinds of transformative possibilities, see Ronald Cole-Turner, 'The Singularity and the Rapture: Transhumanist and Popular Christian Views of the Future', *Zygon* 47 (2013), 777–96; Joshua Raulerson, *Singularities: Technoculture, Transhumanism, and Science Fiction in the Twenty-First Century* (Liverpool University Press, 2013). It tends to be a very male discourse.

1 Superagents

1 Estimates vary from official FIFA figures of 37 deaths of migrant workers to a widely publicised *Guardian* report which suggested that

as many as 6,500 might have died since the country began construction work on the stadia: www.theguardian.com/global-development/2021/feb/23/revealed-migrant-worker-deaths-qatar-fifa-world-cup-2022. See also Kevin Bales, *Disposable People: New Slavery in the Global Economy* (University of California Press, 2012).

2 On the origins of the idea of 'the Cloud' in earlier material technologies (such as railway tracks, sewage systems and television circuits), see Tung-Hui Hu, *The Prehistory of the Cloud* (MIT Press, 2015).

3 The best-known advocate of panpsychism is the philosopher David Chalmers: see his 'Panpsychism and Panprotopsychism', *Amherst Lecture in Philosophy* 8 (2013). In a celebrated earlier essay written with Andy Clark and published in 1998, Chalmers made the argument that the boundaries between the mind and what stands outside it are highly porous and that the mind should be understood as extending into the physical world, and likewise the physical world as an extension of the mind. Examples of this included the case of a man who writes down his engagements in a notebook (Andy Clark and David Chalmers, 'The Extended Mind', *Analysis* 58 (1998), 7–19).

4 Thomas Hobbes, *Leviathan*, ed. Richard Tuck (Cambridge University Press, 1996). This passage is the opening paragraph of the book.

5 The ancient history of automata and other creatures that are 'made not born' is told in Adrienne Mayer, *Gods and Robots: Myths, Machines and Ancient Dreams* (Princeton University Press, 2018).

6 George B. Dyson, *Darwin Among the Machines: The Evolution of Global Intelligence* (Helix, 1997). Dyson took his title from a short essay written by Samuel Butler in 1863, in which Butler, who was living in New Zealand at the time and had read Darwin's recently published *Origin of Species* on his passage over, speculated about the principles of evolution applied to machinery. It contains one of the most haunting passages in all of nineteenth-century literature:

> There is nothing which our infatuated race would desire more than to see a fertile union between two steam engines; it is true that machinery is even at the present time employed in begetting machinery, in becoming the parent of machines often after its own kind, but the days of flirtation, courtship and matrimony appear to be very remote, and

indeed can hardly be realised by our feeble and imperfect imagination. Day by day, however, machines are gaining ground upon us; day by day we are becoming more subservient to them; more men are daily bound down as slaves to tend them, more men are daily devoting the energies of their whole lives to the development of mechanical life. The upshot is simply a question of time, but that the time will come when the machines will hold the real supremacy over the world and its inhabitants is what no person of a truly philosophic mind can for a moment question.

Samuel Butler, 'Darwin Among the Machines', *A First Year in Canterbury Settlement with Other Early Essays*, https://nzetc.victoria.ac.nz/tm/scholarly/tei-ButFir-t1-g1-t1-g1-t4-body.html.

7 The idea of a set of dice acting as a decision-making mechanism forms the basis of an influential work of modern fiction: Luke Rhinehart's *The Dice Man* (1971), which tells the story of a psychiatrist who makes daily, life-changing decisions based on the roll of the dice. The book achieved cult-like status, including among readers who tried to live according to its precepts. If nothing else, it shows that a mechanism does not have to be intelligent in order to make choices: it merely has to have choice-making attributes ascribed to it. Luke Rhinehart was the pen name of the author George Cockcroft, who tried to turn the idea of 'dicing' into a self-help philosophy and an alternative to conventional therapy, with its futile emphasis on making the 'right' decisions. He said of his outlook on life: 'If you ask a human being to explain why he does something, I don't think any one of us is able at all to tell' (Tim Adams, 'Dicing with Life', *Guardian*, 27 August 2000: www.theguardian.com/books/2000/aug/27/fiction.timadams).

8 There have been repeated criticisms of *Leviathan* as a bleak and depressing book ever since it was published in 1651 (see Jon Parkin, *Taming the Leviathan* (Cambridge University Press, 2010)). Influential recent examples of blaming Hobbes for what we don't like about ourselves include Rutger Bregman, *Humankind: A Hopeful History* (Bloomsbury, 2019), which contrasts Hobbes's pessimism with the optimism of Jean-Jacques Rousseau, and David Graeber and David Wengrow, *The Dawn of Everything: A New History of Humanity* (Allen Lane, 2021), which blames

Hobbes *and* Rousseau for having a far too restricted view of human political possibility.

Graeber and Wengrow call *Leviathan* 'the founding text of modern political theory'. They also say its claims are wrong, for three reasons: (1) they simply aren't true, (2) they have dire political implications and (3) they make the past needlessly dull. Their second point – dire! – is the charge most often directed against Hobbes: that he opens the door to a remote and oppressive politics. The first point – not true! – rests on the idea that the state of nature is not as Hobbes described it. We don't in fact have to fight endlessly until a distant political authority rescues us from each other by sparing us from having to take decisions at all. This counterargument is often associated with Rousseau, who described the state of nature in very different terms from Hobbes: as a place where individuals could easily avoid conflict with each other by simply walking away from a fight. For Rousseau, it was only when we were confined by the development of agriculture and industry to fixed places – villages, towns, cities – that we became a threat to each other. The dream of a return to nature is a dream of being liberated from all that. This is why Rousseau appeals to Bregman's view of a more benign human nature. But Graeber and Wengrow think Rousseau was wrong to assume that the choice is either small-scale and natural or big and oppressive.

This is where their third point – dull! – comes in. They believe that setting scalable political organisation in opposition to natural human relationships misses the ways it was once possible to combine them. Rousseau helped create the false impression that the only alternative to the modern state was a return to the simplicity of a natural existence, where equality means that no one owes anyone anything. Not only is this a fantasy – there is no going back to such a simple life – it also ignores the historical record, which shows early human societies constructing sophisticated political arrangements without abrogating their basic humanity. Hobbes created the impression that the only alternative to the modern state was short-lived chaos. This too is a misconception. These early societies – from ancient Mesopotamia to pre-Columbus North America – were not only politically complex; many of them were politically durable too.

Graeber and Wengrow argue that modern politics – the Hobbes project – is built on a series of fake choices: either we are equal *or we* are sophisticated; either we are natural *or* we are intelligent; either we are primitive *or* we operate to scale. Instead, if we can look beyond our modern, Western biases, which predispose us to think the world must be the way we have made it, we will see that the wider history of humanity shows it is possible to be many of these things at once.

It is a compelling critique. It suggests that modern politics has made us fatalistic by allowing us to forget that we chose this way of being. We could choose to do things very differently. But there are also reasons to be doubtful that this is possible. First, if the modern state is a superhuman version of ourselves, then we may have lost the power to recover what we once were. We can restore our humanity only if we can resume being fully human – but by franchising out some of our humanity to a decision-making machine we may have lost that capacity. Dismantling the state might not bring it back. Second, we didn't just make the modern state. The modern state made the world we live in, including much of its technology. It suits the world it has built, and that world suits it. This is not technological determinism. Technological transformation doesn't decide politics. But it does often depend on politics, and then politics comes to depend on it. The artificial relies on the artificial. Once the transformation has happened, there might be no going back.

Graeber and Wengrow's vision of an alternative politics lacks something else. Even if we discover ways of doing politics that are complex and sustainable yet still fully human, that still leaves one attribute missing: replicability. The essence of a human politics is that it is rooted in people and places: we learn to be ourselves by remaining in touch with who we are and where we live. For that reason, these models of politics are not easy to transplant from one place to another, no matter how sophisticated; indeed, the more sophisticated they are, the harder it will be to move them, because their subtleties will be context specific. Artificial modern politics has the advantage that it does not depend on the specific attributes of people and places to function – that's what makes it machine-like. It will be hard for a more human politics to compete. This does not mean that Hobbesian politics is better than the alternatives – it is, after all, inhuman. Perhaps we would be better off without it. But it will be very hard to shake off.

9 A bridge was one of the examples of a 'person by fiction' given by Hobbes. He writes in Chapter 16 of *Leviathan*: 'There are few things

that are incapable of being represented by fiction. Inanimate things, as a church, a hospital, a bridge, may be personated by a rector, master, or overseer. But things inanimate cannot be authors, nor therefore give authority to their actors: yet the actors may have authority to procure their maintenance, given them by those that are owners or governors of those things.' One of the reasons he used these three examples together is that churches and hospitals were often placed at the entrance to bridges, on the assumption that travellers would have need of them.

10 The idea that the state is a kind of nothingness has particular resonance in modern French political thought. For example, the philosopher Claude Lefort argued that the state represents an 'empty space'. The Leviathan tries to fill this space with real power, and as a result ends up in a form of totalitarianism (because ultimately there is nothing but power to fill the space). Lefort believed that democracy, which holds on to the emptiness, can retain room for human creativity, because an empty space is always something we can fill with our imaginations. Once again, Hobbes gets the blame (in this case, for totalitarianism), even though Hobbes was the one who came up with this way of doing imaginative politics in the first place (Claude Lefort, *The Political Forms of Modern Society: Bureaucracy, Democracy, Totalitarianism* (MIT Press, 1986)).

2 Groupthink

1 Almost by definition, there is no definitive account of what went on inside the jury room during its deliberations, only piecemeal recollections, often many years after the event. There is, however, a consensus that the speed of the verdict was a consequence of the early straw vote, and the readiness of the two jurors who had originally been inclined to convict to bow to the multiple reasons given by the majority. Exhaustion seems to have played its part too, along with a sense that the trial had been allowed to go on too long. Gil Garcetti, the Los Angeles District Attorney, said of the verdict in its immediate aftermath: 'Apparently this decision was based on emotion that overlapped reason' (Timothy Egan, 'One Juror Smiled, Then They Knew', *New York Times*, 4 October 1995).

2 The discursive dilemma is discussed extensively in the work of Christian List and Philip Pettit, who make it central to their account of group agency. See Christian List and Philip Pettit, *Group Agency: The Possibility, Design and Status of Corporate Agents* (Oxford University Press, 2011);

Christian List and Philip Pettit, 'Aggregating Sets of Judgments: Two Impossibility Results Compared', *Synthese* 140 (2004), 207–35.

3 The use of Brexit as an example of the discursive dilemma is taken from a blog post written by Anthony McGann in May 2019 at the height of the British government's impasse over how to implement the result of the referendum. McGann's conclusion was that 'the only way out (without disregarding the "will of the people") is to ask the people exactly what they want. That means a referendum where the people are given the choice between the specific Brexit alternatives and remaining in the EU.' In the end, that wasn't the way out; instead, a different kind of vote (a general election) was able to break the deadlock by electing a parliament with a strong majority for whatever deal could be achieved by the new prime minister Boris Johnson. https://blogs.lse.ac.uk/brexit/2019/05/01/deal-or-no-deal-the-only-way-out-is-to-ask-the-people-exactly-what-they-want/.

4 Nagel's argument was primarily designed to establish the philosophical difficulty of reaching firm conclusions about the nature of consciousness. If to be conscious means that it is possible to be like the conscious thing, and if being like some such things (such as bats) is more or less inaccessible to human understanding, then some aspects of consciousness will also be relatively inaccessible to human understanding. At the very least, consciousness on this account cannot be reduced to the domain of the physical, since physical explanations cannot account for what it is like to *be* something like a bat. Critics of Nagel's argument have insisted that sufficiently fine-tuned neuroscience could still explain what it is like to experience the world like a bat. See Thomas Nagel, 'What is it Like to Be a Bat?', *Philosophical Review* 83 (1974), 435–50; for the classic physicalist critique, see Daniel Dennett, *Consciousness Explained* (Little Brown, 1991).

5 The idea that collective decision-making will ultimately be incoherent when it is not subject to dictatorial constraint is particularly associated with the work of the Nobel Prize-winning economist Kenneth Arrow, and subsequently the political scientist William Riker, who helped to popularise Arrow's conclusions. See William H. Riker, *Liberalism Against Populism: A Confrontation Between the Theory of Democracy and the Theory of Social Choice* (W. H. Freeman and Co., 1982). This has also been

described as 'Hobbes's Problem' (Peter Stone, 'Hobbes' Problem', *The Good Society* 24 (2014), 1–14).

6 The idea that democracies can be animated by the collective insight of large groups of people – and that this prospect should determine how we design our democracies – is often termed 'epistemic democracy' (i.e. democracy as a form of knowledge). The case is made in David Estlund, *Democratic Authority: A Philosophical Framework* (Princeton University Press, 2008), and Robert E. Goodin and Kai Spiekermann, *An Epistemic Theory of Democracy* (Oxford University Press, 2018). For a direct application of Condorcet's theorem to democratic possibilities, see Christian List and Robert E. Goodin, 'Epistemic Democracy: Generalizing the Condorcet Jury Theorem', *Journal of Political Philosophy* 9 (2001), 277–306.

7 The jellybeans example comes from James Surowiecki, *The Wisdom of Crowds: Why the Many are Smarter than the Few and How Collective Wisdom Shapes Businesses, Economies, Societies and Nations* (Doubleday, 2004).

8 Just as there is a long tradition of trying to find the intelligence in groups (it goes back to Aristotle), so there is also an equally long tradition of identifying the craziness, scariness and general weirdness of crowd behaviour (it goes back to Plato). Two classic modern texts in this second genre are Charles MacKay, *Extraordinary Popular Delusions and the Madness of Crowds* (1841), and Gustave Le Bon, *The Crowd: A Study of the Popular Mind* (1895).

9 On 13 June 2007 the CIA published on its website a paper entitled 'Using Prediction Markets to Enhance US Intelligence Capabilities'. Though a relatively measured and balanced account of the pros and cons, it is true to say that many of the benefits predicted in this paper have not come to pass: https://web.archive.org/web/20070613045642/www.cia.gov/library/center-for-the-study-of-intelligence/csi-publications/csi-studies/studies/vol50no4/using-prediction-markets-to-enhance-us-intelligence-capabilities.html#_ftn2.

The vogue for prediction markets has for now largely been superseded by the vogue for what are known as 'superforecasters' – individuals who can factor their own propensity for bias into their predictions and correct for it with techniques designed to minimise the role of cognitive biases. Unsurprisingly, these individuals are extremely rare. See Philip E.

Tetlock and Dan Gardner, *Superforecasting: The Art and Science of Prediction* (Crown, 2015).

10 For an account of the turbo-charged, no-holds-barred, Reddit-based version of decisions and answers feeding off (and ultimately eating) each other, see Jason Koebler, 'Send This to Anyone Who Wants to Know WTF is Up With GameStop Stock', *Vice*, 27 January, 2021, www.vice.com/en/article/pkdvgy/send-this-to-anyone-who-wants-to-know-wtf-is-up-with-gamestop-stock.

11 Carville was responding to the 1994 bond market crisis, which prompted a sell-off in long-term US treasury bonds, in response to which the Clinton administration introduced tighter fiscal policies and managed to ride out the storm. In 2022, the premiership of Liz Truss began with a sell-off of UK government bonds following the announcement by her chancellor Kwasi Kwarteng of looser fiscal policy (higher public spending plus tax cuts). She did not survive the fallout – her premiership, at seven weeks, was the shortest in British history. The bond markets can force politicians to adapt, and just occasionally, when they don't, they can force them out of office.

12 Ron Suskind, 'Faith, Certainty and the Presidency of George W. Bush', *New York Times*, 17 October 2004: www.nytimes.com/2004/10/17/magazine/faith-certainty-and-the-presidency-of-george-w-bush.html. Suskind did not confirm the identity of the aide he was speaking to, though it was widely rumoured at the time to be Karl Rove.

13 Suskind compared the mistakes made by the Bush administration to the failings that can beset businesses whose leaders prioritise wishful thinking over market-based realities. Suskind wrote:

> Bush has been called the C.E.O. president, but that's just a catch phrase – he never ran anything of consequence in the private sector. The M.B.A. president would be more accurate: he did, after all, graduate from Harvard Business School … One aspect of the H.B.S. method, with its emphasis on problems of actual corporations, is sometimes referred to as the 'case cracker' problem. The case studies are static, generally a snapshot of a troubled company, frozen in time; the various 'solutions' students proffer, and then defend in class against tough questioning, tend to have very short shelf lives. They promote rigidity, inappropriate surety. This is something H.B.S. graduates,

most of whom land at large or midsize firms, learn in their first few years in business. They discover, often to their surprise, that the world is dynamic, it flows and changes, often for no good reason. The key is flexibility, rather than sticking to your guns in a debate, and constant reassessment of shifting realities. In short, thoughtful second-guessing (ibid.).

14 'Joint enterprise' convictions are increasingly contentious in UK law, following a ruling by the UK Supreme Court in 2016 that the principle had been wrongly interpreted for decades, by equating foresight that a crime might be committed with intent to commit it. Critics have also charged that 'joint enterprise' is predominantly used to prosecute young Black and Asian men as a way of targeting 'gang' culture and is therefore racially discriminatory: www.theguardian.com/law/2022/apr/27/joint-enterprise-ruling-has-not-led-to-fewer-homicide-charges-report-finds.

3 A Matter of Life and Death

1 www.usdebtclock.org/. Many other measures of public and private debt (including student-loan debt and credit-card debt, along with major items government expenditure and income) are calculated in real time on the same site, to a compelling but somewhat spurious degree of second-by-second accuracy.

2 According to the debt clock, current total personal indebtedness in the US stands at more than $24 trillion, which averages out as a personal debt of more than $70,000 per citizen. The national debt, which is larger, would have to be added to this.

3 The relative reliability of certain regime types as creditors, along with the repeated propensity of their governments to squander these advantages, is described in Carmen M. Reinhart and Kenneth Rogoff, *This Time is Different: Eight Centuries of Financial Folly* (Princeton University Press, 2009). The relationship between democracy, 'citizen creditors' and the national debt is also the subject of James Macdonald, *A Free Nation Deep in Debt: The Financial Roots of Democracy* (Princeton University Press, 2006).

4 The capacity of states to renege on debts is a function of their power; the less that power – particularly for those states that have been subject to colonial rule – the harder it is. For an example of this, see Catherine

Porter, Constant Méheut, Matt Apuzzo and Selam Gebrekidan, 'The Root of Haiti's Misery: Reparations to Enslavers', *New York Times*, 20 May 2022, www.nytimes.com/2022/05/20/world/americas/haiti-history-colonized-france.html. For the wider history, see David Graeber, *Debt: The First 5000 Years* (Melville Publishing, 2011).

On a quixotic recent attempt by a relatively poor state to take control of its currency in another way, see David Gerard, 'El Salvador's Bitcoin Law is a Farce: The System Doesn't Work, the Currency Crashed, and the Public Hates It', *Foreign Policy*, 17 September 2021, https://foreignpolicy.com/2021/09/17/el-salvador-bitcoin-law-farce/.

5 The vulture funds pursuing the Argentinian government did have some notable successes in forcing repayment: in 2012 a US court ruled that Argentina had to settle with these funds before it could pay off its other creditors who had accepted an earlier restructuring deal. It is US courts, which can effectively set terms for access to US dollar markets, that have the leverage in these cases, not other branches of the US government (see Martin Guzman and Joseph E. Stiglitz, 'How Hedge Funds Held Argentina to Ransom', *New York Times*, 1 April 2016).

6 Charles Tilly, 'Reflections on the History of European State Making', in Charles Tilly (ed.), *The Formation of National States in Western Europe* (Princeton University Press, 1975). A classic account of the relationship between war and debt financing in the development of the British state is John Brewer, *Sinews of Power: War, Money and the English State, 1688–1783* (Yale University Press, 1990). For a revisionist view which places more emphasis on colonial development, see Steven Pincus and James Robinson, 'Wars and State-Making Reconsidered: The Rise of the Developmental State', *Annales* 71 (2016), 9–34.

7 One of the inspirations for Hobbes's idea of the Leviathan was the Argus Panoptes, the hundred-eyed monster of ancient Greek myth that was eternally vigilant because while some eyes slept, others would always be kept open. It is from this that we get the later idea of 'the Panopticon', which was Jeremy Bentham's name for his experimental prison in which the inmates could always be viewed by the warder; Michel Foucault's overarching label for the workings of modern society; Shoshanna Zuboff's metaphor for the role of surveillance technology in monitoring the world of work; and Edward Snowden's nickname for the NSA.

8 A classic early statement of democratic peace theory is Michael W. Doyle, 'Kant, Liberal Legacies and Foreign Affairs', *Philosophy and Public Affairs* 12 (1983), 205–35. A more recent variant, Thomas Friedman's 'Golden Arches' theory, which states that countries with branches of McDonalds will not go to war with each other (resting the democratic peace on consumerism, convenience and trade rather than enlightened values), was definitively debunked in 2022: there were more than 700 branches of McDonalds in Russia, and more than 100 in Ukraine, when the former invaded the latter.

On the ambivalent public response to the outbreak of war in 1914, see Catriona Pennell, *A Kingdom United: Popular Responses to the Outbreak of the First World War in Britain and Ireland* (Oxford University Press, 2012).

9 On some of the ways in which democracies excel at war, see John Ferejohn and Frances McCall Rosenbluth, 'Warlike Democracies', *Journal of Conflict Resolution* 52 (2008), 3–38. The case is also made – with an emphasis on democratic caution as well as adaptability – in Dan Reiter and Allan C. Stam, *Democracies at War* (Princeton University Press, 2002). That account, however, was written before the US-led invasion of Iraq in 2003 that led to the Iraq War, which puts democratic caution in a somewhat different light.

10 As things stand, the International Criminal Court (ICC) can pursue individuals for war crimes, but not states. The International Court of Justice (ICJ) has jurisdiction over states, but only in limited circumstances. See Ellen Ioanes, 'Here's What the ICC Can Actually Do About Putin's War Crimes', *Vox*, 9 April 2022, www.vox.com/23017838/international-criminal-court-icc-putin-war-crimes.

11 The ranking of corporate indebtedness (at the time of writing) is taken from Statista, 'Companies with the Largest Debt Worldwide in 2002', www.statista.com/statistics/1235574/most-indebted-companies/.

12 For an account of the EIC as 'too big to fail' (and the parallels that suggests with more recent corporate practice) see Nick Robins, *The Corporation that Changed the World: How the East India Company Shaped the Modern Multinational* (Pluto Press, 2012). For a more recent, character-driven study, see William Dalrymple, *The Anarchy: The Relentless Rise of the East India Company* (Bloomsbury, 2019).

13 The alternative is that the state provides them with more cash, which is what happens in the case of corporations that are 'too big to fail'. What may also keep them going – especially under current market conditions – are the vast reservoirs of cash possessed by venture capital, which have in some cases supplanted state funds as the backstop of failed businesses. See Eric Levitz, 'America Has Central Planners. We Just Call Them "Venture Capitalists"', *New York*, 3 December 2020, https://nymag.com/intelligencer/2020/12/wework-venture-capital-central-planning.html.

14 The different models of corporate life and activity in ancient Rome are described in Jeffrey L. Patterson, 'The Development of the Concept of the Corporation from Earliest Roman Times to A.D. 476', *Accounting Historians Journal* 10 (1983), 87–98.

15 The distinction between the two rival Roman models of conceptualising political association is given in Part III of Michael Oakeshott, *On Human Conduct* (Clarendon Press, 1975): 'On the Character of a Modern European State'. The first two parts of the book are concerned with conceptualising what it means to be human and what it means for humans to co-exist in ways that are not simply conditioned by the characteristics of modern politics.

16 In 1946 Oakeshott published a celebrated edition of *Leviathan*, in which he described Hobbes as the pre-eminent philosopher of the 'artificial'. By this, Oakeshott meant that Hobbes uses reason to build the world of politics, and 'reasoning is itself artificial, not natural', i.e. it is a capability we are not born with, but 'acquire'. This would mean, in so far as reason is equated with intelligence, there can be no separate category of artificial intelligence because all intelligence is artificial by definition. What is natural is 'the will', i.e. the capacity that humans are born with to make choices (regardless of their intelligence). This is something humans share with animals. What the state has is an artificial will. But for Oakeshott, despite everything Hobbes says to the contrary, that is not enough to make the state a person, not even an artificial one. Oakeshott's introduction to Leviathan is available at https://oll.liberty-fund.org/page/hobbes-oakeshott-s-introduction-to-leviathan.

17 In Part I of *On Human Conduct* ('On the Theoretical Understanding of Human Conduct'), Oakeshott says that 'human agency does not open

with the unconditional "In the beginning", but the conditional "Once upon a time"'. Our agency, in other words, is defined by our ability to determine the start of our own stories, and when we choose to start them all over again. It is possible that Oakeshott took this idea from Hannah Arendt, who called it 'natality' – the uniquely human ability to begin our lives again.

18 Stephane Garelli, 'Why You Will Probably Live Longer Than Most Big Companies' (2016), www.imd.org/research-knowledge/articles/why-you -will-probably-live-longer-than-most-big-companies/.

19 The story of the early years of Lehman Brothers – and of the relationship between the original brothers themselves – is told in *The Lehman Trilogy*, a play by the Italian author Stefano Massini, which has been performed worldwide, including in the West End and on Broadway. The play was also adapted into a novel in verse form. Stefano Massini, *The Lehman Trilogy* (HarperVia, 2020).

20 In Weber's definition, the 'association' in question is given by the German term *Gemeinschaft*, which is usually translated as 'community', and contrasted with *Gesellschaft*, which covers other kinds of collective organisations founded on rational interest or contract, including modern corporations. Ironically, the modern state is often understood in German thought as a form of *Gesellschaft* – that is, as an instrumental, purposive, rational enterprise, of the kind conceived by Hobbes.

21 The idea of the 'state-nation' was originally conceived to describe certain post-colonial state-building projects of the twentieth century, through which multi-ethnic societies were meant to be turned into political communities; see Alfred Stepan, Juan J. Linz and Yogendra Yadav, *Crafting State-Nations: India and Other Multinational Democracies* (Johns Hopkins University Press, 2011). More recently it has been applied to the earlier history of the United States by Jill Lepore, among others; see Jill Lepore, *This America: The Case for the Nation* (Liveright, 2019). The story of how the French were turned into an entity called France over the course of the nineteenth century is told in Graham Robb, *The Invention of France* (Picador, 2007).

22 The concept of the uncanny valley originated in 1970 in an essay by the Japanese roboticist Masahiro Mori (https://web.ics.purdue.

edu/~drkelly/MoriTheUncannyValley1970.pdf). Some have tried to trace its origins earlier, including to Sigmund Freud's 1919 essay 'The Uncanny', in which he explored the origins of troubled human responses to things that move when we believe they shouldn't, along with the eeriness of lifelike dolls and other inanimate objects that have a soulful appearance. Freud, though, preferred a psychoanalytic explanation:

> Dismembered limbs, a severed head, hands cut off at the wrist, feet which appear to dance by themselves – all these have something peculiarly uncanny about them, especially when, as in the last instance, they prove able to move themselves in addition. As we already know, this kind of uncanniness springs from its association with the castration complex. To many people the idea of being buried alive while appearing to be dead is the most uncanny thing of all. And yet psychoanalysis has taught us that this terrifying fantasy is only a transformation of another fantasy which originally had nothing terrifying about it at all but was filled with a certain lustful pleasure – the fantasy, I mean, of intra-uterine existence (https://web.mit.edu/allanmc/www/freud1.pdf).

23 There has been particular focus on the role of ExxonMobil in both facilitating research into climate change and then working to suppress the results of that research in order to protect its own business model. A detailed account is provided in Neela Banerjee, Lisa Song and David Hasemyer, 'Exxon's Own Research Confirmed Fossil Fuels' Role in Global Warming Decades Ago', *Inside Climate Change*, 16 September 2015, and Neela Banerjee, Lisa Song and David Hasemyer, 'Exxon Believed Deep Dive into Climate Research Would Protect Its Business', *Inside Climate Change*, 17 September 2015.

24 Though often described as its founder, Musk only bought into Tesla nine months after it was created by Martin Eberhard and Marc Tarpenning. A lawsuit in 2009 settled that Musk, along with four others, could be termed one of Tesla's 'co-founders'.

25 The influence of the idea that corporations exist to maximise shareholder value is often traced back to the economist Milton Friedman, and in particular to an article titled 'The Friedman Doctrine: The Social Responsibility of Business is to Increase Its Profits', published in the *New York Times* in September 1970 (www.nytimes.com/1970/09/13/

archives/a-friedman-doctrine-the-social-responsibility-of-business-is-to.
html).

Martin Wolf has recently argued that this doctrine, with its neglect of
the greater capabilities and responsibilities of powerful corporations in
a globalised world, is partly responsible for the current crisis of democratic capitalism. Martin Wolf, *The Crisis of Democratic Capitalism* (Allen
Lane, 2023).

26 A comprehensive history that locates the *Citizens United* ruling
against the long backstory of corporate assertiveness in American political life is provided in Adam Winkler, *We the Corporations: How American
Businesses Won Their Civil Rights* (Liveright, 2019).

27 Maistre, who was strongly influenced by Hobbes, wrote that society
under a mechanical conception was like a watch 'all of whose springs vary
greatly in strength, weight, dimension, form, and position that nonetheless keeps perfect time'. The problems arose when free agents interfered
with its workings, as they must. Joseph de Maistre, *Considerations on
France*, ed. Richard A. Lebrun (Cambridge University Press, 2009).

For a history of the British state over the last two hundred years that
describes the role and conception of the bureaucracy as a 'machine' see
Jon Agar, *The Government Machine: A Revolutionary History of the Computer*
(MIT Press, 2016).

Max Weber uses mechanical imagery throughout his political writings: see particularly 'Parliament and Government in Germany Under
a New Political Order' (1917) and 'The Profession and Vocation of Politics' (1919), both in Max Weber, *Political Writings*, ed. Peter Lassman and
Ronald Speirs (Cambridge University Press, 1994).

4 Tribes, Churches, Empires

1 Harari treats the corporation as a paradigmatic example of a useful
'fiction'. This includes the fiction of the limited liability company. He
writes:

> Such companies were legally independent of the people who set
> them up, or invested money in them, or managed them. Over the last
> few centuries such companies have become the main players in the
> economic arena, and we have grown so used to them that we forget
> they exist only in our imagination. In the US, the technical term for

a limited liability company is a 'corporation', which is ironic, because the term derives from 'corpus' ('body' in Latin) – the one thing these corporations lack. Despite their having no real bodies, the American legal system treats corporations as legal persons, as if they were flesh-and-blood human beings (Yuval Noah Harari, *Sapiens: A Brief History of Humankind* (Vintage, 2014), p. 24).

As the previous chapter here has tried to show, this is too simplistic. Nonetheless, what follows in the first part of this chapter borrows heavily from Harari's account.

2 The figure of 150 (as applied to friends) is commonly known as 'Dunbar's number', after the British anthropologist Robin Dunbar who first enumerated it and then popularised it. See R. I. M. Dunbar, 'Neocortex Size as a Constraint on Group Size in Primates', *Journal of Human Evolution* 22 (1992), 469–93; and Robin Dunbar, *How Many Friends Does One Person Need? Dunbar's Number and Other Evolutionary Quirks* (Faber and Faber, 2010).

3 Harari tells his story of what might happen next in *Homo Deus*, his follow-up to *Sapiens*. Yuval Noah Harari, *Homo Deus: A Brief History of Tomorrow* (HarperCollins, 2015).

4 A notable attempt to emancipate the idea of the sovereign individual from rationalistic and mechanistic state control is James Dale Davidson and William Rees-Mogg, *The Sovereign Individual: Mastering the Transition to the Information Age* (Simon and Schuster, 1999). Part of what makes it notable is that the book has been exceptionally influential among Silicon Valley elites; see, for example, Mark O'Connell, 'Why Silicon Valley Billionaires are Prepping for the Apocalypse in New Zealand', *Guardian*, 15 February 2018, www.theguardian.com/news/2018/feb/15/why-silicon-valley-billionaires-are-prepping-for-the-apocalypse-in-new-zealand.

5 In a profile in the *New Yorker* in 2018, Zuckerberg is reported to have said: 'You have all these good and bad and complex figures. I think Augustus is one of the most fascinating. Basically, through a really harsh approach, he established two hundred years of world peace.' He also said of the honeymoon he took in Rome in 2012: 'My wife was making fun of me, saying she thought there were three people on the honeymoon: me, her, and Augustus. All the photos were different sculptures

of Augustus.' The couple named their second daughter August. Evan Osnos, 'Can Mark Zuckerberg Fix Facebook Before it Breaks Democracy?', *New Yorker*, 10 September 2018.

6 I am indebted to Magnus Ryan for the idea of the Roman Empire as a Death Star.

7 Walter Scheidel, *Escape from Rome: The Failure of Empire and the Road to Prosperity* (Princeton University Press, 2019).

8 On the first 'Great Divergence' see Walter Scheidel, 'From the "Great Convergence" to the "First Great Divergence": Roman and Qin-Han State Formation and its Aftermath', in Walter Scheidel (ed.), *Rome and China: Comparative Perspectives on Ancient World Empires* (Oxford University Press, 2009). A brief summary of how Mediterranean and Chinese empires diverged over the course of the second half of the first millennium CE is available at https://web.stanford.edu/~scheidel/acme.htm.

9 On the possible ephemerality of the nation-state relative to empire, see Niall Ferguson, 'The Unconscious Colossus: Limits of (and Alternatives to) American Empire', *Daedalus*, Spring 2005.

10 The distinction between 'extractive' and 'inclusive' institutions is described in detail in Daron Acemoglu and James A. Robinson, *Why Nations Fail: The Origins of Power, Prosperity and Poverty* (Profile, 2012).

11 The horror of what happened in the Congo under Belgian imperial rule and its legacy for contemporary Belgium are detailed in Adam Hochschild, *King Leopold's Ghost: A Story of Greed, Terror and Heroism in Colonial Africa* (Houghton Mifflin, 1998).

12 Daron Acemoglu and James A. Robinson, *The Narrow Corridor: States, Societies and the Fate of Liberty* (Viking, 2019).

13 The poem, which was first published in Yeats's 1928 collection *The Tower*, is now best-known for its opening line. It is worth reading in full:

> I
> That is no country for old men. The young
> In one another's arms, birds in the trees,
> – Those dying generations – at their song,
> The salmon-falls, the mackerel-crowded seas,
> Fish, flesh, or fowl, commend all summer long

Whatever is begotten, born, and dies.
Caught in that sensual music all neglect
Monuments of unageing intellect.

II
An aged man is but a paltry thing,
A tattered coat upon a stick, unless
Soul clap its hands and sing, and louder sing
For every tatter in its mortal dress,
Nor is there singing school but studying
Monuments of its own magnificence;
And therefore I have sailed the seas and come
To the holy city of Byzantium.

III
O sages standing in God's holy fire
As in the gold mosaic of a wall,
Come from the holy fire, perne in a gyre,
And be the singing-masters of my soul.
Consume my heart away; sick with desire
And fastened to a dying animal
It knows not what it is; and gather me
Into the artifice of eternity.

IV
Once out of nature I shall never take
My bodily form from any natural thing,
But such a form as Grecian goldsmiths make
Of hammered gold and gold enamelling
To keep a drowsy Emperor awake;
Or set upon a golden bough to sing
To lords and ladies of Byzantium
Of what is past, or passing, or to come.

14 The full text of (Thucydides's version of) Pericles' Funeral Oration is in Thucydides, *The History of the Peloponnesian War*, Book 2, 34–46, www.wright.edu/~christopher.oldstone-moore/pericles.htm.

15 I discuss the differences between ancient Greek and modern Greek democracy – including the reasons why modern Greek democracy has

a striking but shallow resilience – in David Runciman, *How Democracy Ends* (Profile, 2019).

16 The story of company-states and their crucial role in modern economic and political development is told in Andrew Philips and Jason Sharman, *Outsourcing Empire: How Company-States Made the Modern World* (Princeton University Press, 2019). The history of the East India Company as a 'company-state' is told in Philip J. Stern, *The Company-State: Corporate Sovereignty and the Early Modern Foundations of the British Empire in India* (Oxford University Press, 2011).

17 The Korean economist Ha-Joon Chang tells 'the Hyundai Story' in this short film: www.youtube.com/watch?v=crS4miW92eA.

5 The Great Transformation

1 The 'great acceleration' is sometimes taken to denote rapid growth since the 1950s across a range of measures of human activity and economic progress, not limited to economic growth: these include population growth, energy use, fertiliser use, water use, foreign direct investment, and international tourism, all of which have shown similar patterns of exponential increase. The term is also frequently used in a pejorative sense, to indicate unsustainability. See https://futureearth.org/2015/01/16/the-great-acceleration/ where the great acceleration is defined as 'the synchronous acceleration of trends from the 1950s to the present day – over a single human lifetime – with little sign of abatement'.

2 There is a vast literature exploring – and disputing – the reasons why the economy of western Europe took off when it did. A classic early account is Douglass C. North and Robert Paul Thomas, *The Rise of the Western World: A New Economic History* (Cambridge University Press, 1973). The specific idea of a 'great divergence' from China was popularised in Kenneth Pomeranz, *The Great Divergence: China, Europe and the Making of the Modern World* (Princeton University Press, 2000) – Pomeranz is one of those who puts a particular emphasis on coal. See also David Landes, 'Why Europe and the West? Why Not China?', *Journal of Economic Perspectives* 20 (2006), 3–22, which prioritises the free market and property rights. For work that emphasises the role of technology and scientific enlightenment culture, see Joel Mokyr, *A Culture of Growth:*

The Origins of the Modern Economy (Princeton University Press, 2016). For the specific role of culture and demography in the case of England, see Gregory Clark, *A Farewell to Alms: A Brief Economic History of the World* (Princeton University Press, 2007). There are many, many other competing accounts – this is just to scratch the surface.

3 The contrasting fates of North and South Korea since 1953 – notwithstanding all that they have in common – is one of the central case studies in Acemoglu and Robinson, *Why Nations Fail*.

4 See Douglass C. North and Barry R. Weingast, 'Constitutions and Commitment: The Evolution of Institutions Governing Public Choice in Seventeenth-Century England', *Journal of Economic History* 49 (1989), 803–32; Douglass C. North, 'Institutions and Credible Commitment', *Journal of Institutional and Theoretical Economics* 149 (1983), 11–23; Douglass C. North, John Joseph Wallis and Barry R. Weingast, *Violence and Social Orders: A Conceptual Framework for Interpreting Recorded Human History* (Cambridge University Press, 2009).

5 J. Bradford DeLong has identified 1870 as the turning point in the story of (American-led) modern economic growth, which he explains through three interrelated innovations: the modern corporation, the research lab, and globalised international trade. The role of the state is less emphasised, though it remains an essential precondition. J. Bradford DeLong, *Slouching Towards Utopia: An Economic History of the Twentieth Century* (Basic Books, 2022).

6 On Argentina's markedly up-and-down modern economic and political history, see José Ignacio García Hamilton, 'Historical Reflections on the Splendor and Decline of Argentina', *Cato Journal* 25 (2005), 521–40; Rok Spruk, 'The Rise and Fall of Argentina', *Latin American Economic Review* 28 (2019), 1–40.

7 Johan Norberg, *Progress: Ten Reasons to Look Forward to the Future* (Oneworld Publications, 2016).

8 The term comes from Matt Ridley, *The Rational Optimist: How Prosperity Evolves* (Harper, 2010). Other works in this genre include Rutger Bregman, *Utopia for Realists: And How We Can Get There* (Bloomsbury, 2016) and Steven Pinker, *Enlightenment Now: The Case for Reason, Science, Humanism and Progress* (Allen Lane, 2018).

9 The Wikipedia page on cognitive biases lists more than 120 different varieties, ranging from the 'end-of-history illusion' to the 'women-are-wonderful effect' (https://en.wikipedia.org/wiki/List_of_cognitive_biases). The most accessible account of the way the brain works to produce these effects remains Daniel Kahneman, *Thinking Fast and Slow* (Farrar, Straus and Giroux, 2011).

10 The contrast between economic growth in the period 1870–1970 relative to the period since is described in Robert J. Gordon, *The Rise and Fall of American Growth: The US Standard of Living Since the Civil War* (Princeton University Press, 2016). See also Ha-Joon Chang, 'The Washing Machine Has Changed the World More than the Internet Has', in his *23 Things They Don't Tell You About Capitalism* (Bloomsbury, 2013).

11 Hannah Arendt, *The Human Condition* (University of Chicago Press, 1958).

12 Thomas Malthus, *An Essay on the Principle of Population*, ed. Donald Winch (Cambridge University Press, 1992). See also Robert J. Mayhew, *Malthus: The Life and Legacies of an Untimely Prophet* (Harvard University Press, 2014).

13 There are a number of hagiographical accounts of Borlaug's life and work. For a revisionist view, see Marci Baranski, *The Globalization of Wheat: A Critical History of the Green Revolution* (University of Pittsburgh Press, 2022).

14 The decline in costs since 2010 has been most notable in solar- and wind-generated energy. A 2022 report on renewable energy costs summed up the reason for the decline in one area as follows:

> Between 2010 and 2021, the global weighted average cost of electricity for onshore wind projects fell by 68% ... This decline occurred as cumulative installed capacity grew from 178GW to 769GW. Cost reductions for onshore wind were driven by falls in turbine prices, and balance of plant costs, as the industry scaled-up, average project sizes increased (notably outside Europe), supply chains became more competitive, and the cost of capital fell (including the technology premium for onshore wind); as well as the higher capacity factors achieved by today's state-of-the-art turbines.

Despite this, formidable challenges remain in integrating solar and wind energy into the grid, along with ensuring continuous supply and storage capacity. www.irena.org//media/Files/IRENA/Agency/Publication/2022/Jul/IRENA_Power_Generation_Costs_2021_Summary.pdf.

15 On the immense political and intellectual challenges of the energy transition, see Daniel Yergin, *The New Map: Energy, Climate and the Clash of Nations* (Penguin, 2020); Helen Thompson, *Disorder: Hard Times in the 21st Century* (Oxford University Press, 2022).

16 The date of 1784 is one suggested in Duncan Kelly, *Politics and the Anthropocene* (Polity Press, 2019). For an account of the destruction wrought on other species by modern humans, see Elizabeth Kolbert, *The Sixth Extinction: An Unnatural History* (Henry Holt and Co., 2014).

17 See John Gray, 'Homo Rapiens and Mass Extinction', in *Gray's Anatomy: Selected Writings* (Allen Lane, 2009).

6 You Didn't Build That
1 Guy Benson, 'No, Conservatives Aren't Taking "You Didn't Build That" Out of Context', *Townhall.com*, 19 August 2012. https://townhall.com/tipsheet/guybenson/2012/07/19/no_conservatives_arent_taking_you_didnt_build_that_out_of_context-n691948.

2 'Remarks by the President', 24 July 2012, https://obamawhitehouse.archives.gov/the-press-office/2012/07/24/remarks-president-campaign-event-0.

3 The threats of trouble included to the American South, which suffered under the Hamiltonian tariff regime because of its reliance on the import of necessities and the export of cotton. There is also considerable controversy about how long protectionism remained essential to American economic growth – longer than many free-marketers would like. The issues remain live ones; see Robert W. Merry, 'Protectionism in America', *National Interest* 146 (2016), 28–36; Benjamin O. Fordham, 'Protectionist Empire: Trade, Tariffs and United States Foreign Policy, 1890–1914', *Studies in American Political Development* 31 (2017), 170–92.

4 House of Commons Committee of Public Accounts, 'Covid-19: Cost Tracker Update', 2 February 2022, https://committees.parliament.uk/publications/8934/documents/152365/default/.

5 Mariana Mazzucato, *The Entrepreneurial State: Debunking Public vs.*

Private Sector Myths (Anthem Press, 2013). A similar argument – drawing on personal experience – is made in William H. Janeway, *Doing Capitalism in the Innovation Economy: Markets, Speculation and the State* (Cambridge University Press, 2012).

6 For a more recent version of the same story – of how unscrupulous private actors piggyback off massive state funding of unprofitable enterprises until they alight on a profitable one – see Michael Lewis, *The Fifth Risk: Undoing Democracy* (W. W. Norton, 2018).

7 Seth Stevens-Davidovich, 'The Rich are Not Who We Think They are. And Happiness is Not What We Think It is Either', *New York Times*, 14 May 2022 www.nytimes.com/2022/05/14/opinion/sunday/rich-happiness-big-data.html. This report is based on Matthew Smith, Danny Yagan, Owen Zidar and Eric Zwick, 'Capitalists in the Twenty-First Century', *Quarterly Journal of Economics* 134 (2019), 1–72.

8 The Amazon story is told in Brad Stone, *The Everything Store: Jeff Bezos and the Age of Amazon* (Little, Brown, 2013) and Brad Stone, *Amazon Unbound: Jeff Bezos and the Invention of a Global Empire* (Simon and Schuster, 2021). For an excellent guide to all things Amazon, see Alina Utrata, 'The Anti-Dystopians' Guide to Amazon', *Substack*, 31 January 2022, https://alinautrata.substack.com/p/the-anti-dystopians-guide-to-amazon.

9 Thiel's intellectual formation is described in detail in Max Chafkin, *The Contrarian: Peter Thiel and Silicon Valley's Pursuit of Power* (Bloomsbury, 2021). Thiel's 'libertarianism', like much else about him, is somewhat idiosyncratic; see Peter Thiel, 'The Education of a Libertarian', *Cato Unbound*, 13 April 2009, www.cato-unbound.org/2009/04/13/peter-thiel/education-libertarian/.

10 Coco Feng, 'Tesla's Elon Musk, Ant Group CEO Write for Magazine of China's Top Internet Watchdog', *South China Morning Post*, 13 August 2022. www.scmp.com/tech/big-tech/article/3188790/teslas-elon-musk-ant-group-ceo-write-magazine-chinas-top-internet.

11 Christopher C. Stacey, 'Getting Started Computing at the AI Lab', MIT Working Paper 235, 7 September 1982, https://dspace.mit.edu/bitstream/handle/1721.1/41180/AI_WP_235.pdf.

12 The Apple story is told in detail in Mazzucato, *The Entrepreneurial State*. For a fuller account of the wider relationship between Silicon

Valley innovation, corporate development and government institutions, see Margaret O'Mara, *The Code: Silicon Valley and the Remaking of America* (Penguin, 2019).

13 Dwight D. Eisenhower, 'Military-Industrial Complex Speech', 17 January 1961, https://avalon.law.yale.edu/20th_century/eisenhower001.asp.

14 For an account of this from the inside – from a former Google employee turned reflective critic – see James Williams, *Stand Out of Our Light: Freedom and Resistance in the Attention Economy* (Cambridge University Press, 2018).

15 On the deliberate slowness of the state, and the growing contrast with the pace of twenty-first-century life, see William E. Scheuerman, *Liberal Democracy and the Social Acceleration of Time* (Johns Hopkins University Press, 2004).

16 In late 2017 I watched Hassabis – visibly awestruck – describe what AlphaZero was capable of at a conference in Los Angeles: it was more like a religious occasion than a corporate presentation. See David Runciman, 'AI', *London Review of Books*, 25 January 2018, www.lrb.co.uk/the-paper/v40/n02/david-runciman/diary.

17 The company's statement of its operating principles is as follows: 'We're solving intelligence to advance science and benefit humanity. At the heart of this mission is our commitment to act as responsible pioneers in the field of AI, in service of society's needs and expectations.' See www.deepmind.com/about.

18 The full transcript of their 'conversation' is given at Blake Lemoine, 'Is LaMDA Sentient? An Interview', *Medium*, 11 June 2022. It is both spooky and quite boring. https://cajundiscordian.medium.com/is-lamda-sentient-an-interview-ea64d916d917.

19 A detailed case against this approach to AI development is made in Emily M. Bender, Timnit Gebru, Angelina McMillan-Major and Shmargaret Shmitchell, 'On the Dangers of Stochastic Parrots: Can Language Models be Too Big?', *FAccT '21, Proceedings of the ACM 2021 Conference on Fairness, Accountability, and Transparency*, 610–23.

7 Beyond the State

1 Carnegie also wrote: 'Looking at the other person's point of view and arousing in them an eager want for something is not to be construed as manipulating that person so that they will do something that is only for your benefit and their detriment.' That might serve as a more modest mission statement for the technology corporations currently leading in AI than their habitually stated intentions to save the world. Dale Carnegie, *How to Win Friends and Influence People* (Simon and Schuster, 1936), a book that since its publication has never been out of print.

2 See Frank Pasquale, *New Laws of Robotics: Defending Human Expertise in the Age of AI* (The Belknap Press of Harvard University Press, 2020).

3 A. J. P. Taylor, *How Wars Begin* (Hamish Hamilton, 1979). The best-known recent account of the origins of the First World War is Christopher Clark, *The Sleepwalkers: How Europe Went to War in 1914* (HarperCollins, 2013), which puts much more emphasis on the human element – and distinctively human failures – including the 'crisis of masculinity' faced by European leaders of the time.

4 Just how dangerous the Cold War was – and how often disaster was narrowly averted by little more than luck – is recounted in Eric Schlosser, *Command and Control* (Penguin, 2014).

5 On the case for regulating Facebook and Google like public utilities, see Josh Simons and Dipayan Ghosh, 'Utilities for Democracy: How and Why the Algorithmic Infrastructure of Facebook and Google Must be Regulated', Brookings Institute, April 2020, www.brookings.edu/research/utilities-for-democracy-why-and-how-the-algorithmic-infrastructure-of-facebook-and-google-must-be-regulated/.

6 Elizabeth Warren, 'How We Can Break Up Big Tech', *Medium*, 8 March 2019, https://elizabethwarren.com/plans/break-up-big-tech.

7 Emily A. Vogels, 'Support for More Regulation of Tech Companies has Declined in US, Especially Among Republicans', *Pew Research Center*, 13 May 2022, www.pewresearch.org/fact-tank/2022/05/13/support-for-more-regulation-of-tech-companies-has-declined-in-u-s-especially-among-republicans/.

8 'How to Understand China's Common Prosperity Policy',

China Briefing, 21 March 2022, www.china-briefing.com/news/ china-common-prosperity-what-does-it-mean-for-foreign-investors/.

9 Gan Yang, '"Unifying the Three Traditions" in the New Era', in *Voices from the Chinese Century: Public Intellectual Debate in Contemporary China*, eds. Joshua Fogel, Timothy Cheek and David Ownby (Columbia University Press, 2019).

10 Sometimes this is done admiringly – *Remaking the Chinese Leviathan* (a book from 2002) – sometimes critically – 'The Specter of Leviathan: A Critique of Chinese Statism' (an essay from 2018) – and sometimes despairingly: 'Don't expect anything from Leviathan; there's no point in appealing either ... In the end, we have to help ourselves' (from Li Yuan, 'With "Zero Covid" China Proved It's Good at Control. Governance is Harder', *New York Times*, 26 December 2022, www.nytimes. com/2022/12/26/business/china-covid-communist-party.html.

11 For details of EU legislation in this area, see 'The Digital Services Act Package', https://digital-strategy.ec.europa.eu/en/policies/ digital-services-act-package.

12 For a personal account of the weirdness of working in this (deeply male) business culture as it tries to make the shift away from fetishising the founder, see Anna Weiner, *Uncanny Valley: A Memoir* (Fourth Estate, 2020).

13 Benoit Berthelot, 'Amazon Europe Unit Paid No Taxes on $55 Billion Sales in 2021', *Bloomberg UK*, 20 April, 2022, www. bloomberg.com/news/articles/2022-04-20/amazon-europe-unit-paid-no-taxes-on-55-billion-sales-in-2021.

14 Dominic Cummings, 'Regime Change #3: Amazon's Lessons on High-Performance Management for the Next PM', *Substack*, 22 February 2022, https://dominiccummings.substack.com/p/ amazons-lessons-on-high-performance.

15 Ibid.

16 Dominic Cummings, '"People, Ideas, Machines" 1: Notes on "Winning the Next War"', *Substack*, 10 March 2022, https://dominic-cummings.substack.com/p/people-ideas-machines-i-notes-on.

17 Victor describes the whole idea, appropriately, on a single poster

sheet in primarily visual form: http://worrydream.com/SeeingSpaces/ SeeingSpaces.jpg.

18 James C. Scott, *Seeing Like a State: How Certain Schemes to Improve the Human Condition Have Failed* (Yale University Press, 1998). For recent updates of Scott's framework for thinking about the state in the digital age, see Marion Fourcade and Jeffrey Gordon, 'Learning Like a State: Statecraft in the Digital Age', *Journal of Law and Political Economy* 1 (2020), which argues that 'the turn to dataist statecraft facilitates a corporatist reconstruction of the state'; Henry Farrell, 'Seeing Like a Finite State Machine', *Crooked Timber*, 16 November 2020, https://crookedtimber. org/2019/11/25/seeing-like-a-finite-state-machine/, in which Farrell writes:

> In short, there is a very plausible set of mechanisms under which machine learning and related techniques may turn out to be a disaster for authoritarianism, reinforcing its weaknesses rather than its strengths, by increasing its tendency to bad decision-making, and reducing further the possibility of negative feedback that could help correct against errors. This disaster would unfold in two ways. The first will involve enormous human costs: self-reinforcing bias will likely increase discrimination against out-groups, of the sort that we are seeing against the Uighur today. The second will involve more ordinary self-ramifying errors, that may lead to widespread planning disasters, which will differ from those described in Scott's account of High Modernism in that they are not as immediately visible, but that may also be more pernicious, and more damaging to the political health and viability of the regime for just that reason.

19 The story of Project Cybersyn is told in Eden Medina, *Cybernetic Revolutionaries: Technology and Politics in Allende's Chile* (MIT Press, 2011). See also George Eaton, 'Project Cybersyn: The Afterlife of Chile's Socialist Internet', *New Statesman*, 22 August 2018 www.newstatesman.com/culture/observations/2018/08/ project-cybersyn-afterlife-chile-s-socialist-internet.

20 The 'Project Cybersyn' quote is from Evgeny Morozov, 'The Planning Machine', *New Yorker*, 14 October 2014, www.newyorker.com/ magazine/2014/10/13/planning-machine.

21 Georgia Frances King, 'The Venn Diagram Between

Libertarians and Crypto Bros is so Close it's Basically a Circle', *Quartz*, 23 May 2018, https://qz.com/1284178/almost-half-of-cryptocurrency-and-bitcoin-bros-identify-as-libertarian.

22 On the deeper relationship between the appeal of blockchain technology and growing mistrust in the state, see William Magnuson, *Blockchain Democracy: Technology, Law and the Rule of the Crowd* (Cambridge University Press, 2022).

23 The cost of crypto can also be measured in its environmental effects: it is enormously energy intensive. The US currently hosts about a third of all global crypto-asset operations, which consume between 0.9 and 1.7 per cent of the total US electricity usage. This level of energy usage is equivalent to the amount consumed by all home computers or all domestic lighting in the US. Worldwide, crypto consumes the equivalent of the entire energy usage of countries such as Australia or Argentina. Office of Science and Technology Policy, 'Climate and Energy Implications of Crypto-Assets in the United States', September 2022, www.whitehouse.gov/wp-content/uploads/2022/09/09-2022-Crypto-Assets-and-Climate-Report.pdf.

8 Who Works for Whom?
1 Carl Benedikt Frey and Michael A. Osborne, 'The Future of Employment: How Susceptible are Jobs to Computerisation?', *Technological Forecasting and Social Change* 114 (2017), 254–80.

2 The demise of the professions in the face of automation has been predicted for a while. One of the most influential accounts is Richard Susskind and Daniel Susskind, *The Future of the Professions: How Technology Will Transform the Work of Human Experts* (Oxford University Press, 2015).

3 See Carl Benedikt Frey, *The Technology Trap: Capital, Labour, and Power in the Age of Automation* (Princeton University Press, 2019).

4 This list of horse-related occupations comes from Brad Smith and Carole Ann Browne, 'The Day the Horse Lost Its Job', *Microsoft Today in Technology*, 22 December 2017, https://blogs.microsoft.com/today-in-tech/day-horse-lost-job/.

5 The contrast between the speed of Cohen's and Dylan's writing

methods is the subject of a celebrated anecdote, recounted in an episode of Malcolm Gladwell's *Revisionist History* podcast www .simonsaysai.com/blog/hallelujah-with-malcolm-gladwell-e7-s1-revisionist -history-podcast-transcript-2bcc8c9fb467:

> **Alan Light (music journalist):** Well, there's a famous story that, uh, you know, Leonard Cohen and Bob Dylan have this kind of mutual admiration thing and, apparently, they met up in the 80s at some point. They were both in Paris and they went to meet at a cafe and Dylan said, 'Oh, I like that, that song *Hallelujah*,' which is a fascinating piece of the story that, really, the first person who paid attention to *Hallelujah* as an important song was Bob Dylan. But he said to Leonard, you know, 'I like that song. How long did you work on that?' And Leonard said, 'I told him that I'd worked on it for 2 years.'
>
> **Malcolm Gladwell:** Which was a lie. Cohen later confessed it took him much longer. Then, Cohen asks Dylan how long it took him to write the song *I and I*.
>
> **AL:** And Bob said, 'Yeah, 15 minutes.'

6 On the politics of UBI, see Guy Standing, *Basic Income and How We Can Make It Happen* (Pelican, 2017); on the sometimes-surprising history of that politics, see Peter Sloman, *Transfer State: The Idea of a Guaranteed Income and the Politics of Redistribution in Modern Britain* (Oxford University Press, 2019).

7 Will Ensor, Anderson Frailey, Matt Jensen and Amy Xu, 'A Budget-Neutral Universal Basic Income', AEI Economics Working Paper, May 2017, www.aei.org/wp-content/uploads/2017/05/UBI-Jensen-et-al-working-paper.pdf.

8 Chandrayan Gupta, 'Dealing with Loneliness Using an AI Chatbot', *Medium*, 26 February 2021, https://medium.com/invisible-illness/dealing-with-loneliness-using-an-ai-chatbot-4f86488caf2d.

9 'A Vision of "Nursing Care in 2040", Future Care Lab in Japan', https://futurecarelab.com/en/news/nursing-care-in-2040-from-future-care-lab-in-japan.

10 There is a growing literature on the end of globalisation. Examples include Finbarr Livesey, *From Global to Local: The Making of Things and the End of Globalisation* (Profile, 2017); Stephen D. King, *Grave New World:*

The End of Globalization, the Return of History (Yale University Press, 2017). On the impact of the Ukraine war, see Adam S. Posen, 'The End of Globalization?', *Foreign Affairs*, 17 March 2022, www.foreignaffairs.com/articles/world/2022-03-17/end-globalization.

11 The classic argument that animals' rights are based on their capacity to suffer remains Peter Singer, *Animal Liberation: A New Ethics for Our Treatment of Animals* (HarperCollins, 1975). There is an ongoing debate as to what rights for robots or AIs might mean. Present scepticism that they don't have rights does not necessarily translate into future certainty that they won't. See David J. Gunkel, *Robot Rights* (MIT Press, 2018); John Basl and Joseph Bowen, 'AI as a Moral Right-Holder', in *The Oxford Handbook of Ethics of AI*, eds. Markus D. Dubber, Frank Pasquale and Sunit Das (Oxford University Pres, 2022).

12 There are many enjoyable skewerings of Davos man. See, for example, Anand Giridharadas, *Winners Take All: The Elite Charade of Changing the World* (Penguin, 2020).

Conclusion: The Second Singularity

1 On the full range of existential risk scenarios, see Toby Ord, *The Precipice: Existential Risk and the Future of Humanity* (Hachette, 2020).

2 Martin Rees writes about the relative – and pressing – risks of bio terror/error in *On the Future: Prospects for Humanity* (Princeton University Press, 2018). Rees took a famous bet in 2017 with Steven Pinker (one of the 'rational optimists') about whether bio terror or error would lead to one million casualties from a single event before the end of 2020 (see https://longbets.org/9/ for the detailed terms). The outcome of this bet hangs on the agreed causes of the Covid pandemic.

3 Many of the worst-case scenarios for humans in relation to AI – including over the very long term – are described in Nick Bostrom, *Superintelligence: Paths, Dangers, Strategies* (Oxford University Press, 2014).

4 The vastly outsize responsibility of a small number of states and corporations for possible doomsday scenarios is discussed in Luke Kemp, 'Agents of Doom: Who is Creating the Apocalypse and Why', *BBC Future*, 26 October 2021, www.bbc.com/future/article/20211014-agents-of-doom-who-is-hastening-the-apocalypse-and-why.

5 Ross Douthat, 'How Seriously Should We Take Putin's Nuclear Threat in Ukraine?', *New York Times*, 24 September 2022, www.nytimes.com/2022/09/24/opinion/ukraine-war-putin-russia.html.

6 William MacAskill, *What We Owe the Future: A Million-Year View* (Oneworld, 2022).

7 https://80000hours.org/start-here/.

8 On the fallout for EA from the SBF fiasco see Jennifer Szalai, 'How Sam Bankman-Fried Put Effective Altruism on the Defensive', *New York Times*, 9 December 2022, www.nytimes.com/2022/12/09/books/review/effective-altruism-sam-bankman-fried-crypto.html.

For a timely moral and philosophical critique of the Effective Altruism movement, see Carol J. Adams, Alice Crarey and Lori Gruen (eds.), *The Good It Promises, the Harm It Does: Critical Essays on Effective Altruism* (Oxford University Press, 2022).

9 The case for relying on the wise for political choice-making ('epistocracy') is made in Jason Brennan, *Against Democracy* (Princeton University Press, 2016).

LIST OF ILLUSTRATIONS

1. Avocados chairs created by OpenAI, DALLE-E (6/6/2023)   2
2. 'Crossing the river', a corporate bridge-building exercise   12
3. Charles Ogle in *Frankenstein* (1910). Photo: © TCD/ Prod.DB/Alamy   15
4. Detail from the frontispiece to Thomas Hobbes' *Leviathan* (1651). Photo: Public domain   20
5. Discursive dilemma 1   41
6. Discursive dilemma 2   42
7. Scene from *Twelve Angry Men* (film, 1957). Photo: Allstar Picture Library Ltd / Alamy Stock Photo   45
8. Condorcet's paradox   50
9. The Lehman Durr & Co. offices in Montgomery, Alabama, 1874. Photo: The Picture Art Collection/Alamy Stock Photo   91
10. Former Lehman Brothers Chairman and CEO Richard Fuld testifies before the House Financial Services Committee about the collapse of Lehman Brothers, 20 April, 2010 in Washington, DC. Photo: © Chip Somodevilla/Staff/Getty Images   98
11. Chart showing global economic growth over two millennia. Source: World GDP – Our World In Data based on World Bank & Maddison (2017): CC BY   133
12. Chart showing disaggregated economic growth over 700 years, from unchartedterritories.tomaspueyo.com. Reproduced with the permission of Tomas Pueyo   134
13. Chart showing population growth since the agricultural revolution. Source: Our World in Data based on estimates by the History Database of the Global Environment (HYDE) and the United Nations: licensed under CC-BY-Sa and by the author Max Roser   151

14. 'Escaping the Malthusian Trap', from Professor Bedir
Tekinerdogan, *Engineering Connected Intelligence: A Socio-
Technical Perspective*, (fig 5), on researchgate.net, open access   153
15. Planet Earth at night-time with city lights in space with stars.
Oceania side. Photo: © Leonello Calvetti/Alamy Stock
Photo   159
16. Original Trabant 601 deLuxe brochure. Photo: John Lloyd/
flickr   166
17. Regional Government Headquarters nuclear bunker,
Perthshire. Photo: Joseph Trevaskis, TayScreen   199
18. This image is from a presentation by Bret Victor called
'Seeing Spaces', and was drawn by David Hellman   216
19. Cybersyn Ops room, from 99percentinvisible.org. Photo:
Gui Bonsieppe   220
20. NBA Replay centre, Secaucus, New Jersey, USA. Photo:
© Andy Marlin – USA TODAY NETWORK   227
21. Robotic heathcare assistants, Japan. Photo: JIJI PRESS/
JIJI PRESS/AFP via Getty Images   243
22. David Cameron during a session at the World Economic
Forum (WEF) annual meeting in Davos, 21 January, 2016.
Photo: © Fabrice Coffrini/Staff Getty Images   251
23. Still from *Rise of the Planet Apes* (film, 2011). Photo:
Pictorial Press Ltd/Alamy Stock Photo   257
24. Former prime minister Boris Johnson visits a boxing academy
in London. Photo: © PA Images /Alamy Stock Photos   260
25. Internet meme showing adaptation of Michelangelo's
'David' meeting a robotic hand. Photo: Public domain   272

While every effort has been made to contact copyright-holders of illustrations, the author and publishers would be grateful for information about any illustrations where they have been unable to trace them, and would be glad to make amendments in further editions.

INDEX

A

accountability 63–7, 96–100, 259
  AI and 270–71
  robots and 67, 251–2, 270
  wars and 75–6, 78
accountancy 229, 236
Acemoglu, Daron 123, 124, 125, 126
acting 31–3, 63
addiction 183, 211
adoption 89
advertising 180, 181, 210
Africa 154
agricultural revolution 106–7
AI-state 207
algorithms 2, 5, 6, 7, 16
  accountability and 66
  answers and 61
  culture and 195
  state as 21, 31
Alibaba 190, 204
Alice Through the Looking Glass
  (Carroll) 125
Allende, Salvador 219
Alphabet 174, 181, 202, 210
AlphaFold 186
AlphaGo 190
AlphaZero 83, 186–7, 190, 192, 196,
  232
altruism 160–61

Amazon 4, 86–7, 102, 131–2, 171–2,
  174, 181–2, 195
  advertising 181, 210
  Alexa 251
  in China 190
  CIA, work with 172, 202
  cloud computing 87, 172, 202
  Cummings on 212–15
  Luxembourg fine (2021) 210
  shareholders 182
  tax avoidance 210–11
American Enterprise Institute
  240
androgyny 204
animal rights 249
answers vs decisions 56–62, 268–9
Ant Group 204
Anthropocene epoch 8, 158–62
Apple 144, 174, 176–7, 210
Arendt, Hannah 146–50, 217, 233
Argentina 74, 92
Aristotle 107
Arkhipov, Vassili 197
Arnault, Bernard 172
ARPANET 176
artificial general agency (AGA)
  23–38, 55, 83, 84, 138, 188, 192, 271
artificial general intelligence (AGI)
  84, 191, 255, 262–3

artificial intelligence (AI) 2–3, 83–6,
186–93
arms race 190, 195
automation 226–53
autonomous weapons 196–200
chess / Go playing 83, 186–7, 190,
196, 232
DeepMind 83, 186–7, 190, 192, 196,
232
general 84, 191, 255, 262–3
Malthusian trap and 156–8
narrow 83–4, 191
OpenAI 2, 189
storytelling and 86
Athens, ancient 123–8, 149, 194
audiences 63–4
Augustus, Roman Emperor 114
Austen, Jane 86
autocracies 25, 28, 50, 74, 75, 137
public opinion and 205
risk and 167
real-time data and 217
wars and 74, 76, 77
automation 226–53
agency and 232–3
creativity and 228
division of labour 241–4
education and 243–5
healthcare and 229–30, 241–5
sports and 226–7
universal basic income 238–41
automotive industry 131–2, 231–2
electric vehicles 175
self-driving vehicles 3, 4, 66, 83,
176, 233
autonomous weapons 196–200
average income levels 122–3
avocado-chairs 2

B

Babylon 106
Baidu 4, 190–1, 204
Bank of England 88
Bankman-Fried, Sam 224, 265
bankruptcy 80
bar examinations 3
Barings 92
Bartleby, the Scrivener (Melville) 235
basketball 227, 228–9
bats 47–8
battery technology 189
Battle of Waterloo (1815) 88
beauty, concept of 60
de Beauvoir, Simone 102
Beer, Stafford 219
Belgium 120, 122–3
Belt and Road initiative 246
Bender, Emily 192
Berlin Wall, fall of (1989) 167
betting markets 53
beverage distributors 171
Bezos, Jeffrey 171–2, 175, 182, 213–14
biases 51, 52, 53, 54, 143, 150
availability heuristic 143
loss aversion 150
Biden family 116
Biden, Hunter 209
Biden, Joseph 203, 209
biological disasters 255, 257
birth rates 150–58, 204
Bitcoin 223
Black Death (1346–53) 152
black-box decision-making 68, 180
Blair, Anthony 'Tony' 97
Blitzscale 171
blockchain 223–5
Blue Origin 175

BMW 79, 87, 165
bodies 17, 145
Boeing 202
bond market 58–9, 70, 72, 74
boom and bust cycles 53
Borlaug, Norman 154
Boston Dynamics 186
Boyd, John 215
BP 4
brain 48
  consciousness and 48
  franchising out of 17
Brazil 140–41
Brexit 42, 43–4, 53, 59, 65, 85, 212, 245
bridge building exercise 11–13, 32–3
Brin, Sergey 172–3, 210
British East India Company 79, 129–31, 139, 181–2
British Empire 120, 122
  Indian colonies 79, 122, 129–31, 136, 181–2
Bush family 116
Bush, George Walker 61
Butler, Samuel 17
ByteDance 190
Byzantine Empire (330–1453) 119, 124

C
Cameron, David 251
Canada 137
cancer 3, 177, 229
capitalism 8, 101, 140
care bots 100
Carnegie, Dale 196
carpenters 234
cars *see* automotive industry
Carville, James 58, 72

Catholic Church 7, 116–17, 118
Cats (2019 film) 95
Cayman Islands 90
Central Intelligence Agency (CIA) 172, 174, 202, 220
chair-avocados 2
ChatGPT 2, 86, 192
chess 83, 186–7, 192, 196, 232
Chicago School 221
Chile 219–22
China 4, 9, 246
  AI research 189–90, 194–5
  AI-state 207
  Belt and Road initiative (2013–) 246
  birth rates 154, 155, 204
  cities in 107, 109
  civilisation vs state 93, 94
  colonialism 121
  common prosperity doctrine 204–5, 206
  corporations in 4, 139–40, 201, 203–8, 218
  Covid-19 pandemic (2019–23) 204
  economic growth 120, 136, 137, 139–40
  employment and 234
  entertainment industry 204
  famines in 142
  gaming in 204
  great divergences 120
  imperial dynasties 113, 114, 115, 116, 120
  institutions 137
  Maoist period (1949–76) 30, 206
  one-child policy (1980–2013) 154, 155
  online tutoring industry 204

population 107, 109, 113, 154
protectionism 190
social media in 205
Tesla 175
three systems 206
Uighur genocide (2014–) 195
US, relations with 189–90, 194–5,
    201, 203, 206, 247
vertically integrated model 205
China Wangxin 175
cities 106–7, 109
citizen juries 259
Citizens United vs FEC (US, 2010)
    98–9
City of London 36–7, 74
civil service 100
civil society 124–9
climate change 96–7, 156, 246,
    254–5, 257, 260
Clinton family 116
Clinton, William 'Bill' 58
cloud computing 16, 87, 172,
    202
co-operatives 102
co-option 201, 203–8, 218
coal 136, 137, 159
Cochran, Johnnie 40
coding 3
cognitive biases *see* biases
cognitive revolution 104–6
Cohen, Leonard 233
CoinDesk 224
Cold War (1947–91) 176, 177, 194,
    197–200, 254
colonialism 120–21, 129–31, 136
Comcast 202
committees 46, 64, 65, 72
communes 102

communism 102
    see also Marxism
'company men' 235
company-states 129–32, 139
competition 201–3, 206
'computer says no' 61
de Condorcet, Nicolas de Caritat,
    Marquis 49–51, 57
Confucianism 206, 207, 208
Congo 122, 134
consciousness 48, 84
conspiracy theories 203
Constantinople 119
constitutions 28, 85, 88, 233–4
consultancy 229
contraception 154–5
Cook, Timothy 210
Cooley, Armanda 43
corporate bridge-building 11–13,
    32–3
corporate malpractice 179
Corporation of the City of London
    36–7, 74
corporations 4–10, 35–8, 39, 79–82,
    94, 107, 110–13
    accountability and 63–4, 96–100
    as artificial agents 37
    co-option 201, 203–8, 218
    competition 201–3
    debt 79–81
    destruction of 89–90, 92, 93
    durability of 37, 64, 87, 89–92, 94,
        266
    employment *see* labour
    as fictions 109, 110–13
    growth and 139–41
    Hobbes on 36
    humanisation of 98–100

lifespans 87, 89–92
limited liability 80–81, 117–18
long-term challenges and 267
Malthusian trap and 155–7
monopolies 171, 174, 178–86,
  202–3
partnerships 82
profit maximisation 99
remits 81, 85, 86–7
Rome and 117
sovereignty and 37
states and 35–8, 80, 85–6, 131, 139,
  171–93, 201–25, 248, 258, 270–71
storytelling and 85–7
tax avoidance 90
uncanny valley and 95–100
vertically integrated model 189,
  205, 237, 246
corruption 116, 124, 178
Covid-19 pandemic (2019–23) 28, 79,
  128, 168, 203, 204, 210, 238, 255
credible commitment 138
credit 72
cricket 227
crowds
  accountability of 62–7
  answers vs decisions 56–62, 268
  feelings of 63
  madness of 52, 54, 55–6
  wisdom of 6, 51–69, 77
cryptocurrencies 223–5, 265
Cuban Missile Crisis (1962) 197
Cummings, Dominic 212–15,
  217–18
cybernetics 219–22
cyberwarfare 195
Czechia 93
Czechoslovakia 93

D
DALL-E 2, 189
dancing 3, 186, 228
DARPA 176
Darwin Among the Machines (Dyson)
  21
data centres 16
Davos man 250, 265
Death Star 118, 122
debt
  corporations 79–81
  states 70–75, 78, 80, 81, 88, 89,
    240
decisions vs answers 56–62, 268–9
Declaration of Independence (US,
  1776) 88
DeepMind Technologies 83, 186–7,
  188, 190, 192, 196, 232
Delaware, United States 90, 91, 96
democracies 25, 28, 123, 148, 202
  answers vs decisions 59, 268–9
  collective responsibility and 65
  Condorcet's paradox and 49–51
  corporations, comparison with
    212–18
  discursive dilemma and 42, 43–4
  elections 28, 77, 116, 137, 202, 205,
    206, 240, 253
  fiscal policies and 73
  generations and 247
  humanisation and 148, 261
  intelligence and 268–9
  long-term challenges and 184
  prosperity and 123, 126, 137
  risk and 167, 259–61
  real-time data and 217
  robots and 253
  wars and 74, 76–8

wisdom of crowds and 51, 53, 59, 268–9
Democratic Party, US 202
democratic peace theory 76–8
Democratic Republic of the Congo 122–3, 133
demographic transition 150–58, 204, 241–8
Dengism 206
Denmark 8, 137
Department of Energy, US 175
deterrence 77–8, 197
dialectical materialism 109
dictatorships *see* autocracies
Digital Markets Act (EU, 2022) 208
digital revolution 109
Digital Services Act (EU, 2022) 208
discursive dilemma 41–4
disease 108, 152
    Black Death (1346–53) 152
    Covid-19 pandemic (2019–23) 28, 79, 128, 168
    horse flu epidemic (1872) 230
    Plague of Athens (430 BCE) 127
division of labour 106, 139, 241–6
doctors 229
Douthat, Ross 258
Dutch East India Company 129–30, 136, 139
Dylan, Bob 233
Dyson, George 21
dystopias 256

E
East Germany (1949–90) 93, 165–6, 167
East India Company
    British 79, 129–31, 139, 181–2

Dutch 129–30, 136, 139
Eastern Roman Empire (330–1453) 119, 124
economics
    advertising 180, 181
    bond markets 58–9, 70, 72, 74
    boom and bust cycles 53
    cybernetics 219–22
    free markets 163–5, 220–22
    global financial crisis (2008) 60
    growth 8, 133–41
    markets 52–4, 58, 60, 101, 109, 163–93, 221–5
    monopolies 171, 174, 178–86, 202–3
    national debts 70–75, 78
    protectionism 166–7, 190
    start-ups 171–3, 211–18
    vertical integration 189, 205, 237, 246
    war and 74–5, 167–8, 170
education 243–5
effective altruism 263–7
efficient markets 52
egotists 161, 170
Egypt, ancient 13, 115
80,000 Hours, 263–4, 266–7
Eisenhower, Dwight 178
elections 28, 77, 116, 137, 202, 205, 206, 240, 253
electric vehicles 175
empires 104, 107, 110, 112, 113–22
    coercion 114–15
    colonialism 120–21, 129–31, 136
    company-states and 129–32
    durability 115–16
    innovation and 118–19, 122
    scalability 115, 117–20
    states, transition to 120–22

energy 108, 189, 205

England 88, 119, 134, 136, 138, 139, 142, 194

English Civil War (1642–49) 22, 36

Enlightenment 108

Entrepreneurial State, The (Mazzucato) 169, 170

Erewhon (Butler) 17

Escape from Rome (Scheidel) 119–20

Essay on the Principle of Population (Malthus) 152–3

European Organization for Nuclear Research 215

European Union (EU) 9, 85
Brexit 42, 43–4, 53, 59, 65, 85, 212, 245
tech companies, regulation of 208–11

Ex Machina (2014 film) 14

exams 3

existential risk movement 263–4

F

Facebook 105, 114, 173, 174, 179, 190, 195, 201

failed states 93

families 35, 89

famines 108, 141–2, 152

feminism 102

Fiat 140

fictions 104
corporations and 109, 110–13
empires as 115
states as 31–5, 104, 109, 110–13

fiefdoms 107

FIFA World Cup 13

5G 195

First Singularity 8, 272

Food and Drug Administration (US) 212

food production 108, 152, 154

football 39, 227

Ford 189, 231–2

'Forever Young' (Dylan) 233

fossil fuels 156, 159

Foucault, Michel 102

France 88–9, 93–4, 119
colonialism 120
economic growth 135, 138
England, relations with 194
institutions 88–9
population 107, 155
Revolution (1789–99) 88–9, 93–4, 100

franchising out of brain 17

Frankenstein (Shelley) 15–16, 18, 35

free market economics 163–5, 220–25

'freedom dividend' 239

Freud, Sigmund 102

Frey, Carl Benedikt 226, 228

Friedman, Milton 221

friendships 105–6, 148

FTX 224, 265

Fuld, Richard 'Dick' 97

Future of Humanity man 265

G

gaming 204

Gan Yang 205–6

Gates, William 'Bill' 173, 210

General Data Protection Regulation (EU, 2016) 210

General Motors 181, 182, 189

generations 246, 247

Generative Pre-trained
 Transformer 2, 86, 192
 GPT-3 2
 GPT-4 3, 189
Germany 79, 87–8, 89, 93, 119, 120,
 148
 East Germany (1949–90) 93,
 165–6, 167
 Nazi period (1933–45) 79, 89, 148,
 166, 177
 UK, relations with 194
 Weimar Republic (1918–33) 223
Ghana 136
global financial crisis (2008) 60, 90,
 178, 222
globalisation 8, 188–9, 245–6
Glorious Revolution (1688) 88
Go 83, 190
Goldman Sachs 89
Google 21, 60, 132, 172–3, 174, 179,
 195
 advertising 179, 180, 181
 in China 190
 DeepMind Technologies 83,
 186–7, 190
 LaMDA 191–2, 249
 lobbying 201–2
 staff numbers 181
Gray, John 160
Great Acceleration 135, 159
Great Depression (1929–39) 147
great transformations 120, 133–62
 corporations and 139–41
 human experience of 141–50
 inequality and 134, 140
 institutions and 137–41
 replications 135, 137
 population and 150–58

Greece 123–8, 149
green energy 189, 205
Green Revolution 154
greenwashing 97
gross domestic product (GDP) 123,
 133–41
group choice, theories of 49–69
 Condorcet paradox 49–50
 Jury Theorem 50–51, 57
 wisdom of crowds 6, 51–69
group identity 45–9, 65
 accountability and 62–7
 incoherence and 49
 states and 30, 46–7
groupthink 45, 51, 52, 53, 62
guilds 107, 116

H
H-4 Hercules 170
'Hallelujah' (Cohen) 233
Hamlet (Shakespeare) 31, 33
Han Empire (202 BCE – 220 CE)
 113, 120
Harari, Yuval 104, 109, 110, 111, 112,
 271
Harvard University 173
Hassabis, Demis 186–8
Hawk-Eye systems 226–7
Hayek, Friedrich 221
healthcare 146, 168, 240, 241–5
HITS 173
Hobbes, Thomas 18–38, 50, 62, 73,
 83, 126–7, 148, 207, 241, 261, 271
hockey stick 133–41
Holocene epoch 158
Holy Roman Empire (800–1802) 113
Homo Deus 111, 271
Homo faber 233

Homo rapiens 160, 170
Homo sapiens 104
Hong Kong 129
horses 231–2
hospitals 143, 229–30
How to Win Friends and Influence People (Carnegie) 196
Huawei 195
Hughes, Howard 170
Human Condition, The (Arendt) 146–50
human intelligence (HI) 16, 26, 172, 187–8, 199–200, 271
humanisation 97, 98–100, 148, 184, 260–61
hunter-gatherer societies 105
Hussein, Saddam 59
Hyundai 131, 166

I
IBM 173
identity
    group *see* group identity
    personal 109–10
ideological conflicts 195
immigration 155, 245, 246–7
India 4, 9, 79–80, 121
    British colonies in 79, 122, 129–31, 136, 137, 181–2
    economic growth 136, 137, 140
    population 113, 154
individuality 6
Industrial Revolution (*c.*1760–*c.*1840) 8, 135, 136, 167, 229–30
inequality 122–3, 134, 140
inheritance tax 240
innovation 118–19, 122, 167–93
    corporations and 171–93

risk and 167–71, 176
states and 167–93
wars and 167–71, 177
Instagram 179, 181, 183, 195
institutions 88–9, 101, 116–19, 122, 124, 131, 137
    growth and 137–41
intergenerational tensions 246, 247
International Trade Union Confederation 172
Internet
    addiction and 183, 211
    ARPANET 176
    Internet of Things 195
    monopolies 178–86, 202–3
    search engines 52, 60, 172–3, 179, 180, 270
    social media 180, 184–5, 195
investment funds 251–2
iPad 177
iPhone 144, 176
Iraq 59, 61–2, 106
Ireland 142
Iron Giant, The (1999 film) 35
Israel 128, 214
Italy 119, 120, 140–41

J
Japan 89, 128, 155, 242–3, 244, 245
Jassay, Andrew 210
jellybean guessing game 51–3, 54, 56–7, 58, 84
jobs *see* labour
Jobs, Steve 176–7, 210
Johnson, Alexander Boris 212, 214, 260
Johnson, Samuel 147
Johnson & Johnson 89

joint enterprise 66
Joint Stock Companies Act (UK,
 1844) 80
joint stock companies 80, 117–18
Jordan 106
JP Morgan Chase 89
juries 39–41, 43, 44–5, 50–51, 57, 62,
 68
Jury Theorem 50–51

K
Kennedy family 116
Kim Jong-un 115, 137
Kleinberg, Joel 173

L
labour; jobs 146–50, 226–53
 automation of 226–53
 benefits 237, 238
 careers 235
 durability and 147, 233, 236
 exploitation and 237
 jobs 147
 time and 233
 progression 235
 retirement 238
 self-employment 238
 shortages of 238
 stability 147, 233–5, 236
 tasks 228, 231–2, 233–4, 236–8
LaMDA 191–2, 249
language 83, 85, 105
law; legal systems 32–3
 automation and 229, 236
 bar examinations 3
 joint enterprise 66
 juries 39–41, 43, 44–5, 50–51, 57, 62,
  68

leagues 107
Lee Sedol 190
Leeson, Nicholas 92
Lehman Brothers 89–90, 91–2, 97
Lemoine, Blake 191–2
Leviacene epoch 162
Leviathan (Hobbes) 18–38, 50, 62, 83,
 126, 127, 148, 207, 241, 261, 271
liberation projects 102
libertarianism 174–5, 222–5
life expectancy 8, 25, 87, 108, 135,
 145, 206
lifespan 87, 145, 273
Lima, Peru 109
Limited Liability Act (UK, 1855) 80
limited liability companies 80–81,
 117–18
Liu Xiaofeng 205–6
lobbying 201–2
London, England 107, 109, 188
long-term challenges 184, 262–8
Los Angeles, California 109
loss aversion 150, 240
Louis Vuitton 172
Louis XIV, King of France 137
Louisiana Purchase (1802) 92
Luxembourg 210
LVMH 172
lynch mobs 55

M
Ma, Jack 204
MacAskill, William 262–3
Macmillan, Maurice Harold 219
madness of crowds 52, 54, 55–6
de Maistre, Joseph 100
Malthus, Thomas 152–3, 154
Malthusian trap 152–8

Manhattan Project (1942–6) 218
Mao Zedong 30, 206
markets 52–4, 58, 60, 101, 109, 163–
    93, 220–25
  betting markets 53
  Blitzscale 171
  bond markets 58–9, 70, 72, 74
  free market economics 163–5,
    220–25
  monopolies 171, 174, 178–86, 202–3
  prediction markets 53
  states and 60, 163–93
Marxism 82, 86, 102, 109, 222–3
masks 23–4, 31
Massachusetts Institute of
  Technology (MIT) 186
Mazzucato, Mariana 169, 170
mechanisation 112
Medicaid 240
medicine 211–12, 229–30
Melville, Herman 235
Meta 114, 132, 174, 179, 181, 182, 185,
  201
Metaverse 114, 185
Microsoft 173, 174, 210
microwaves 168
military-industrial complex 178,
  205
Mind Sports Olympiad 187
Ming Empire (1368–1644) 113
modernity 112, 116, 129, 132, 205
Moët Hennessy 172
monarchy 22
monopolies 171, 174, 178–86, 202–3
monopoly on violence 92–3, 102,
  138
moral hazard 64
Mossad 214, 215

murder 66, 76
Musk, Elon 97, 110, 144, 171–2, 175

N
Nadella, Satya 210
Nagel, Thomas 47
Napoleonic Wars (1803–15) 88
narcissists 161, 170
Narrow AI 83
narrow corridor 122–9, 141
Narrow Corridor, The (Acemoglu
  and Robinson) 123, 124, 125, 126
National Aeronautics and Space
  Administration (NASA) 173, 175,
  215, 227
National Basketball Association
  (NBA) 227, 228–9
national debt 70–75, 78, 88, 89, 169
National Institutes of Health (NIH)
  170
natural disasters 108
Nazi Germany (1933–45) 79, 89, 148,
  166, 177
Neanderthals 104, 160
Netherlands 129–30, 134, 136, 139
New York Times 61, 171
New York, United States 230
New Zealand 128
Norberg, Johan 141–2, 143, 144
North Korea 115, 137
North, Douglass 138
Norway 128
nuclear weapons 77–8, 149, 168,
  197–200, 254, 256–7, 258, 260

O
Oakeshott, Michael 82–5
Obama, Barack 163–4, 178

oil industry 96
On Human Conduct (Oakeshott) 82–5
OpenAI 2, 189
organised crime 36
Osborne, Michael 226, 228
Ottoman Empire (1299–1922) 119
outliers 132

P
Page, Larry 172–3, 210
PageRank system 173
Palantir 174
panpsychists 17
Paris, France 107
Parliament 46
Patagonia 74
patriarchy 101
PayPal 144, 174
penicillin 168
per capita GDP 123
performance 31–5
Pericles 125, 127, 149
personality 23
Peru 109
Petrobras 140–41
physical bodies 17, 145
Pichai, Sundar 210
plagues 127, 152
Planet of the Apes films 105, 256, 257
Pleistocene epoch 158
poisonous river exercise 11–13, 32–3
politics
    answers vs decisions 59, 268–9
    coercion and 30, 31
    automation and 246, 247
    intergenerational tensions and 246, 247

parties 39, 100, 149
    as performance 31
    prediction markets and 53
    state and 18–38
populations 150–58
    cities 106–7, 109
    demographic transition 150–58, 204, 241–8
    empires 113–14
    Malthusian trap 152
    risk and 259–61
Portugal 121
postmodernism 102
prediction markets 53
prejudice 54
price fixing 179
primary guessing 52
principalities 107
Procter & Gamble 89
profit maximisation 99
Progress (Norberg) 141–2, 143, 144
Project Cybersyn (1971–3) 219–22
prosperity 122–9, 133–62
    corporations and 139–41
    human experience of 141–50
    inequality and 134, 140
    institutions and 137–41
    replications 135, 137
    population and 150–58
protectionism 166–7, 191
psychoanalysis 102
psychopaths 161, 170
Public Accounts Committee 168
public opinion 28
Putin, Vladimir 29, 97–8, 115, 258

Q
Qatar 13

R

Rabbit, Run (Updike) 235
racism 54
radar 168
Ralph Lauren 227
Rand, Ayn 174, 178
rational optimists 142, 256
real-time data 216–25
realpolitik 62
recklessness 168
Rees, Martin 255
Reformation 119
religions 7, 36, 82, 104, 107, 112, 117,
    143
Renaissance 108
revolutions 88
riots 22, 54, 55, 96
risk 167–71, 176
river crossing exercise 11–13, 32–3
Roanoke, Virginia 163, 178
Robinson, James 123, 124, 125, 126
Robocop (1987 film) 35
robots 248–53
    accountability and 67, 251–2, 270
    care bots 100, 241–3, 245, 248
    dancing 186, 228
    labour and 155
    sex bots 4, 100
    state as 5, 18–21, 31, 35, 83
    uncanny valley 95
    voting rights 253
Roman law 81
Rome, ancient 7, 110, 113–20, 131
    average income levels 123
    coercive authority 114–15
    corporations in 117
    fall of 119, 124
    population 106, 107, 113

religious bodies in 117
republicanism 116
scalability and 117–19
Romney, Willard Mitt 164
Royal Society of Statisticians 219
rule of law 28, 122, 137
Russia 29, 30, 74, 78, 97–8, 115, 245,
    246, 254, 258

S

S&P 500 index 89
sacrifice, concept of 196
'salary men' 235
salesmen 235
San Francisco, California 122
Sapiens (Harari) 104, 109, 110, 111,
    112, 271
scalability 67, 115, 117
Scheidel, Walter 119–20
schools 143
scientific revolution 8, 108–9, 111,
    112
Scotland 93
Scott, James 216–17
search engines 52, 60, 172–3, 179,
    180, 270
second guessing 52
Second Singularity 9, 254–73
secular churches 82
Seeing Like a State (Scott) 216–17
seeing spaces 215–16
self-driving cars 3, 4, 66, 83, 176
semiconductors 205
server farms 16
sex 4, 100, 168
sexism 54
Shakespeare, William 31, 33
Shanghai, China 109

shareholders 80–81, 99, 180, 181, 182
shark-infested river exercise 11–13,
  32–3
Shelley, Mary 15–16, 18, 35
Silicon Valley 171–93, 201–3
Simpson, Orenthal James 40–41, 43,
  62, 68
Singapore 92, 137, 214–15
Singularity 8–9, 145, 254–73
  First 8, 272
  Second 9, 254–73
slavery 107, 123, 149, 252
Slovakia 93
Snap 195
soccer *see* football
social care 241–3
social machines 100–103
social media 180, 184–5, 195, 205
socialism 206, 208, 219–23
societas 81–2, 117, 218
soft power 195–6
South Africa 129
South China Sea 194
South Korea 8, 128, 131, 135, 136, 151,
  155, 190
South Sudan 93, 128
sovereign individuals 112
Soviet Union (1922–91) 30, 82, 176,
  197–200
space travel 175
SpaceX 175
Spain 119, 121
Sparta 123, 125, 194
sports 226–7
Spruce Goose 170
Sputnik 176, 190
stability 46, 124–5, 126, 137–8
Stalin, Joseph 30

Stanford University 173
Star Wars films 118
start-ups 171–3, 211–18
states 4–10, 18–38, 94, 110–13
  accountability and 75–6, 259
  as algorithms 21, 31
  as artificial agents 23–38, 55, 83,
    84, 138
  belief in 34–5, 37
  binding decisions and 24, 27
  civil society and 124–8
  coercion and 30, 31, 35, 60, 81, 93,
    183, 221
  constitutions 28, 85, 88
  corporations and 35–8, 80, 85–6,
    131, 139, 171–93, 201–25, 248, 258,
    270–71
  debts 70–75, 78, 80, 81, 88, 89, 169,
    240
  as decision-making mechanism
    24, 26
  destruction of 92–3
  durability of 24–6, 33, 72–6, 87–8,
    89, 92–3, 94, 247, 262, 266
  economic growth 133–41
  empires, transition from 120–22
  employment and 234, 237, 238, 245
  failed states 93
  as fictions 31–5, 104, 109, 110–13
  as general purpose 81, 84
  generations and 247
  governments and 72, 124
  humanisation of 97, 148, 184,
    260–61
  innovation and 167–93
  lifespans 87–8, 89, 92–3, 262
  long-term challenges and 184,
    262–7

Malthusian trap and 155–7
markets and 60, 164–93
monopoly on violence 92–3, 138
as partnerships 82, 85–6
peoples and 93–4
prosperity of 122–9, 133–62
revolutions 88
as robots 5, 18–21, 31, 35, 83
risk and 167–71, 176, 183, 259–61
as secular churches 82
real-time data and 216–25
sovereignty of 37
as start-ups 211–18
storytelling and 85–6
uncanny valley and 95, 96, 97–8
violence of 30, 75, 92–3, 96, 97,
  102
wars and 24, 29, 74–9, 167–71, 177,
  240
wisdom of crowds and 53, 55
steam engine 159
stock exchanges 136
storytelling 85–6, 109
supply chains 188–9
Supreme Court, US 98–9, 202
surveillance systems 174, 258
Suskind, Ronald 61–2
Sweden 141–2, 143
Switzerland 168

T
Taiwan 137, 194
Tanzania 93
Tata 4
tax avoidance 90, 91, 210–11
taxidermy 95
Taylor, Alan John Percivale 197
Tencent 190, 204

tennis 226
terrorism 53, 144, 256–7
Tesla 58, 97, 175, 188–9, 190, 237
Thailand 129
theatre 31, 63
Thiel, Peter 144, 174–5, 179
thieves 36
Thirty Years' War (1618–48) 22
3D-printing 246
three systems 206
Thunderbirds (TV series) 221
Thurlow, Edward 63
TikTok 114, 183, 190, 195
Tilly, Charles 75
'Too big to fail' 165
Toy Story films 95
Trabant 165–6, 167, 168
trade unions 147
Trans World Airlines 170
treaties 76
tribes 104, 110, 112, 161
Trump family 116
Trump, Donald 53, 175, 184, 203,
  209, 245
Turkey 106, 121
Twelve Angry Men (1957 film) 44–5
Twelve Monkeys (1995 film) 256
Twitter 144, 163

U
Uighurs 195
Ukraine 29, 74, 78, 203, 245, 246, 254
uncanny valley 95–100
United Kingdom 4, 88
  AI research 188
  Brexit 42, 43–4, 53, 59, 65, 85, 212,
    245
  civil service 100

colonialism 79, 120–22
cybernetics in 219
economic growth 135–6, 138
Germany, relations with 194
immigration 245
national debt 73
Parliament 46
population growth 153
Scotland 93
start-up state and 212–15, 217–18
United Nations 90, 92, 93
United States 4, 7, 9, 102, 110, 149
    China, relations with 189–90,
        194–5, 201, 203, 206, 247
    Citizens United vs FEC (2010)
        98–9
    Cold War (1947–91) 176, 177, 194,
        197–200
    constitution (1787) 234
    corporations in 139, 171–93, 201–3
    corruption in 116, 178
    Cuban Missile Crisis (1962) 197
    DARPA 176
    Declaration of Independence
        (1776) 88
    economic growth 135, 138, 139
    free market economics in 163–4,
        166
    horse flu epidemic (1872) 230
    Louisiana Purchase (1802) 92
    Manhattan Project (1942–6) 218
    military-industrial complex 178,
        205
    NASA 173, 175, 215, 227
    national debt 70–71, 73, 78
    National Institutes of Health
        (NIH) 170
    Navy 186

population 113
presidential election (2012) 163–4
presidential election (2016) 53, 175,
    245
presidential election (2020) 239
protectionism in 166–7
Rome, comparison with 7, 116
Second World War (1939–45) 168,
    170
Silicon Valley 171–93, 201–3
universal basic income (UBI) 238–41
universitas 81, 116, 218
University of Chicago 221
unsexy businesses 171
Uruguay 128
Uruk 106, 107

V
vertically integrated model 188,
    205, 237, 246
Vichy France (1940–44) 89
Victor, Bret 215–16
video assistant referee system
    (VAR) 227
violence
    crowds and 22, 55, 57, 66
    scientific revolution and 108–9
    states and 30, 75, 92–3, 96, 97, 102
    wars 4, 24, 29, 74–9
Volkswagen 79, 166
vulture funds 74

W
Wall Street Journal 224
Warren, Elizabeth 202
wars 4, 24, 29, 74–9, 240
    accountability for 75–6, 78
    autonomous weapons 196–200

democratic peace theory 76–8
deterrence 77–8, 197
innovation and 167–71, 177
national debt and 74–5
nuclear weapons 77–8, 149, 168,
    197–200, 254, 256–7, 258, 260
washing machines 144
Watt, James 159
weapons of mass destruction 59
Weber, Maximilian 92, 100
WeChat 195
weddings 105–6
Weimar Germany (1918–33) 223
Weingast, Barry 138
welfare state 75, 135, 146, 156
'What is It Like to be a Bat?'
    (Nagel) 47
What We Owe the Future (MacAskill)
    262–3
Wilson, James Harold 219
Wimbledon 227
Winklevoss, Cameron and Tyler
    173
wisdom of crowds 6, 51–69
    accountability and 62–7

answers vs decisions 56–62, 268
    wars and, 62 77
women 149, 151
work *see* labour
World Economic Forum 250
World War I (1914–18) 73, 197
World War II (1939–45) 168, 170

X
Xi Jinping 115, 137, 204–5, 209
Xinjiang, China 195

Y
Y Combinator 214
Yang, Andrew 239
Yeats, William Butler 124
'You didn't build that!' speech
    (Obama, 2012) 163–4, 178

Z
Zanzibar 93
Zelenskyy, Volodymyr 29
Zuckerberg, Mark 114, 173, 182, 201,
    210